TWO STUDIES IN
ATTIC PARTICLE USAGE

MNEMOSYNE

BIBLIOTHECA CLASSICA BATAVA

COLLEGERUNT

A.D. LEEMAN · H.W. PLEKET · C.J. RUIJGH

BIBLIOTHECAE FASCICULOS EDENDOS CURAVIT

C.J. RUIJGH, KLASSIEK SEMINARIUM, OUDE TURFMARKT 129, AMSTERDAM

SUPPLEMENTUM CENTESIMUM VICESIMUM NONUM

C.M.J. SICKING and J.M. VAN OPHUIJSEN

TWO STUDIES IN ATTIC PARTICLE USAGE

TWO STUDIES IN ATTIC PARTICLE USAGE

LYSIAS AND PLATO

BY

C.M.J. SICKING

AND

J.M. VAN OPHUIJSEN

WITHDRAWN

E.J. BRILL

LEIDEN · NEW YORK · KÖLN

1993

The paper in this book meets the guidelines for permanence and durability of the Committee on Production Guidelines for Book Longevity of the Council on Library Resources.

Library of Congress Cataloging-in-Publication Data

Sicking, C. M. J.
    Two studies in attic particle usage : Lysias & Plato / C.M.J. Sicking and J.M. van Ophuijsen.
        p.   cm. — (Mnemosyne, bibliotheca classica Batava. Supplementum. ISSN 0169-8958 ; 129)
    Includes bibliographical references and index.
    ISBN 9004098674
    1. Attic Greek dialect—Syntax.   2. Greek language—Particles. Lysias—Language.   4. Plato—Language.   I. Ophuijsen,   J.M. van, 1953-   . I. Title.   III. Series.
    PA526.S65   1993   486—dc20   93-15296
                                                                                    CIP

Die Deutsche Bibliothek - CIP-Einheitsaufnahme

Two studies in attic particle usage : Lysias & Plato / by C. M. J. Sicking and J. M. van Ophuijsen. - Leiden ; New York ; Köln : Brill, 1993
    (Mnemosyne : Supplementum ; 129)
    ISBN 90-04-09867-4
NE: Sicking, C. M. J. ; Ophuijsen, J. M. van; Mnemosyne / Supplementum

ISSN   0169-8958
ISBN   90 04 09867 4

PRINTED IN THE NETHERLANDS

CONTENTS

PART ONE

DEVICES FOR TEXT ARTICULATION
IN LYSIAS I AND XII

by C.M.J. Sicking

General

Special

Appendix

PART TWO

OYN, APA, ΔH, TOINYN:
THE LINGUISTIC ARTICULATION OF ARGUMENTS
IN PLATO'S *PHAEDO*

by J.M. van Ophuijsen

General

Special

PREFACE

The two studies which follow were not originally designed as parts of one structure. Yet they share a number of characteristics in their general approach to the subject of Greek particle usage, and to a not negligible extent supplement each other in the choice of particles, the aspects under which these particles are considered, and the types of context discussed. It therefore seemed to make sense to publish them in one volume.

We have not attempted to achieve complete uniformity. Such minor discrepancies as there are between our views have been allowed to stand, and we have tried to help our readers in referring from each text to the other.

CMJS
JMvO

ABBREVIATIONS

as in LSJ, with the following exceptions and additions:

Denniston   J.D. DENNISTON, *Greek Particles*. Oxford 1934, 1954[2]
Des Places   E. DES PLACES, *Etudes* (see Bibliography)
GP   = Denniston
KG   R. KÜHNER & B. GERTH, *Ausführliche Grammatik der griechischen Sprache, Zweiter Teil: Satzlehere*, I (1898[3]) and II (1904[3]) (cited by page number)
LSJ   H.G. LIDDELL & R. SCOTT, *A Greek-English Lexicon*. Revised (…) by H.S. JONES (…). Oxford (1925-)1940

(Pl.)   *Charm.*   *Charmides*
        Euthyd. *Euthydemus*
        Euth.   *Euthyphro*
        Gorg.   *Gorgias*
        La.   *Laches*
        Ly.   *Lysis*
        Parm.   *Parmenides*
        Phd.   *Phaedo*
        Phdr.   *Phaedrus*
        Polit.   *Politicus*
        Prot.   *Protagoras*
        Resp.   *Respublica*
        Soph.   *Sophistes*
        Symp.   *Symposium*

BIBLIOGRAPHY

Editions

Herodoti Historiae recognovit (...) *Tom.* I, II C. HUDE. Oxford 1908
Lysiae Orationes recognovit (...) C. HUDE. Oxford 1912 (the edition used except where otherwise stated)
——, Lysias *Discours*. Texte établi et traduit par L. GERNET & M. BIZOS. Tome I (I-XV) Paris 1924
Lysias *Orationes* recensuit T. THALHEIM. Maior ed. alt. corr. Leipzig 1913
Platonis Opera recognovit (...) I. BURNET. Tom. I-V, Oxford 1900-1907

Studies

E.J. BAKKER, *Linguistics and Formulas in Homer.* Thesis Leiden. Amsterdam & Philadelphia 1988
——, 'Boundaries, Topics and the Structuring of Discourse', *Studies in Language* 17 (1993) *(forthcoming)*
——, 'Whose Point of View?' *(unpublished MS)*
J. BLOMQVIST, *Greek Particles in Hellenistic Prose.* Lund 1969
L. BRANDWOOD, *A Word Index to Plato.* Leeds 1976
J.D. DENNISTON, *The Greek Particles.* Second edition, Oxford 1954
R. EUCKEN, *De Aristotelis dicendi ratione.* Pars I: *Observationes de particularum usu.* Göttingen 1866
E. DES PLACES, *Etudes sur quelques particules de liaison chez Platon*: OYN *et ses composés*, APA, TOINYN. Paris 1929
MATTH. DEVARIUS, *Tractatus de Graecae linguae particulis.* Rome 1588
S.C. DIK, *Coordination: Its Implications for the Theory of General Linguistics.* Amsterdam 1968
——, *Functional Grammar.* Amsterdam 1979
DIONYSIUS THRAX, ΤΕΧΝΗ ΓΡΑΜΜΑΤΙΚΗ (*Ars Grammatica*), ed. G. Uhlig. Leipzig 1883
A. HELLWIG, 'Zur Funktion und Bedeutung der griechischen Partikeln', *Glotta* 52 (1974) 145-71
H. HOOGEVEEN, *Doctrina particularum linguae Graecae.* Leiden 1769 (The *Praefatio* is cited by r(ecto) and v(erso) of f(olium).)
——, In *Epitomen* redegit C.G. SCHÜTZ. Second edition, Leipzig 1786
C. KROON, 'Causal Connectors in Latin: The Discourse Function of *nam, igitur* and *ergo*', in: M. Lavency & D. Longree, *Proceedings of the Vth Colloqium on Latin Linguistics*, CILL (1989) 231-243
H. KURZOVÁ, *Der Relativsatz in den indoeuropäischen Sprachen.* Hamburg 1981
G. LEECH, *Principles of Pragmatics.* London & New York 1983
H. PINKSTER, *On Latin Adverbs.* Amsterdam 1972
——, *Latijnse Syntaxis en Semantiek.* Amsterdam 1984
C.J. RUIJGH, *Autour de "TE épique": études sur la syntaxe grecque.* Amsterdam 1971
A. RIJKSBARON, *Temporal & Causal Conjunctions in Ancient Greek.* Amsterdam 1976
D.M. SCHENKEVELD, 'From *particula* to Particle: the Genesis of a Class of Words', in: Irène Rosier (ed.), *L'Héritage des grammairiens latins de l'antiquité aux Lumières.* (Actes du Colloque de Chantilly 2-4 septembre 1987). Bibliothèque de l'Information Grammaticale, Société pour l'Information Grammaticale, Paris 1988

E. SCHWYZER, *Griechische Grammatik*, zweiter Band, *Syntax und syntaktische Stilistik*, vervollständigt (...) von A. DEBRUNNER. München 1959[2]

C.M.J. SICKING, 'Griekse partikels: definitie en classificatie', *Lampas* 19 (1986) 125-41

——, 'The Distribution of Aorist and Present Stem Forms in Greek, Especially in the Imperative', *Glotta* 59 (1991) 14-43, 154-172

S.R. SLINGS, '"KAI *adversativum*": some thoughts on the semantics of coordination', in: *Linguistic Studies Offered to Berthe Siertsema* ed. D.J. van Alkemade *et al.* Amsterdam 1980, 101-25

PART ONE

DEVICES FOR TEXT ARTICULATION
IN LYSIAS I AND XII

C.M.J. SICKING

ACKNOWLEDGEMENTS

I wish to record a debt to my late wife. What understanding I may have won has been greatly increased by her knowledge of Greek and acute sensitivity to the nuances of the language of Lysias and Aristophanes. I am conscious that there is much in what follows which she could have improved.

My thanks are due to Dr Egbert J. Bakker for some stimulating conversations drawing from his knowledge of discourse organisation and to Dr Jan M. van Ophuijsen for his meticulous care in translating and, in the process, correcting and clarifying my in many ways messy Dutch text.

CMJS

DEVICES FOR TEXT ARTICULATION
IN LYSIAS I AND XII

1. *Introductory*

A considerable section of the *Praefatio* to H. HOOGEVEEN's *Doctrina particularum linguae Graecae*[1] is devoted to refuting the notion that a number of Greek particles are strictly speaking dispensable (*otiosae*). This notion had by then already had a long vogue, dating back as it did at least to DIONYSIUS THRAX,[2] who assigned quite a few particles to a class of σύνδεσμοι παραπληρωματικοί ('expletive' conjunctions), which μέτρου ἢ κόσμου ἕνεκα παραλαμβάνονται without adding to the content of the sentence. Hoogeveen rejects the suggestion that the use of superfluous matter in good classical authors might be to contribute to the virtue of *elegantia*, and sets himself the task of showing that what appears to be superfluous does in reality serve a purpose.

For Hoogeveen all those words count as particles which *ipsae, per se solae spectatae, nihil significant*. Effectively his list is the same as that of Dionysius. When the nouns and verbs, the participles and adverbs derived from them, as well as articles, pronouns and prepositions have been excluded, what remains are

– the comparatively clear-cut sets of (1) words subservient to the *orationis structura* (e.g. conjunctions) and (2) words whose omission would alter the truth conditions of the sentence in which they occur (such as negations, ἄν, interrogatives),

– a rather less well-defined set of (3) adverbs such as πάλιν, αὖτις, ἀτέχνως, ἀμέλει, δηλονότι, etc., all of which at least bear a clear referential meaning, and

– finally (4) the allegedly otiose σύνδεσμοι παραπληρωματικοί familiar from Dionysius, whose use in Hoogeveen's opinion is to be looked for in the same sphere as that of the *vultus, gestus, vocis ductus* accompanying an utterance: among the concepts invoked in explaining them are *emphasis, confirmatio, affirmatio, limitatio*, and *perspicuitas*, the latter e.g. for 'apodotic δέ' and other items addressed by ancient grammarians and scholiasts in such phrases as ἐκ περιττοῦ κεῖται, ἐκ περιουσίας, and πλεονάζει.

---

[1] Leiden 1769: f. (7) v.-(11) r.; in the *Epitome* by C.G. Schütz, 2nd ed. Leipzig 1786: p. xiii-xviii.

[2] 20.8/p. 96-100 Uhlig.

1.1. *State of the Question*

Compared to Hoogeveen's the inventory of particles recognized by J.D.
DENNISTON[1] shows some significant deviations. Classes of words left out
of account are those whose omission does not leave truth conditions unaffected, such as negations and interrogatives; furthermore conjunctions introducing subordinate clauses, not because they do not in Denniston's
view count as particles but on the ground that 'their importance is grammatical rather than stylistic';[2] and likewise the majority of such semantically more or less transparent adverbs as αὖ, αὖτε, αὖθις, εἶτα, ἔπειτα,
ὅμως, ἀμέλει, ἀτέχνως, etc. What remains is, in Hoogeveen's terms
quoted above, the sum of the quasi-*otiosae* plus the particles taken to
support the *orationis structura*, with the exception of the subordinating
conjunctions. The resulting set coincides by and large with what KÜHNER
GERTH subsume under 'Adverbien'[3] and under 'kopulative',[4] 'adversative',[5] and 'kausale Beiordnung';[6] their 'disjunktive Beiordnung'[7] is passed
over in silence.

Denniston's working definition and classification of the word class
accords with this demarcation: particles may be either 'connecting particles' or 'particles of emphasis and nuance', also known as 'adverbial
particles'. His introduction as well as his actual discussion of individual
particles show the boundaries between these two subclasses to be decidedly fleeting, both from a synchronic and from a diachronic point of view.
In plainer words we are dealing with a class of vocables which are not
covered by the categories of traditional grammar, which in many cases
cannot be translated,[8] and whose omission does not leave the text incom-
prehensible or affect the truth conditions of the statements contained in it.

Notwithstanding minor discrepancies in how individual items are assigned to the various categories, the general outline of the subject has
remained unchanged from the days of Hoogeveen, indeed of Dionysius,

---

[1] *Greek Particles*, Oxford 1934, 1954[2].

[2] P. xl. This motivation brings out what many of Denniston's discussions imply, that
the category of style is a basic constituent of his frame of reference, on a par with lexical
meaning, grammar, and logic—indeed the principal consideration where the particles are
concerned. Compare his characterization (p. xxxvii) of the outcome of the later 'evolution
of particles' in the metaphor 'less body, more bouquet'.

[3] R. Kühner–B. Gerth, *Griechische Grammatik*, Satzlehre (hereafter: KG), II 116-78.

[4] II 235-61.

[5] II 261-95.

[6] II 317-47.

[7] II 295-316.

[7] Hoogeveen already felt the need to argue that the fact that a Greek word does not
have an equivalent in Latin is not enough to prove that it is redundant: cf. esp. his f. 9 r. (=
Epitome p. xvi).

onwards: no account is given of things indispensable to either *orationis structura* or cognitive meaning, but devices operative in the 'connection' between main, or at least co-ordinate, clauses, or otherwise unconcerned with the meaning of the clause or clauses itself are explained. The semantic apparatus too (*perspicuitas* and *emphasis*, *confirmatio*, *affirmatio* respectively) remains basically unchanged and, as the considerable overlap between different items in Denniston's description alone suffices to show, remains inadequate.

1.2. *Desiderata*

This situation can be understood from a point of view of traditional grammar as applied to Greek which is eloquently expressed near the beginning of the most influential modern syntax of the language: 'Da die Sprache Ausdruck der Gedanken ist, die Gedanken aber durch Sätze ausgedrückt werden, so springt in die Augen, dass die Grammatik nichts anderes ist als Satzlehre.'[1] Such a point of departure does not help towards appreciating two considerations which are particularly vital to an understanding of the particles.

First, the structure of a text is not exhaustively described as the sum of the 'connections' between successive sentences: a structure made up of larger segments, and the devices by which its articulation and coherence are effected, have to be taken into consideration.

Secondly, language is not so much a medium for the unilateral expression of thoughts (nor of feelings, or desires, &c.) as a means of communicating with and acting upon an audience, in the use of which the speaker takes into consideration, exploits and manipulates the perceptive capacities, previous information, supposed opinions, feelings &c. of his audience.

Existing descriptions of the field show another limitation which favours a tendency to reduce features of use and distribution of particles to an author's individual style, in that they classify the material according to different periods, literary genres and the division between prose and verse, rather than by different types of text, such as narrative, exposition, argument, dialogue, and the situations to which these belong.

These observations are all the more relevant as the large majority of Greek texts written before the Hellenistic period constitute a μίμησις of speech and are meant to appeal to the ear rather than to the eye.[2] Oral

---

[1] KG I 344.2 / 1. In his footnote Gerth disclaims responsibility for the statement.

[2] The otherwise vital distinction between oral *production* and oral *presentation* rightly made by E.J. BAKKER, 1993, does not bear on the Greek prose discussed here.

communication makes special demands on the speaker in terms of enabling his audience to assign successive items of information to their proper
place within the larger unity they should contribute to. Moreover these
texts are generally directed to a definite audience in a particular situation,
which explains the comparatively high incidence of features whose use is
bound up with this communication even in texts which do not take the
form of monologue or dialogue.[1]

1.3. *Purpose and plan*

What follows are the results of an attempt to describe and explain, from
the position outlined above, for two speeches transmitted under the name
of Lysias—i.e. for texts destined for a single hearing at one juncture—the
articulation effected by devices marking the beginning of sentences. This
gives rise to a tentative definition of the value and function of the particles
discussed,[2] and to an assessment of the motives which presumably guided
the author in choosing them. To this end it has been registered for every
independent sentence in Lysias I and XII which particle marks its beginning, or in the absence of any such marker, whether we find a connecting
relative[3] or the situation known as asyndeton.[4] For the purpose of this
investigation all those sections of texts have been counted as independent
sentences which in the Oxford text edited by Hude extend from one colon
or question mark or full stop to the next. In a number of instances Hude's
punctuation could be questioned; however, a different decision in any of
these instances would not affect the material foundation of the following
arguments.

The exposition is primarily based on Lysias I. Recourse has been had
to Lysias XII insofar as it contains (1) particles not found in or (2) uses of
particles which could not, or not equally fully, be illustrated from Lysias
I. The order adopted for the individual articulating devices is to deal with
the most frequent (δέ, καί, γάρ, οὖν) first, except that relative connection
has been subjoined to the treatment of καί on the grounds of their shared
characteristic of enhancing continuity. The remainder fall into place as
one account leads organically to the other: first τοίνυν after οὖν on account of its relation with that particle as well as with δέ, then καίτοι and

---

[1] It is a telling fact that both the frequency and the diversity of particle use are seen to
decrease in Hellenistic prose: cf. BLOMQVIST p. 132 ff.

[2] To the extent that they cover the same ground the following pages may be taken to
supersede their author's previous statement on the subject (in *Lampas* 19 (1986) 125-41).

[3] See 18 ff. below.

[4] See 40 ff. and 78 below.

μέντοι as sharing a semantic component with τοίνυν; next to μέντοι comes ἀλλά, which has in common with it, and with none of the other particles treated, that its use involves restrictions with regard to the content of what precedes and what follows it. Finally a discussion of asyndeton is followed by a summing up.

Lysias' first speech in the Oxford edition by Hude is punctuated by a full stop, a colon or a question mark in 124 places. In addition four independent clauses, all introduced by γάρ, have been enclosed within round brackets, which brings the total number of sequences recognized by Hude as self-contained sentences to 128. The beginning of these sentences is marked as follows:

Lysias I	proem	narration	proof	epilogue	total
§	1-8	9-26	27-46	47-50	
(number of lines)	27	121	113	16	277
δέ	1	28	15	1	45
καί	1	13	4	–	18
relative	–	–	2	–	2
γάρ	3	13	10	3	29
οὖν	–	3	1	–	4
μὲν οὖν (...δέ)	1	2	–	–	3
μὲν οὖν	–	–	2	–	2
τοίνυν	1	3	–	–	4
καίτοι	–	–	3	–	3
ἀλλά	–	–	1	–	1
ἔπειτα	–	–	2	–	2
εἶτα	–	–	1	–	1
'asyndeton'	1	7	3	3	14
total	8	69	44	7	128
1:	3.4	1.8	2.6	2.3	2.16

For Lysias' twelfth speech the corresponding figures are:

Lysias XII	proem	narration	proof I	proof II	epilogue	total
§	1-4	5-21	22-40	41-80	81-100	
(n. of lines)	21	103	115	224	118	581
δέ	3	24	12	32	13	84
μηδέ	–	–	–	3	–	3
καί	–	7	4	10	5	26
relative	–	1	2	3	3	9
γάρ	1	6	15	17	7	46
οὖν	1	6	2	3	1	13
τοίνυν	–	–	1	5	1	7
καίτοι	–	–	1	4	2	7
καὶ μήν	–	–	1	–	–	1
μέντοι	1	–	1	–	2	4
ἀλλά	–	1	–	1	4	6
ἀλλὰ γάρ	–	–	1	1	1	3
ἔπειτα	–	–	1	–	–	1
εἶτα	–	–	2	–	–	2
ἔτι δέ	–	–	1	–	–	1
'asyndeton'[1]	1	4	[2]4	4	6	28
total	7	49	57	83	45	241
1:	3.0	2.1	2.0	2.7	2.6	2.41

2. δέ *and* καί

Denniston's characteristic way of understanding 'connexion' primarily as connexion between the contents of sentences leads to the assumption of a continuity and gradual transition between an 'adversative' δέ and a 'connective' καί. Thus in his discussion of δέ: 'As a connective, δέ denotes either pure connexion, 'and', or contrast, 'but', with all that lies between. (…) The former sense preponderates where no μέν precedes, and in such cases there is no essential difference between δέ and καί'.[3] And on καί:

---

[1] Including instances of ὥστε.

[2] Excluding nine changes of speaker in a series of questions and answers in XII.25.

[3] *GP* 162, where in a footnote Hartung's explanation in terms of 'duality' versus 'unity' is too easily discarded as being 'hardly of practical importance'.

'(…) its primary force is, beyond all reasonable doubt, addition. Like δέ, it is used both as a connective and as a responsive particle'.[1] A further corollary is that the 'neutral' particle δέ in certain contexts in which a well-defined relation between sentence contents appears to obtain, is supposed to stand for γάρ, οὖν, or ἤ[2]—just as καί may occur 'instead of ἤ'.[3]

A related view is held by Kühner-Gerth, who assign δέ to a middle ground between on the one hand *copulative* particles (such as καί and τε), and on the other hand *adversative* particles (such as ἀλλά), 'indem es sowohl kopulative als adversative Kraft in sich vereinigt und daher einen Gedanken einem anderen entweder entgegenstellt oder nur gegenüberstellt'. The use of δέ is taken to be that with this particle a new idea 'als ein von dem vorhergehenden verschiedener diesem gegenübergestellt wird'.[4] The use of καί is defined in a contrast with that of τε as follows: 'τε und καί bedeuten beide *und*, unterscheiden sich aber so, dass das erstere Zusammengehöriges verbindet und die verbundenen Gedanken und Begriffe als eine Einheit darstellt, das letztere hingegen die verbundenen Begriffe oder Gedanken als Verschiedenes bezeichnet'.

Neither of these approaches is capable of accounting for the distribution of the two particles—unless one is prepared to accept, in explanation of the greater frequency of δέ, appeals to 'stylistic' considerations, such as Denniston makes,[5] or even to such personal characteristics as an alleged naïvety or lack of logical sophistication in individual authors; or, at the other extreme, such generalisations as the claim that 'the Greeks have a predilection for contrasts'.

One of the few authors to have addressed this question of the distribution is C.J. RUIJGH.[6] In his opinion δέ is 'l'outil banal de la coordination des phrases indépendantes qui se succèdent à l'intérieur d'un récit', corresponding to what he calls 'asyndetic coordination' in languages like Latin and French.[7] It marks the 'transition à un fait nouveau', whereas items linked by καί *together* make up 'un seul membre de la série'.

It is here proposed that the difference between δέ and καί at the beginning of independent sentences as it is found in Lysias I and XII can be accounted for as a difference between (καί) *including*[8] a further item within the context of that which precedes, and (δέ) *opening* a new section of

---

[1] *GP* 289.
[2] *GP* 169.
[3] *GP* 292.
[4] KG 262.
[5] P. of ref. supra.
[6] Ruijgh 1971, § 127 ff.
[7] Ruijgh 1971, § 129.
[8] Cf. E.J. Bakker 1993.

the text. The use of δέ therefore results in a certain *discontinuity*, unlike
that of καί, which establishes a *connection* between what precedes and
what follows:[1] an instance of δέ placed after a constituent indicates the
beginning of a new section, an instance of καί placed before a constituent
is a mark of continuity.

2.1. δέ

To the use of δέ in Lysias I the following more detailed observations
apply:
  1.   Wherever a clause introduced by δέ is preceded by one introduced
by μέν, the entire structure is at the beginning marked as one complex:
e.g. by οὖν at 7 in ἐν μὲν οὖν τῷ πρώτῳ χρόνῳ ... ἐπειδὴ δέ μοι ἡ μήτηρ
ἐτελεύτησε ..., by δέ at 12 in ἡ δὲ τὸ μὲν πρῶτον οὐκ ἤθελεν ... ἐπειδὴ
δὲ ἐγὼ ὠργιζόμην ..., by γάρ at 38 in εἰ μὲν γὰρ ... μετελθεῖν ἐκέλευον
ἐκεῖνον ἠδίκουν ἄν· εἰ δέ (...). It may be suspected that it is above all
these contexts, in which δέ marks the beginning of a second member
previously announced by μέν, which have given rise to the attribution to
δέ of an 'adversative' force, since two such members can be said to balance each other and to that extent form counterparts. Still, the fact that
'but' is often appropriate at the corresponding place in an English sentence does not establish it as the *meaning* of δέ; a translation employing
an adversative 'connector', e.g. (12) 'She at first was unwilling, *but* when
I became angry ...', seems to add an element which is not expressed in
the Greek, and this makes it at best an *interpretation* by the translator.[2]
That the adversative relation is not given with μέν ... δέ by themselves
appears e.g. from 9, where πρῶτον μέν (οὖν) introduces background information consisting in the arrangement of Euphiletus' house, and ἐπειδὴ
δέ continues the narrative; and from 4 (ἡγοῦμαι δέ ...), where the only
contrast with the preceding sentence, introduced by (3) περὶ μὲν οὖν, is
that between what does not need proof (the culpability of the offence) and
what does (Eratosthenes' having committed it). The predominant use, then,
of μέν ... δέ (... δέ) appears to be that of marking two (or more) successive sections within a larger whole.
  2.   The discontinuity attending the use of δέ is confirmed by the observation that often sentences are marked by δέ which feature other char-

---

[1] It will be noted that reference to 'coordination', including a somewhat self-contradic-
tory 'asyndetic coordination', of 'members' is avoided.
[2] It is relevant to note that *some* marker is required if only to prevent a misunderstanding of the clause as a postponed subordinate clause such as those found in 40 (ἵνα...), and
47 (ἐάν...).

acteristics serving as 'boundaries' to structure a larger stretch of discourse:[1] out of 44 δέ-sentences in Lysias I there are fourteen beginning with a dependent clause (ἐπειδὴ δέ 8 x,[2] εἰ δὲ (μή) 4 x,[3] ἐὰν δέ and ἵνα δέ one each) and six beginning with a participle (predicative in nominative 4x,[4] absolute genitive twice[5]), and such phrases as καὶ πρότερον δέ 12, μετὰ δὲ ταῦτα 15, πρῶτον δέ 22, and ὅμως δέ in 14 likewise serve a purpose of structuring. In a further ten instances we have a topic switch (e.g. ἡ δέ in 12, αὕτη δέ 15, ἐγὼ δέ 26, 29), and in five an imperative (ἀνάγνωθι 30 & 31, σκέψασθε 37, 39, & 43) likewise marking a shift to new information. There remain five instances of δέ with a finite verb at the beginning of a sentence.[6]

3.   As a means towards articulation of the structure *within* a sentence δέ has been used more sparingly.[7] The typical situation is that of two topics in one connection distinguished by μέν and δέ.[8]

4.   The structure of the rhetorical question at I.27 is worth noting. Beginning with πῶς γὰρ ἄν (sc. κατέφυγεν), it is expanded by a relative clause ὅστις ... κατέπεσεν εὐθύς which is in turn continued by περιέστρε-ψα δ' αὐτοῦ τὼ χεῖρε, ἔνδον δὲ ἦσαν &c., i.e. by a series of clauses not formally included within the scope of ὅστις. Here the choice of αὐτοῦ as opposed to a demonstrative pronoun such as ἐκείνου shows that the question should not be taken to end with a question mark, i.e. the syntactic equivalent of a full stop, after εὐθύς; it follows that we here have one instance of δέ marking a clause continuing a sentence without a preceding μέν.[9]

---

[1]   For the use in discourse organization of subordinate clauses and participles marked by δέ see Bakker 1993.

[2]   I.6, 7, 9, 12, 14, 19, 21, 23.

[3]   I.21, 36, 38, 48.

[4]   I.18, 22, 24 (*bis*).

[5]   I. 11, 14.

[6]   I.18 ψεύσῃ δέ; 4 ἡγοῦμαι δέ and 21 ἀξιῶ δέ; 14 ἔδοξε δέ μοι; and 16 ἐστι δέ.

[7]   This raises questions of punctuation which, however, do not affect the account given here. At 18 after ἐλθὼν δὲ οἴκαδε ἐκέλευον ἀκολουθεῖν μοι τὴν θεράπαιναν εἰς τὴν ἀγοράν and before ἀγαγὼν δ' αὐτὴν κτλ it would be possible to replace the comma printed by Hude and Thalheim with a full stop.

[8]   Thus I.9 ἐγὼ μέν ... αἱ δὲ γυναῖκες, 23 & 33 τοὺς μέν ... τοὺς δέ, 24 οἱ μὲν πρῶτοι ... οἱ δ' ὕστερον, 36 τοὺς μὲν νόμους ... τὸν δὲ ψῆφον, 48 τοὺς μὲν κειμένους ... ὑτέρους δέ and τοὺς μὲν φυλάττοντας ... τοῖς δὲ βουλομένοις. Cf., without a change of topic, I.17 ἐνθυμούμενος μέν ... ἀναμιμνησκόμενος δέ, and with balancing clauses rather than phra-ses 42 ἵν' ὡς ἀσφαλέστατα μὲν αὐτὸς εἰσῆα ... ὡς μετὰ πλείστων δὲ μαρτύρων τὴν τιμωρίαν ἐποιούμην. Without any balancing μέν-phrase 38 (εἰ μὲν γὰρ) λόγων εἰρημένων ἔργου δὲ μηδενὸς γεγενημένου (μετελθεῖν ἐκέλευον ἐκεῖνον ἠδίκουν ἄν, εἰ δὲ ἤδη πάν-των διαπεπραγμένων κτλ.).

[9]   Just as an instance of δέ marking a phrase continuing a compound absolute genitive without a preceding μέν was found at I.38, quoted in n. 8 above.

2.2. καί *and* καί μήν

A comparison of the distribution of δέ with that of καί shows that καί is regularly employed, as δέ is not, to include several predicates within a context sharing the same subject, or at least topic: thus at 3 in ἅπαντας ὑμᾶς νομίζω ... ἔχειν καὶ οὐδένα οὕτως ... διακεῖσθαι, 4 ὡς ἐμοίχευεν ... καὶ (ἐκείνην τε διέφθειρε καὶ τοὺς παῖδας τοὺς ἐμοὺς ᾔσχυνε καὶ ἐμὲ αὐτὸν ὕβρισεν ...) καὶ (οὔτε ... οὔτε ... οὔτε ...), 19 (κἀκείνη τὸ μὲν πρῶτον) ἔξαρνος ἦν καὶ ποιεῖν ἐκέλευεν ὅ τι βούλομαι, and 36 ἐὰν ... λέγωσι καὶ ... φάσκωσι. This may be taken to confirm the hypothesis of the two particles effecting *continuity* and *discontinuity* respectively.

2.2.1. With καί it helps to distinguish its contribution to narrative contexts from that to exposition or argument. Thus in 2 καί introduces the *expansion* and *amplification* of the thesis with which the preceding sentence ended: '(1) ... you will all consider the punishment for such a grave crime to be light, (2) and (καί) this (ταῦτα) is the prevalent assessment not just here but in the whole of Greece'. The whole complex, after an explanation marked by γάρ, is concluded by οὕτως ... ἡγοῦνται, and the parallel construction of the two sections on either side of καί by means of οὐκ ἂν εἴη ... ἀλλά stresses the cohesion. A similar context is 31 (30 τούτου μὴ καταγιγνώσκειν φόνον ὃς ...) καὶ οὕτω σφόδρα ὁ νομοθέτης ἐπὶ ταῖς γαμεταῖς γυναιξὶ δίκαια ταῦτα ἡγήσατο εἶναι ὥστε καὶ ἐπὶ ταῖς παλλακαῖς κτλ., where δέ would be equally inappropriate: we have an extension strengthening by means of an implicit argument *a fortiori* the previous claim, rather than the introduction of a fresh point.

Besides expansion and amplification καί frequently introduces an *alternative description* or expression with the same reference as that which precedes. Thus in 29 τὸν δὲ τῆς πόλεως νόμον ἠξίουν εἶναι κυριώτερον καὶ ταύτην ἔλαβον τὴν δίκην ἣν κτλ. the second clause represents the speaker's actions as the practical consequence of his acknowledgement of the superior authority of the law: '... and *so* ...', '... which *means* that ...' are ways of expressing what καί in these contexts leaves to be understood.

2.2.2. In I.10 three instances of καί, besides that in καὶ μὴ βοᾷ, are found in a passage beginning with ἵνα δὲ μή which[1] supplies background information to the continuation of the story in (11) προϊόντος δὲ τοῦ χρόνου κτλ. The use of καί to accumulate the constituents of this background may be said to cement the internal cohesion of the passage.

---

[1] Two of them are preceded by a full stop and one (the last) by a comma in Hude's edition.

2.2.3. καὶ μήν

In Lysias XII.27 one instance is found of the collocation καὶ μήν, whose function on the strength of its constituent parts[1] should be to include in a given connection a point which the speaker wishes to uphold at any cost and regardless of the feelings of his audience. Here it is followed by οὐδὲ (τοῦτο). This alone would have sufficed to fit the point in, but by including it within the scope of the previous one the speaker is able to increase the coherence of his argument: Eratosthenes' claim to have *objected* to *orders* is unconvincing not only as to the objecting itself, but even more incontestably (μήν) because on the assumption of his having objected (εἴπερ ἀληθῆ λέγει φάσκων ἀντειπεῖν) it becomes all the more improbable that he was given the order in the first place.

2.3 δέ *and* καί *compared*

In the use of δέ and καί at 12-4 a more complex motivation is carried to a subtle effect. This part of the narration is presented in eight periods, four of which are introduced by δέ and three by καί, and the last one is 'asyndetic'. Those beginning with καί all three detail the speaker's response to events on which he subsequently learnt to put a different construction from the way he understood them at the time. This misguided response in fact, as it turns out, enabled his wife, her lover and their maid to carry on with their plot: '(11) After dinner our child began to cry: it was hurt by the maid on purpose just to do that. (12) καί I told her to go and feed it. She δέ at first refused. When δέ I became angry she began to tease me. (13) καί I laughed. She δέ got up and went, and locked the door [2] in jest. καί I went to sleep. (14) When δέ day approached she came back, unlocking the door.[3] As δέ I asked about the sound of the door I had heard in the night, she claimed the light had gone out and she had gone to our neighbours' to light a torch. I (ø) did not reply, believing her.' The paraphrase is meant to bring out that the choice of καί here serves to characterize the speaker's response as the consistent and natural behaviour of a man who, himself *bona fide,* is unaware that he is only a pawn in a game played by others, the successive stages of which are marked by δέ.

In 19 καί introduces both of the contrary responses of the maid to her interrogation by the speaker, characterising them not as successive steps on *her* part but as wholly determined by *his* successive ploys, the latter of

---

[1] For μήν see *Appendix* p. 54 below.

[2] The instance of καί which connects the verbs sharing the same subject προστίθησι and ἐφέλκεται is on a different level of organization from those here compared.

[3] The καί between ἧκεν and ἀνέῳξεν likewise is not on a par with the others.

which is introduced by δέ: (18) ἔφην … (19) κἀκείνη τὸ μὲν πρῶτον …
ἐπειδὴ δὲ ἐγὼ … ἐξεπλάγη … καὶ τότε ἤδη …[1]
The dramatic conclusion to the narrative is given in I.23-6.[2] The structure of this section may be represented schematically as follows:[3]

ὁ δ᾽ Ἐρατοσθένης, ὦ ἄνδρες, εἰσέρχεται,
    καὶ ἡ θεράπαινα
        ἐπεγείρασά με
        εὐθὺς φράζει ὅτι ἔνδον ἐστί.
    κἀγὼ
        εἰπὼν ἐκείνῃ ἐπιμελεῖσθαι τῆς θύρας,
        καταβὰς σιωπῇ
        ἐξέρχομαι,
    καὶ ἀφικνοῦμαι ὡς τὸν καὶ τόν,
    καὶ
        τοὺς μὲν ⟨οὐκ⟩ ἔνδον κατέλαβον,
        τοὺς δὲ οὐδ᾽ ἐπιδημοῦντας ηὗρον. (24:)
παραλαβὼν δ᾽ ὡς οἷόν τε ἦν πλείστους ἐκ τῶν παρόντων ἐβάδιζον.
    καὶ
        δᾷδας λαβόντες ἐκ τοῦ ἐγγύτατα καπηλείου
        εἰσερχόμεθα (ἀνεῳγμένης τῆς θύρας καὶ ὑπὸ τῆς ἀνθρώπου
                                   παρεσκευασμένης).
ὤσαντες δὲ τὴν θύραν τοῦ δωματίου
    οἱ μὲν πρῶτοι εἰσιόντες ἔτι εἴδομεν αὐτὸν κατακείμενον παρ τῇ
                                          γυναικί,
    οἱ δ᾽ ὕστερον ἐν τῇ κλίνῃ γυμνὸν ἑστηκότα. (25:)
ἐγὼ δ᾽, ὦ ἄνδρες,
        πατάξας
    καταβάλλω αὐτόν
    καὶ
        τὼ χεῖρε περιαγαγὼν ἐς τοὔπισθεν
        καὶ δήσας
    ἠρώτων διὰ τί ὑβρίζει εἰς τὴν οἰκίαν τὴν ἐμὴν εἰσιών
    καὶ ἐκεῖνος
        ἀδικεῖν μὲν ὡμολόγει
        ἠντεβόλει δὲ
        καὶ ἱκέτευε μὴ ἀποκτεῖναι ἀλλ᾽ ἀργύριον πράξασθαι
ἐγὼ δὲ (…).

---

[1] The full stop printed by Hude and Thalheim before the latter instance of καί somewhat obscures this connection.
[2] An instance of καί at 22 is hard to assess owing to the lacuna which follows.
[3] By courtesy of E.J. Bakker.

Here the distribution of δέ and καί serves to differentiate between five principal steps separated by δέ, and the subdivisions of each of these connected by καί: (I) Eratosthenes arrives, *exit* Euphiletus; (II) return of Euphiletus and company; (III) Eratosthenes caught in the act; (IV) first and last confrontation and verbal exchange between the two men; (V) summary execution. Each of these stages is relevant to the charge laid against the speaker: (i) it was Eratosthenes who trespassed on Euphiletus' house and home, not Euphiletus who was the aggressor; (ii) Euphiletus has taken care to provide for eye-witnesses;[1] (iii) Eratosthenes was caught *flagranti crimine*; (iv) he pleaded guilty and implicitly admitted that Euphiletus was justified in killing him for his offence; and (v) Euphiletus effectively made himself the instrument of the law.

3. εἶτα, ἔπειτα *and* ἔτι δέ

The set of particles discussed by Denniston does not include εἶτα and ἔπειτα. Yet in Lysias I.40-1 these two words serve to articulate a sequence, opening with καίτοι πρῶτον, of three rhetorical questions which convey as many εἰκός arguments refuting the claim that Eratosthenes did not come to Euphiletus' house of his own accord but was trapped: if this were, it is retorted, Euphiletus would not have (1) invited a guest for that evening, nor have (2) allowed his guest once he was there[2] to leave but have asked for his assistance, nor would he have (3) left it to the last minute to provide himself with helpers and witnesses. The three probabilities are mentioned in the order in which the supposed different options come to bear on the course of events rather than in that in which they would *ex hypothesi* have suggested themselves to Euphiletus, and their force as proof is cumulative: they supplement each other in that the second and third of them each presuppose that the preceding one had not been realised, i.e. that the situation had developed as it has in fact, rather than as the incriminating hypothesis would make it likely to have developed. In 46 too ἔπειτα subjoins an independent rhetorical question: 'what other motive for exposing myself to such a risk? ἔπειτα (assuming such ἀσέβεια on my part) would I have invited witnesses to my own outrageous action?'.

In Lysias XII εἶτα and ἔπειτα likewise introduce rhetorical questions. Two of these in 26 form a taunting continuation of the questioning of

---

[1] The point is exploited at 46.

[2] With δέ the hearer might have failed to grasp that he should imagine a new situation, differing from that evoked by the previous supposition; in other words using εἶτα saves an explicit '(his guest)—*once he was there*—'.

Eratosthenes in 25, which is designed to reveal the inconsistencies—i.e.
the lack of εἰκός—in the other's replies: 'And then, if that is so (εἶτα),
you protested in order to save, but arrested in order to kill him? And in
addition (καί) you protested when it was not in your power to save, but
arrested when it was? And then, if that is so (εἶτα), you lay claim to praise
for your ineffectual protest but disclaim punishment for your effective
misdoings?' The order of the questions is such that anyone who swallows
the first thereby places himself before the obstacle of the next one as a
consequence of it; it also happens to be that of the actual course of events.
In 27 ἔπειτα introduces another εἰκός-argument phrased as a rhetorical
question, this time supplementing a comparable argument in the form of a
(negative) assertion.

3.1. The one instance of ἔτι δέ in our sample at XII.28 marks the beginning of another argument which is in a special sense an εἰκός-argument,
again a subsidiary one, and now adopting the jury's point of view: 'this
line of defence would be acceptable from any other Athenian citizen, but
what εἰκός is there in your accepting it from among the Thirty themselves?'.

3.2. Judging from our sample εἶτα, ἔπειτα, and ἔτι δέ characteristically
introduce *subsidiary* arguments in a train of argumentation from εἰκός.
This use could not be served by δέ, since the speaker does not so much
proceed from one point to the next as offer an *alternative* for the previous
point; nor by ἀλλά, which would *replace* the preceding point by the following one,[1] nor by ἤ, which would invite the hearer to *choose* between
the two. One factor in determining the choice of εἶτα and ἔπειτα seems to
be the speaker's adopting the chronological order of the events recounted,
whereas our one instance of ἔτι δέ in addition marks a change of viewpoint, from defendant to jury, i.e. from speaker to hearer.

4. *'Relative connection'*

By what is called 'relative connection' a strong cohesion between the
preceding and the following section is achieved. A comparatively simple
case is XII.13: 'there we found Theognis guarding other men': ᾧ παρα-
δόντες ἐμὲ πάλιν ᾤχοντο. The relative here serves to incorporate Θέογνιν
ἑτέρους φυλάττοντα, i.e. the antecedent together with what was predicated of it, into the new statement. A more complicated situation is found
in I.36 (35 οὗτοι – sc. οἱ νόμοι – τοίνυν περὶ τῶν τοιούτων τοῖς ἀδικου-

---

[1] See p. 35-6 and 49-50 below.

μένοις τοιαύτην δίκην λαμβάνειν παρακελεύονται.) οἷς ὑμᾶς ἀξιῶ τὴν αὐτὴν γνώμην ἔχειν. The relative here does not refer back to the nearest constituent which would be grammatically capable of serving as its antecedent,[1] nor even to the nearest but one, but to the subject and topic of the preceding clause, with all that was stated about it: 'it is with *these* laws that I expect you to agree'. And in I.33 the neuter relative (ἀνθ'[2]) ὧν refers back not to one particular grammatical antecedent but to the complex of considerations just specified in explanation of the severe punishment for fornication: 'to compensate for all *this* the legislator has prescribed the death penalty for these men'.[3]

4.1. According to Kühner-Gerth, the relative pronoun 'does not only serve to connect a subordinate clause to a main clause, but also to subjoin sentences which *should properly have been* expressed in the form of a paratactic main clause. The relative in these cases *deputizes for* a personal or a demonstrative pronoun accompanied by a connective such as καί, ἀλλά or δέ, γάρ, οὖν, ἄρα'.[4] A description such as this shows how the phenomenon of relative connection eludes the categories of traditional grammar, a situation which leaves the motives of Greek speakers for adopting constructions of this type in the dark. The decisive considerations seem to be two:

1. certain clauses introduced by a relative pronoun do not serve to define or describe the antecedent,[5] but to connect with it a new comment of independent interest. The information contained in this may be *either* (a) previously known to the hearer, as at XII.65, to be quoted presently, *or* (b) new,[6] as at XII.13, and at Pl. *Meno* 89 E 9-10 in εἰς καλὸν ἡμῖν Ἄνυτος ὅδε παρεκαθέζετο· ᾧ μεταδῶμεν τῆς ζητήσεως[7] and

2. the choice of a relative pronoun rather than an anaphoric demonstrative pronoun attended by a connecting particle appears to be moti-

---

[1] This incidentally makes it impossible to replace the full stop by a comma, as one might feel inclined to do at XII.13.

[2] The preposition, which calls for a neuter, rules out the immediately preceding τῶν μοιχῶν as a possible antecedent.

[3] Compare XII.94 and 96 ἀνθ' ὧν: 'and in reprisal for all this', as well as 43 ὧν: 'it is to this company that Eratosthenes and Critias belonged', and 56 ᾧ καί ...: 'and by doing so they also demonstrated...'.

[4] 'Das Relativpronomen dient nicht allein zur Verbindung eines Nebensatzes mit einem Hauptsatze, sondern auch zur Anknüpfung solcher Sätze, welche *eigentlich* als beigeordnete Hauptsätze *hätten* ausgedruckt *werden sollen*. Das Relativum vertritt dann die Stelle eines Demonstrativ- oder Personalpronomens in Verbindung mit einem Bindeworte, wie καί, ἀλλά od. δέ, γάρ, οὖν, ἄρα...'—KG II.434, italics CMJS.

[5] In the way that e.g. Xen. *An.* I.3.15 τῷ ἀνδρὶ ὃν ἂν ἕλησθε πείσομαι does.

[6] H. Kurzova (1981) 47 takes account of the first but not of the second possibility.

[7] Any decision whether to punctuate a comma, a colon or a period seems arbitrary.

vated by a desire to include what has been stated of the referent in the new clause without any rupture or discontinuity. The new clause does not so much offer new, *additional* information, or an extension or *expansion* of that contained in the previous one, as information that is *inseparable* from that which we had. The complementary halves are linked by the relative, which brings out to the full that what has been said and what is about to be said have reference to the same object. The speaker leaves it to the imagination of his audience to conceive of the reason for this emphasis on the ascription of two predicates to one subject. An example in which this is highly effective is XII.65 ὥσπερ πολλῶν ἀγαθῶν αἰτίου ἀλλ' οὐ μεγάλων κακῶν γεγενημένου. ὃς πρῶτον μὲν τῆς προτέρας ὀλιγαρχίας αἰτιώτατος ἐγένετο (...). To paraphrase: 'as though he ... (*They are speaking of the very man* who...').

5. γάρ

Anyone who marks the beginning of a section of his text with γάρ is subordinating the stretch which comes within the scope of the particle to a (preceding or following) item in his narrative or argument. In an extreme case we have a parenthesis, i.e. a syntactic continuum is interrupted by the clause containing γάρ. In Lysias I this happens three times.[1] The common factor of nearly all γάρ-clauses as to content is that they supply information in answer to a question which might be raised in the minds of the audience by what has just preceded or is about to follow.

5.1.   In I.6 γάρ marks the beginning of the narration, announced by the speaker in 5, which is only concluded with οὕτως in 27, and so in its entirety falls within the scope of the particle: by means of the information which he presents in the form of a narrative the speaker acquits himself of a promise made in 5. In 37, 39 and 44 the sentence containing γάρ follows upon a request addressed to the jury to consider certain points more closely (37, 39 & 43 σκέψασθε δέ). In 39 the speaker has just concluded the section of his plea devoted to the interpretation of the relevant laws, after which the words σκέψασθε δέ mark the beginning of a new section. The γάρ-sentence identifies the first point which he wishes to draw attention to: the accusation that he has deliberately had his victim lured to the scene of the assault. His first defence is that, even if this had been the case, it would not have detracted from the justness of his action. The second is that it is in fact not the case: σκέψασθε that here again their claim is false. Having affirmed that the jury will easily perceive this, the speaker presents

---
[1] In I.9, 41 & 42.

in a clause containing γάρ the facts, which have been stated before, required for understanding his argument. In both instances, then, the γάρ-clause supplies information which should enable the audience to follow what is coming.

In 43 σκέψασθε δέ, as in 39, introduces a new stage in the argument, now in the form of an oblique question: whether the speaker was prompted by some other motive to kill his adversary? The first clause containing γάρ makes explicit the presupposition underlying the preceding question: οὐδεμίαν γὰρ εὑρήσετε '(I may confidently dare you to scrutinize me:) you are not going to find any'. A sentence introduced by another γάρ offers the argument which we have been led to expect, in the form of a check-list of possible motives with a series of no's.

5.1.1 In I.9 the parenthetic sentence containing γάρ anticipates the question of the relevance of the information about the arrangement of the speaker's house to the story: the audience might wonder what this was leading to, which is what the speaker wishes to prevent. Elsewhere information required for a correct understanding of what is being said is supplied afterwards: in 8 the speaker explains in what sense it is that he calls his mother's death the origin of all his misfortunes: it was at her funeral (γάρ) that his wife was first noticed by Eratosthenes, and from there he led her astray. The speaker then anticipates the obvious query 'in what way (sc. do you mean that, or did he do so)?' by specifying (γάρ) that Eratosthenes found himself an opportunity to seduce his wife by watching and approaching her maid. And in 11 the words ὕστερον γὰρ ἅπαντα ἐπυθόμην furnish a reply to the question 'how do you know?' which might rise in the minds of the audience. Two comparable instances are, in 41, οὐ γὰρ ἤδη, reminding the hearer of the circumstances explaining why the speaker was trying to call on neighbours who, as it turns out, are not in town, and in 42 τί γὰρ ἤδη εἴ τι κἀκεῖνος εἶχε σιδήριον; explaining why it would in fact have been safer to have provided for assistance beforehand: he could not tell whether his rival was armed.

5.2. Within the use of γάρ two categories are distinguished by Denniston. Such cases as were discussed in the last section he calls 'explanatory';[1] the large majority of uses, however, he brings under the heading of 'confirmatory or causal, giving the ground for belief, or the motive for action'.[2] He points out that this usage of γάρ is 'commoner in writers whose mode of thought is simple than in those whose logical faculties are more

[1] P. 58 ss.
[2] P. 58.

fully developed. The former tend to state a fact before investigating its reason, while the latter more frequently follow the logical order, cause and effect (...)'.[1] He refers[2] to observations on 'the commonness of γάρ in Homer and Herodotus, and (...) the comparative rarity in Herodotus of the syntactical conjunctions, ἐπεί, ἐπειδή, ὅτι, ὡς', implicitly suggesting a connection.[3]

This seems hardly the most promising frame of reference towards an account of the use of γάρ, as may be seen from an example in which the two forms of expression implicitly compared by Denniston appear in one context in Thuc. VII.34.7 ... οἵ Κορίνθιοι εὐθὺς τροπαῖον ἔστησαν ὡς νικῶντες, ὅτι πλείους τῶν ἐναντίων ναῦς ἄπλους ἐποίησαν καὶ νομίσαντες αὐτοὶ οὐχ ἡσσᾶσθαι δι' ὅπερ οὐδ' οἱ ἕτεροι νικᾶν· οἵ τε γὰρ Κορίνθιοι ἡγήσαντο κρατεῖν εἰ μὴ καὶ πολὺ ἐκρατοῦντο, οἵ τ' Ἀθηναῖοι ἐνόμιζον ἡσσᾶσθαι ὅτι οὐ πολὺ ἐνίκων.

Here the clauses introduced by ὅτι and by δι' ὅπερ contain the *justification* of a claim on the part of the subject: 'they conducted themselves as victors, regarding themselves as such *because*"&c.; 'they did not consider themselves defeated *for the same reason that* their adversaries did not claim a victory'; these adversaries, on the other hand, 'considered themselves defeated *because* they could not boast a clear victory'. By contrast the sentence introduced by γάρ offers an *explanation*: 'the notions of victory and defeat underlying the response of each party were ... respectively'. In the case of the causal clauses[4] to dispute these in themselves ('It was the other party that put most ships out of action') or to dispute the causal connection ('It takes more to be proclaimed victorious') would effectively be to dispute the claim they are meant to justify; with the γάρ-sentence disputing either its truth or its relevance would imply that the attempt at explanation had failed but would not thereby impugn the statement which was to be explained.

---

[1] P. 58. The frequent occurrence of clauses introduced by ἐπεί &c. allowing a causal interpretation *following* the main clause is ignored.

[2] P. 58.

[3] Such a connection is in any case not confirmed by the observation that γάρ is quite common in Thucydides, who presumably is to count among the writers 'whose logical faculties are more fully developed'.

[4] This is not the place to deal with the subject of the causal clause in Greek as a whole, which involves (1) differences between on the one hand cognitive discourse, in which causal explanation is itself the central concern (e.g. Pl. *Prot.* 326 E 6-7 διὰ τί οὖν τῶν ἀγαθῶν πατέρων πολλοὶ ὑεῖς φαῦλοι γίγνονται;), and on the other hand contexts in which explanation and argument serve ulterior purposes, and includes (2) distinctions between ὅτι, ὡς, ἐπεί, διότι, &c. as well as, with regard to ὡς, (3) the demarcation between what are to count as 'causal' and what as 'final' clauses—questions broached but hardly exhausted by Rijksbaron 1976 and well deserving further study. For a difference between ἐπεί and ὡς in narrative contexts see Bakker, 'Whose point of view?'.

This use of γάρ can be exemplified from Lysias I. The speech opens with (I.1) 'I would wish you to judge in my case as you would judge if you yourselves were in my position. εὖ γὰρ οἶδ' ὅτι every punishment would seem light to you.' The sentence beginning with γάρ does not serve in some way to justify the speaker's wish from his own point of view, but to make his audience understand why it is his wish. At I.5 the speaker states his intention of 'telling you from the beginning all that has happened to me'. ταύτην γὰρ ἐμαυτῷ μόνην ἡγοῦμαι σωτηρίαν, 'you can see why: I consider this as my only chance'.[1] At I.11 he has understood that the maid was making his child cry on purpose: ὁ γὰρ ἄνθρωπος ἔνδον ἦν, 'you can see why: that man was in the house'. In I.16 he is told that his rival 'has corrupted many wives in addition to yours': ταύτην γὰρ [τὴν] τέχνην ἔχει, 'you see, it's his specialty'. The speaker as an honest man would not, or so he makes the woman imply, understand and believe her statement if it had not been explained to him that there are people who make a regular practice of such conduct. At I.44 it is the audience which is supposed to need a similar explanation from the speaker: 'I have not acted in hopes of (lucre &c.)': ἔνιοι γὰρ τοιούτων πραγμάτων ἔνεκα θάνατον ἀλλήλοις ἐπιβουλεύουσι, 'for you must realise there are people who do make designs on each other's lives from such motives'. Finally, at I.21 he demands that his rival should be taken red-handed; ἐγὼ γὰρ οὐδὲν δέομαι λόγων ἀλλὰ κτλ.: 'Let there be no mistake about the point of my demand: I have no use for talk, it's the plain fact that I want brought out into the open'.

5.3. So far, we have been trying to show that the received distinction in the description of γάρ between 'explanatory' and 'causal' (Denniston[2]), or between 'adverbial' and 'kausal' or 'begründend' (Kühner-Gerth[3]) cannot do justice to the facts. The purpose of sentences introduced by γάρ is primarily explanatory: they provide answers to all sorts of questions raised by the speaker's utterances, e.g. 'how will he make good his promise', 'why is he saying what he is saying', or 'what makes a man do what x is

---

[1] For the need to explain the insertion of a full διήγησις at this point see below p. 29 on τοίνυν.

[2] P. 58. Cf. LSJ s.v. I.b. 'in simple explanations' as distinct from (a.) 'introducing the reason or cause of what precedes' (and 'c. to introduce a detailed description...' &c.).

[3] Vol. II p. 331 ('Adverbiale Geltung hat γάρ ferner, wenn es in der Weise des deutschen *nämlich* eine Erläuterung oder Erklärung einleitet') & 335 ('dient γάρ als entschieden kausale Konjunktion dazu, den vorausgehenden (zuweilen auch nur gedachten) Satz zu begründen'). Cf. Schwyzer-Debrunner, who (p. 560) accommodate *within* the 'überwiegend kausalen Bedeutung' a subordinate distinction between '(nur) erklärend' and 'begründend', apparently as a difference of degree or a (privative) binary opposition rather than a(n equipollent) dichotomy.

said to have done', &c. In translating γάρ one should in general avoid a suggestion that the speaker is trying to substantiate a claim by rational argument; it should rather appear that the explanation brings out the truth and inherent persuasiveness of the other statement.[1]

5.4.   Even when a γάρ-clause does in fact provide the grounds for a claim, as it occasionally does, it should still not simply be equated with a 'causal' clause. A case in point is Lysias XII.27: 'It is not εἰκός to grant my opponent's plea that he was carrying out orders; οὐ γὰρ δήπου ἐν τοῖς μετοί-κοις πίστιν παρ' αὐτοῦ ἐλάμβανον.' If we were to rewrite this in the form of a causal clause as 'because they did not put his loyalty to the test in the matter of the metics', the rhetorical effect of Lysias' presentation of the 'argument' gets lost in the process: γάρ supplies the self-evidently adequate answer to the question 'why indeed is it unreasonable to believe him?' which might arise among the audience, whereas a causal clause by explicitly offering an argument would draw attention to the *onus probandi* resting upon the speaker and so might sooner provoke contradiction. The explanation of Lysias' wording is not that his 'mode of thought is simple'; it is that this is the most effective wording rhetorically.[2]

5.5.   Those who consider that γάρ by itself introduces a reason or cause are regularly faced with the need to supply (in thought) from the context the statement which is supposed to call for such causal explanation. According to Kühner-Gerth 'γάρ most often as a decidedly causal conjunction serves to give the grounds for the preceding, at times merely notional, sentence'.[3] Their example is Pl. *Euth.* 2 B: τί φής; γραφὴν σέ τις, ὡς ἔοικε, γέγραπται ; οὐ γὰρ ἐκεῖνό γε καταγνώσομαι, ὡς σὺ ἕτερον, which they paraphrase by '(so I have to assume,) since I cannot suspect you &c.'[4] It seems preferable, however, to understand γάρ as anticipating a suppositious question 'why do you think so?' or '… ask that?' by making explicit a presupposition of the previous sentence which might suggest this question. 'I put my question in this way as (1) I cannot assume that it is the other way round, and (2) there is no alternative'. Lysias I.44

---

[1] It is relevant to note that sections with γάρ may not only serve to explain the content of *what* the speaker is saying, but also to explain the fact *that* he is saying it, as it were answering his own question 'why I do say this'.

[2] It is relevant to note that the claim is an (οὐκ) εἰκός (αὐτῷ πιστεύειν), rather than e.g. οὐ πιστεύω, μὴ πιστεύετε, or οὐκ ἀληθές. The audience is required to appreciate that the possibility of their πίστιν παρ' αὐτοῦ λαμβάνειν is on the face of it incompatible with the condition ἐν τοῖς μετοίκοις, therefore the conjunction of the two has not occurred.

[3] KG II.335.

[4] Ib. '(ich muss dies annehmen) denn das kann ich dir doch nicht zutrauen u.s.w.'

quoted above[1] is comparable: here too the speaker answers questions regarding the previous sentence, and its relevance to his proof in particular, by making explicit what he began by leaving implied. To arrive at an adequate interpretation it is more helpful to make explicit which *question* the γάρ-sentence is supposed to answer, than to assume an ellipse and supply a 'suppressed' or 'missing' *statement*.

6. οὖν

Lysias I contains four instances of simple οὖν. In I.16 προσελθοῦσα οὖν μοι ἐγγὺς ἡ ἄνθρωπος resumes a statement made in 15 in προσέρχεταί μοί τις πρεσβῦτις ἄνθρωπος.[2] Again in 16 with ἐὰν οὖν λάβῃς τὴν θεράπαιναν ... ἅπαντα πεύσει ('Just ask your maid, she can tell') the speaker proceeds from her opening remark ('Don't think I'm meddlesome—we have a common enemy') towards what she has to say to Euphiletus. In 18 after a summary in ἔλεγον ὅτι ἐγὼ πάντα εἴην πεπυσμένος τὰ γιγνόμενα ἐν τῇ οἰκίᾳ he comes to the point in direct speech accompanied by οὖν in σοὶ οὖν ... ἔξεστι δυοῖν ὁπότερον βούλει ἑλέσθαι ἢ (...) ἢ (...). Together with the preceding summary this sentence could be said to make up one 'act' as this term is used in pragmatics. And in 45 the sentence (τί ἂν οὖν βουλόμενος ἐγὼ κτλ.) marked by οὖν is as a QED to the section beginning in 43, the *demonstrandum* being that the speaker has not been led by any other motive besides the ἀδίκημα suffered (43 σκέψασθε δέ... ζητοῦντες εἴ τις ἐμοὶ καὶ Ἐρατοσθένει ἔχθρα πώποτε γεγένηται πλὴν ταύτης· οὐδεμίαν γὰρ εὑρήσετε): as in the first of the two instances in I.16 we return to the main line of thought.

In all four instances, then, there is a difference in what may be called 'status' between the section marked by οὖν and that which precedes it, with the speaker proceeding or returning from an introduction[3] or an excursion or explanation[4] to his principal message. A characteristic situation is that of a sentence with οὖν following one with γάρ, where the speaker returns from a subsidiary explanation to the main line of his story or argument, e.g. in XII.7 'they had no difficulty in persuading their audience (sc. to ransack the metics), *for* killing meant nothing to them but making money meant a lot to them; *so* they decided to arrest ten of them'. This use has contributed to the notion that οὖν at this stage in the develop-

---

[1] P. 23.
[2] The intervening sentence αὕτη δέ κτλ. is marked by δέ. Here αὕτη refers anaphorically (via the predicative adjunct ὑπὸ γυναικὸς ὑποπεμφθεῖσα) to the mistress of the πρεσβῦτις, whose role is defined in this sentence; with αὕτη δέ she is marked as its *topic*.
[3] Cf. XII.14.
[4] Cf. XII.36, 64, and 88.

ment of the language can be credited with an 'inferential' force.[1] In fact the train of thought is not 'killing meant nothing to them, and *therefore* they...'; the sentence containing γάρ has been inserted so as to explain the qualification οὐ χαλεπῶς in the previous sentence, and with ἔδοξεν οὖν αὐτοῖς the speaker returns to his story and rounds off one stage in it.[2]

In XII.9 two instances of οὖν are found in succession. We have (in 8-9) five sentences with alternating subjects, 'I asked Peison (μέν) ..., he (δέ) replied ...; I (οὖν) told him ..., he (δέ) agreed to ..., I (οὖν) knew ... (μέν), yet it seemed to me (δέ) ...'. The story is presented from the perspective of the speaker: the use of οὖν twice serves to maintain this perspective.

6.1.   Lysias I contains three instances of οὖν marking the beginning of a complex of two sentences articulated by μέν and δέ. In his opening paragraph the speaker has stated his conviction that the jury will consider the customary punishment inadequate to the crime of his opponent, and in 2 has confirmed and amplified this by pointing out that elsewhere the same view is taken of this crime as in Athens. In 3 he concludes what he has to say about the punishment, resuming τὰς ζημίας μικράς of 1 in περὶ μὲν οὖν τοῦ μεγέθους τῆς ζημίας, and in 4 with ἡγοῦμαι δέ proceeds to his next point.

At the beginning of his διήγησις in 6 Euphiletus distinguishes between the earlier days of his marriage, when he was still keeping an eye on his wife, and the period, announced by ἐπειδὴ δέ, from the birth of his child onwards, when he put full trust in her. He then (7) subdivides this latter period into two stages divided by the death of his mother: ἐν μὲν οὖν τῷ πρώτῳ χρόνῳ ... ἐπειδὴ δέ κτλ. The occurrence of οὖν at the beginning of this subset marks the beginning of the story in a narrower sense, to which the preceding paragraph supplies just a background, heightening the inherent drama of the situation and implying at once that the speaker was sufficiently cautious and that his wife was not depraved from the outset.

The interpretation of μὲν οὖν in 9 is hindered by a lacuna at the beginning of 8, which has deprived the sentence ἐπειδὴ δέ ending 7 of its apodosis, but so much is clear: this sentence is followed by two γάρ-clauses declaring how the death of the speaker's mother led to all his κακά, after which 'flash-forward' a more circumstantial narrative is opened with an-

---

[1] Cf. vO infra 89 f.

[2] Cf. XII.24: 'I wish to make him step up and question him, *for* I feel that it is permitted to do so; *so* step up (ἀνάβηθι οὖν) and answer me'. Here οὖν clearly does not mark any inference, but marks both (1) the return to the intention expressed previous to the γάρ-sentence, and (2) the speaker's proceeding to carry his intention into effect.

other (9 πρῶτον) μὲν οὖν, which fills in the detail whose relevance has now been anticipated and with ἐπειδὴ δὲ τὸ παίδιον ἐγένετο ἡμῖν a point is reached which we already passed in 6.

6.2. In the view of Denniston,[1] οὖν by the time to which Lysias I belongs has attained 'its commonest, connective meaning'. The nature of the implied 'connection' is taken to vary from 'progressive' or 'proceeding to a new point, or a new stage in the march of thought'[2] to 'inferential'.[3] An obvious defect of this account is its failure to specify the difference between οὖν and other allegedly progressive particles such as δέ on the one hand, and other allegedly inferential particles on the other hand.[4]

It seems nearer to the heart of the matter to say that οὖν marks a difference in what may be called 'status' between what precedes and what follows, where this status may be defined in terms of a relation of *relevance*: the speaker marks what precedes as relevant, and for the present purpose subsidiary, *to what follows*, and by extension to the story or argument as a whole. Often this takes the form of the speaker marking that which precedes the particle as somehow introductory, explanatory, or providing background. This account does away with the need to assume a separate 'resumptive' force as Denniston does:[5] returning from a digression is just one of the ways in which the general description here given may work out.

6.3.1. μὲν οὖν

When οὖν marks a section which is articulated internally by μέν and δέ, the part containing μέν may either constitute a return to an element from the preceding context, rounding off one step before proceeding to the next one with δέ, as at I.3 in περὶ μὲν οὖν τοῦ μεγέθους τῆς ζημίας ... ἡγοῦμαι δέ ...;[6] or it may itself contain new information, balanced by that in the part containing δέ.[7]

6.3.1.1. Twice in Lysias I do we find μὲν οὖν without any following δέ balancing the μέν. In 28 the speaker with the imperative πρῶτον μὲν οὖν

---

[1] P. 416.

[2] P. 426.

[3] Ib.

[4] It would not make for conceptual clarity to qualify as 'progressive' the use, described above (p. 25), of οὖν in resuming the main thread of his narrative or argument after an excursion or an explanation, and so *proceeding with* or *continuing* it.

[5] P. 428.

[6] Cf. e.g. Pl. *Phdr.* 246 A 3, 250 C 7-8, and 253 C 2-6.

[7] Cf. e.g. Pl. *Phdr.* 250 B 1-5, 250 E 1-251 A 1, and 256 A 7-B 7.

ἀνάγνωθι τὸν νόμον proceeds to having the laws which justify him in executing his wife's lover recited. When after the reading of the first law he speaks again—i.e. after a change of speaker—this continuation of his speech follows 'asyndetically'. In 47 μὲν οὖν comes at the beginning of the peroration: ἐγὼ μὲν οὖν ὦ ἄνδρες οὐκ ἰδίαν ὑπὲρ ἐμαυτοῦ νομίζω ταύτην γενέσθαι τὴν τιμωρίαν ἀλλ' ὑπὲρ τῆς πόλεως ἁπάσης, followed by a γάρ-sentence explaining in what sense this is so.

This use is to be compared not with those uses of μὲν οὖν … δέ in which, as in I.3 quoted in the previous section, the part containing μέν harks back to an earlier statement and thereby concludes a subject,[1] and that containing δέ opens a new one, but with those in which the member containing μέν offers new information. Where μὲν οὖν is not balanced by δέ the speaker appears *at once* to conclude what precedes *and* to proceed to what is next on his agenda. It thus effects a deeper incision than δέ would do. In I.28 the speaker is concluding his narration with a discussion (27-8) of some disputed issues: contrary to the accusation he has not, he assures the jury, dragged his enemy into his own house, nor killed him when he had taken refuge by the hearth, where it would be an unholy act to do so: 'this said' (μέν), 'I now come to (οὖν) the reading of the law'.[2] It is worth comparing XII.47 πρὸς μὲν οὖν τούτους τοσαῦτα λέγω, τοὺς δὲ μάρτυράς μοι κάλει, where the same movement as in I.28 is executed in two steps rather than one: the first clause rounds off, with the second one the questioning of witnesses is continued. The use of οὖν aptly marks the speaker's proceeding to make good his promise of 46 μάρτυρας ὑμῖν παρέξομαι. It may be surmised that, but for a wish to mark the return to the witnesses from the aside to the συμπράττοντες, *τοὺς μὲν οὖν μάρτυράς μοι καλεῖ would have sufficed.[3]

7. τοίνυν

Of τοίνυν four instances occur in Lysias I, seven in XII.

7.1. In I.5 the sentence containing τοίνυν announces the διήγησις in the words ἐγὼ τοίνυν ἐξ ἀρχῆς ὑμῖν ἅπαντα ἐπιδείξω κτλ., a type of con-

---

[1] Cf. KG. II 158: '… dient die Verbindung von μὲν οὖν dazu, den vorangegangenen Gedanken *abzuschliessen*'.

[2] I.e. the first of the laws which were mentioned at the beginning of I.27, just before the present excursion about the moot points.

[3] The method adopted here does not accommodate diachronic considerations. It may be observed, however, that there is no *need* to assume, as Denniston (p. 475) does implicitly, that in μὲν οὖν an older, affirmative use of μέν is involved.

text in which elsewhere δέ is found.[1] The difference is that the narration in I is spoken by the *defendant*. An account of events by his accuser has preceded,[2] but the speaker feels the need to retail his own significantly different version in full.[3] Preliminary to his story he defines in I.5 the burden of his proof, affirming explicitly in a clause introduced by γάρ the vital importance for him of telling the whole story. The use of τοίνυν, then, seems to be motivated by the narration being as unexpected as it is crucial.

An analogous interpretation seems to apply to the remaining instances in Lysias I. In I.34 the speaker is discussing the laws bearing on the case, recited in 29-32. What is especially pertinent is that a man in his position is not just *authorized* by these laws to execute the death penalty—which presumably was not disputed—but is in fact *compelled* to do so—which presumably was. It is significant that both the particle and the point which it serves to mark are repeated in I.35. To paraphrase: '(34) Mind you, the laws have not just acquitted me of any *in*justice, but actually ordered me to exact the *just*[4] requital that I have. It is for you to decide whether to uphold these laws or not; (35) my conviction is that they are there for cases to be referred to them. These laws, mind you, positively *exhort*[5] the injured party to exact such a just requital'.

In I.45 the refutation of an idea that the speaker might have been motivated by an old grudge is being concluded. With τοίνυν he fires his Parthian shot: what clinches the matter is that, far from entertaining any feud, he had never so much as set eyes on his rival.

7.2.   In Lysias XII.50 the speaker explicitly raises the issue whether a hypothetical plea on the part of Eratosthenes would be acceptable to the audience, and τοίνυν serves to bring home to those inclined to accept this plea what amounts to a sufficient condition for the refutation of it: 'if you buy that, you cannot at the same time allow it to appear that *p*', in other words 'if it turns out that *p*, then this excuse is null and void'.[6] And in XII.55 the particle adds relief to a statement about how those who ex-

---

[1] E.g. XIII.4 δεῖ δ᾽ ὑμᾶς (...) ἐξ ἀρχῆς τῶν πραγμάτων ἁπάντων ἀκοῦσαι and XXXII. 3 ἐξ ἀρχῆς δ᾽ ὑμῆς περὶ αὐτῶν διδάξαι πειράσομαι. In both of these speeches a narration is provided by the plaintiff, just as was to be expected of him, and all that the proem is required to convey is his excellent motive for suing.

[2] It is referred to at I.27.

[3] The anomaly is brought into relief by the use of the personal pronoun ἐγώ as well as by the particle.

[4] The antithesis exploits the connection between ἀδικεῖν and δίκην.

[5] The position of the verb at the end of the sentence yields focus.

[6] For τοίνυν in *ad hominem* arguments in Plato see 160 below.

pected Peison and his set to aid the refugees in the Piraeus were disap-
pointed.

7.3.   In Lysias XII it can be observed that—predictably—τοίνυν is in
'competition', i.e. overlaps in distribution, with οὖν as well as with δέ. In
XII.43 the speaker after calling his witnesses continues with τὸν μὲν τοίνυν μεταξὺ βίον αὐτοῦ παρήσω· ἐπειδὴ δέ κτλ. The transition invites
comparison with that made in I.7 by means of μὲν οὖν ... δέ. The next
topic is Eratosthenes' co-membership with Critias of a committee preparing to overthrow democracy. Having described the intentions and activi-
ties of this committee the speaker announces that he is going to call witnesses to Eratosthenes' membership of it: (XII.46) ὡς τοίνυν τῶν ἐφόρων
ἐγένετο μάρτυρας ὑμῖν παρέξομαι. Here οὖν for the return, after (45)
γάρ, to a topic in the preceding context would have qualified; as it is our
attention is pointed to the new element that the speaker is able to substantiate this incriminating association by means of witnesses: 'Mind you,
that he *was* one of these ἔφοροι is a fact that I shall provide witnesses to'.
The explicit exclusion of the συμπράττοντες, with the admission οὐ γὰρ
ἂν δυναίμην, confirms that this was not expected or obvious.[1]

At XII.79 too τοίνυν occurs in a type of context in which οὖν is familiar. One section of the speech is concluded by the words περὶ μὲν τοίνυν
Θηραμένους ἱκανά μοι ἐστι τὰ κατηγορημένα. In the next sentence, introduced by δέ, he urges that now is the opportunity for justice and requital rather than mercy and pardon. The heavy stress laid on this in the
words ἥκει δ' ὑμῖν ἐκεῖνος ὁ καιρός, ἐν ᾧ... seems to call for a somewhat more emphatic incision than οὖν would have yielded.[2] In XII.84 the
protasis ἐπειδὴ τοίνυν πάντα ποιοῦντες ⟨ἱκανὴν⟩ δίκην παρ' αὐτῶν οὐκ
ἂν δύναισθε λαβεῖν, resuming (82) παρ' ὧν οὐδ' ... λάβοιτε, has to
support the claim that it would be nothing less than αἰσχρόν to settle for
any but the severest punishment—a strong claim, which needs all the
momentum that τοίνυν can lend to it so as not to turn itself against the
speaker.

---

[1] The committee of ἔφοροι is known to us from no other sources, and the way in which
it is introduced at XII.43 in πέντε ἄνδρες ἔφοροι κατέστησαν—without the article—suggests that it was not familiar to the audience either. Yet the proof that Eratosthenes belonged to it is essential to the posthumous character assassination; a more moderate and
marginal partisan of the oligarchy might afterwards have escaped censure sooner than a
close associate of Critias himself.

[2] And the need for this insistence may in turn be explained by a presumed reluctance
on the part of the jury to turn against Theramenes, who had resisted the more extreme
outrages of the Thirty; compare the remarks of Gernet in his introduction to the speech in
the Budé edition (p. 158-9).

7.4. In sum, by τοίνυν as used in Lysias I and XII the speaker marks a new section of the text as being outside or beyond the expectations of his audience in content, or indeed by its very presence. This will usually apply to sections of particular importance to the argument.[1]

8. καίτοι

Of καίτοι according to Denniston[2] 'the primary *force* is, no doubt," and I would have you know"'. This is at once differentiated into a less common 'connective –' and a 'secondary, adversative *sense*',[3] after which his treatment of the particle is divided into 'adversative',[4] 'continuative',[5] and 'logical'[6] or 'syllogistic, or argumentative'[7] '*use*'.[8] Instances are assigned to each of these classes on the basis of relations between the content of successive sentences primarily, i.e. of a consideration which is external to the use of the particle as such. This, as well as the heterogeneous nature of the classes of instances thus constituted—most conspicuously that of the allegedly 'rare'[9] 'continuative' use—suggests that a more unified description might be worth attempting.

8.1. In Lysias I from 37 onwards the speaker is engaged in refuting the charge that he had laid a snare to catch his rival red-handed. His preliminary argument that he would as a matter of fact have been justified in doing so is followed in 39 by a proof that his opponents do not speak the truth, which begins with a reminder of facts mentioned earlier,[10] followed by an appeal to the jury to share his thoughts in the words (I.40) καίτοι … ἐνθυμήθητε. He then offers three considerations (πότερον … ἢ …; εἶτα …; (41) ἔπειτα[11]), submitting what would have been consistent with his opponents' hypothesis, and with μᾶλλον ἢ once more driving home the contrast with the actual facts, before renewing with the help of (I.42) another καίτοι his appeal to his audience to draw the obvious conclusion.

---

[1] For τοίνυν employed to correct or forestall a discrepancy between the pragmatical information (…) of the speaker and that of the hearer in Plato see vO 164 below.

[2] *GP* 555; italics CMJS.

[3] Ib., id.

[4] P. 556.

[5] P. 559.

[6] P. 561.

[7] P. 559.

[8] P. 556, 559; italics CMJS.

[9] P. 559.

[10] ὅπερ καὶ πρότερον εἶπον: in I.22-3.

[11] Cf. above at p. 17.

In both instances καίτοι marks the transition from agreed fact to an indispensable experiment in thinking *ex hypothesi*.

At I.31 the speaker has just had the summary execution of his rival justified by the reading of an Areopagitic law. This law, however, did not discriminate between the corruption of a married woman and of a παλλακή. Anticipating an awkwardness in that this might be construed as detracting from the gravity of the offence, the speaker turns the point to good account by claiming that this is so only for want of a more severe punishment to be applied in the case of a married woman. His assumption that the legislator would have imposed a heavier penalty if one had been available is introduced by καίτοι, and a return to actual reality is pointed by νῦν δέ. It is true that it would be possible to establish a contrast between what follows καίτοι and what precedes it, since this is another statement of the equality before the law of adulterers in relation to both classes of women; it is also true that the sentence following καίτοι can be made to enter as a premise into an argument leading to the conclusion that the corrupter of a married woman deserves the severest punishment available; but these do not appear to be the decisive considerations motivating the choice of καίτοι. As in I.40 & 42 the particle serves to invite the audience to interpret their observations of fact in the light of a compelling conception.

8.2.   At XII.31 the preceding context has recalled the audience's resentment at the intrusion of the agents of the Thirty into their homes. With καίτοι the speaker submits the hypothetical consideration that *if* anyone might be exculpated on account of *force majeure*, it should in justice be these agents sooner than Eratosthenes, who could have gone scot-free. In XII.47 the speaker is taking for granted the impossibility of calling the accomplices of the ἔφοροι to witness, but volunteers the supposition, introduced by καίτοι, that if they were sane (εἰ ἐσωφρόνουν *bis*) they *would* in fact testify against their former masters. Similarly at XII.48 a simple statement of the fact that Eratosthenes ἀγαθοῦ μὲν οὐδενὸς μετέσχεν is followed by the counter-factual supposition of what he would have done if he *were* an ἀνὴρ ἀγαθός. At XII.57 the ascertained fact that Pheidon's party opposed *both* the Thirty *and* the demos is confronted with the two-fold consequence that (1) *if* it was right that the Thirty should have left Athens, then it was not right that the demos had, and (2) *if* it was right that the demos should have done so, then it was not right that the Thirty had—so that (58 ὥστε) Pheidon is put in the wrong either way.

In XII.62 the speaker faces the slightly awkward need to discredit Theramenes, anticipating Eratosthenes' claim to have been his associate (ὅτι ἐκείνῳ φίλος ἦν καὶ κτλ.). With καίτοι he then draws a rather far-fetched analogy between Eratosthenes' claim specifically to have 'participated in the same works' (...καὶ τῶν αὐτῶν ἔργων μετεῖχε) as Theramenes, and a purely suppositious claim to have participated in the same works as Themistocles which Eratosthenes might have made had he been a contemporary of that politician, and goes on to point out the difference between the ἔργα involved. At XII.88 the very act of appearing as a witness for the defence has been represented as an insult to the jury, and καίτοι adds this objection against acquitting members of the Thirty, that these men, *if* acquitted, would be able once more to ruin their city. In 89 the particle marks another confrontation (and contrast) of fact ('Their claim is ...') with supposition ('I take it to be a lot easier to ... than to ...'), but here with the supposition in front.

8.3.   On the basis of the instances of καίτοι occurring in Lysias I and XII, and taking into account the primary value of its component parts, it seems possible to hypothesize that the speaker by means of this particle marks a statement as one that is to be *included* with the preceding context, and directs the particular *attention* of his audience to it, and to specify that he is apt to do so while confronting agreed *fact* with potentially controversial *supposition*, and more often than not when suggesting that there is a *discrepancy* or downright *inconsistency* between these two.

9. μέντοι

Of μέντοι, which is not found in Lysias I, the first of four instances in Lysias XII occurs in the proem at 2: after the somewhat paradoxical statement that in the present case it is not for the accuser to explain his grudge against the defendant, but for the defendant to explain the grudge against the community which made him act as he did, a statement introduced by μέντοι serves to take away any suggestion as though the accuser did not in fact have his own private injuries to compain of. This statement does not so much offer independent new information as form part of the explanation beginning with γάρ of the statement of the paradox opening 2;[1] but within this connection it does not so much add to the explanation as forestall a misunderstanding: 'I am upholding the claim' (μέν) 'in contrast to what you might have been led to surmise' (τοι) is a paraphrase which

---

[1] The transition from this explanation to the next section is made by means of μὲν οὖν in 3 ἐγὼ μὲν οὖν ὦ ἄνδρες δίκασται οὔτ' ἐμαυτοῦ πώποτε οὔτε ἀλλότρια πράγματα πράξας κτλ. Cf. p. 28 above.

aims at bringing out both what μέν retains of the force of the original μήν,[1] and why the speaker feels a need to appeal to his audience by means of τοι.

At XII.34 the speaker has from 26 onwards been discrediting the claim of his opponent to have protested against the order he was given to arrest Polemarchus, arguing that whereas in the absence of witnesses it is easy for the defendant to speak well of himself, it is necessary for the jury to base themselves on the actual facts. He then with μέντοι again secures a correct understanding: 'This (sc. claim of yours),[2] however, I do not deny: I grant, if you wish, that you did in fact protest'— enabling him to drive home his most devastating retort—'I just wonder what you might have done had you agreed, when while claiming to have protested you have killed Polemarchus'.

In XII.81 the speaker anticipates that the accused will in his turn put the blame on his associates and accomplices, and with μέντοι points out that this should not be taken to imply any analogy between Eratosthenes' position and that of the πόλις. And at 86 a similar anticipation of a line of defence to be taken by men 'representing their own virtue as outweighing the infamy <of those men, i.e. the party of the accused>' is countered with 'I would μέντοι wish they had been as anxious to save the πόλις as those (other) men were to ruin it'. In these two instances, then, the statement introduced by μέντοι is to eliminate what is supposed to be suggested by the opposition, whereas at XII.2 & 34 it serves to eliminate the possibility of a misunderstanding suggested by the speaker's own words.

9.1.   The feature of eliminating a suggestion which is common between these instances in Lysias XII would bring them under a heading, in Denniston's terminology,[3] of 'adversative' μέντοι, existing besides allegedly 'emphatic' and 'progressive' μέντοι. It seems possible, however, to accommodate the instances of the particle coming under the latter two headings within a slightly enlarged general description of 'correcting possible misconceptions and/or frustrating expectations', as a brief digression from Lysias into other authors quoted by Denniston may illustrate.

Instances of allegedly 'emphatic' μέντοι are Aristophanes, *Frogs* 171

καὶ γάρ τιν' ἐκφέρουσι τουτονὶ νεκρόν·
οὗτος, σὲ λέγω μέντοι, σὲ τὸν τεθνηκότα

---

[1] Cf. *Appendix* p. 54 below.

[2] The demonstrative appears to refer backwards, ultimately to the reply ἀντέλεγον in the course of the interrogation in 25, as well as forwards to ἀντειπεῖν.

[3] P. 399 ss.

'... you there, yes it's you I'm talking about (sc. though you might not expect me to),[1] the dead man...'; and *Thesm.* 9

πῶς μοι παραινεῖς; δεξιῶς μέντοι λέγεις

which approximates to 'Which way are you urging me? – Well, one way I *do* make out: by talking cleverly', exploiting the ambivalence of πῶς, which is most naturally taken with the object or content of the παραίνεσις, but is syntactically capable of being taken to qualify the act of παραινεῖν itself.

Instances of allegedly 'progressive' μέντοι are Xen. *Hell.* III.2.1: (Dercyllidas is deliberating ὅπως ἂν μὴ ... μηδ' αὖ Φαρνάβαζος ... κακουργῇ τὰς Ἑλληνίδας πόλεις, πέμπει οὖν πρὸς αὐτὸν καὶ ἐρωτᾷ πότερον βούλεται εἰρήνην ἢ πόλεμον ἔχειν. ὁ μέντοι Φαρνάβαζος ... σπονδὰς εἵλετο 'Pharnabazus, however, (i.e. frustrating a suggestion implicit in Dercyllidas' scheme) opted for a treaty';[2] and Pl. *Charm.* 155 C 5: (earlier I had confidently suggested to his cousin Critias τί οὐκ ἐπέδειξάς μοι τὸν νεανίαν καλέσας δεῦρο.) ὁ δ' ἐλθὼν μεταξὺ ἐμοῦ τε καὶ τοῦ Κριτίου ἐκαθέζετο· ἐνταῦθα μέντοι, ὦ φίλε, ἐγὼ ἤδη ἠπόρουν καί μου ἡ πρόσθεν θρασύτης ἐξεκέκοπτο '... at that moment—believe me—I was bowled over...'.

9.2.   The fact that μέντοι, unlike the particles treated earlier, is regularly found in sentences whose relation to the previous context has been marked by other means, as e.g. in Ar. *Clouds* 126 ἀλλ' οὐδ' ἐγὼ μέντοι (...) & *Birds* 100 τοιαῦτα μέντοι (...), and Xen. *Oec.* I.8 οὐδὲ ἡ γῆ μέντοι (...) places the particle rather outside the primary scope of the present discussion. For the present purpose then, what precedes may suffice.

10. ἀλλά

Descriptions of ἀλλά are varied. Between the extremes of an *adversative* use, found e.g. in Soph. *Ant.* 523 οὔτοι συνεχθεῖν, ἀλλὰ συμφιλεῖν ἔφυν, and that of *cutting short*, as found e.g. in Ar. *Thesm.* 457

(νῦν οὖν ἁπάσαισιν παραινῶ καὶ λέγω
τοῦτον κολάσαι τὸν ἄνδρα πολλῶν οὕνεκα·
ἄγρια γὰρ ἡμᾶς, ὦ γυναῖκες, δρᾷ κακά,
ἅτ' ἐν ἀγρίοισι τοῖς λαχάνοις αὐτὸς τραφείς.)
ἀλλ' εἰς ἀγορὰν ἄπειμι· δεῖ γὰρ ἀνδράσιν
πλέξαι στεφάνους συνθηματιαίους εἴκοσιν.

---

[1] Denniston's 'call to attention' (p. 400) is infelicitous.
[2] Denniston's "Well, Ph. chose a truce" (p. 406) is rather bland.

the range of terms used by Kühner-Gerth, Denniston, Ruijgh and others includes 'eliminative',[1] sometimes glossed as 'substituting the true for the false',[2] 'correcting',[3] and 'limiting' ἀλλά.[4] A fairly common presupposition seems to be that ἀλλά is properly 'at home' in genuine or strong oppositions of the type 'not A but –A' (or 'A, not –A'); uses of the particle in the absence of such an opposition are accommodated by considering difference as a form of opposition.[5] What follows is an attempt to arrive at a more unified description of the use of the particle from the point of departure of *substitution*[6] rather than of (stronger or weaker) *oppositions*.

10.1. In such instances as Soph. *Ant.* 523 οὔτοι συνεχθεῖν, ἀλλὰ συμφιλεῖν ἔφυν, Pl. *Phdr.* 229 D 2 ὡς ἐκεῖθεν ἀλλ' οὐκ ἐνθένδε ἡρπάσθη, and Lys. XIV.16 ὡς ἐκεῖνον πολλῶν ἀγαθῶν ἀλλ' οὐχὶ πολλῶν κακῶν αἴτιον γεγενημένον, the same statement is expressed twice, once in affirmative form and once in the negative, 'substituting the true for the false'[7] in the sense that the speaker replaces an incorrect predication which his audience might entertain, by the correct one which he hopes in this way to gain acceptance for. In each of these cases the mutual exclusion between the affirmative and the negative phrase is given with the meaning of the terms involved, but the basic structure is not different from that in contexts in which no negation is found, such as that of Xen. *Mem.* I.2.2, where the claim requiring to be demolished is given in the form of a rhetorical question: 'How (πῶς οὖν) could such a man have corrupted others?' ἀλλ' ἔπαυσε μὲν τούτων πολλοὺς ἀρετῆς ποιήσας ἐπιθυμεῖν κτλ. '*On the contrary*, he has set many men on the path to virtue'.

---

[1] *GP* p. 1; 'la valeur éliminative est … la valeur fondamentale de ἀλλά' Ruijgh (1971) 136.

[2] *GP* p. 1.

[3] 'On pourrait désigner cet emploi de ἀλλά par le terme de 'correctif', puisque la particule sert à introduire la mention du fait correct après la mention d'un fait qui, aux yeux de l'interlocuteur, est incorrect'. Ruijgh p. 136.

[4] '… sodass das erstere Glied durch das letztere nur teilweise aufgehoben, d.h. nur *beschränkt* wird' KG II.283.

[5] Cf. Ruijgh (1971) 136: 'Les autres emplois de ἀλλά sont moins fréquents, et il est possible de les expliquer à partir de l'emploi éliminatif'. The distinction in Schütz' *Epitome* p. 1 between *usus discretivus et (usus) adversativus*, in which the particle marks *diversitas* and *oppositio* respectively, is related, though it is worth noting that the underlying distinction between a διαφορική and an ἐναντιωματική force for which the original Hoogeveen invokes the authority of *Grammatici* (I.I.ii-iii & viii-ix, pp. 2 & 5 respectively) made the διαφορική the *primaria potestas* and *princeps notio*.

[6] As quoted from Denniston, but with a rather wider reference, not to truth and falsity alone.

[7] *GP* p. 1.

10.2. In other contexts of ἀλλά what we have is not one simple statement worded in two ways, but a complex statement in which the addition of a second predicate serves to eliminate a suggestion which might be raised by the first one.[1] Examples are Eur. *El.* 293 λόγους ἀτερπεῖς ἀλλ' ἀναγκαίους κλύειν, Pl. *Resp.* 348 A 3 ἤκουσα, ἔφη, ἀλλ' οὐ πείθομαι and, more convoluted, *Crat.* 431 C 12 οὐκοῦν ὁ μὲν ἀποδιδοὺς πάντα, καλὰ τὰ γράμματα τε καὶ τὰς εἰκόνας ἀποδίδωσιν, ὁ δὲ ἢ προστιθεὶς ἢ ἀφαιρῶν, γράμματα μὲν καὶ εἰκόνας ἐργάζεται καὶ οὗτος, ἀλλὰ πονηράς; where the second predicate πονηράς is not on the same level with the first predicate ἐργάζεται, but a specification of, and as it were grafted upon it. In the last of these passages this way of presenting the information serves a characteristically didactic explicitness and unambiguous clarity, exemplified also e.g. by Arist. *Rhet.* 1372 a 8 ἢ μὴ λαθόντες μὴ δοῦναι δίκην ἢ δοῦναι μὲν ἀλλ' ἐλάττω τὴν ζημίαν εἶναι τοῦ κέρδους, but in the earlier two the purpose seems to be to add relief to the principal information contained in the section following ἀλλά, as in Pl. *Euth.* 3 A 6 βουλοίμην ἄν, (...) ἀλλ' ὀρρωδῶ μὴ τοὐναντίον γένηται, where Euthyphro's preference for things to develop as Socrates supposes they will, makes all the more poignant his fear that the opposite may in fact take place.

10.3. The difference between ἀλλά and μέντοι is illustrated by Denniston[2] from Thuc. VIII.86.2-3 οἱ δὲ στρατιῶται τὸ μὲν πρῶτον οὐκ ἤθελον ἀκούειν, ἀλλ' ἀποκτείνειν ἐβόων τοὺς τὸν δῆμον καταλύοντας, ἔπειτα μέντοι μόλις ἡσυχάσαντες ἤκουσαν. οἱ δ' ἀπήγγελλον ὡς οὔτε ἐπὶ διαφθορᾷ τῆς πόλεως ἡ μετάστασις γίγνοιτο, ἀλλ' ἐπὶ σωτηρίᾳ κτλ. Here ἀλλά *replaces* one predication with another: the negative statement helps to delimit the scope of the affirmative one, and adds relief to it by providing a contrastive foil. The motive for thus presenting as two statements what is effectively a single one may be a desire for just this kind of highlighting,[3] as in the first instance in this passage: 'far from being willing to listen, they shouted "Kill the καταλύοντας"'; or the speaker may feel the need to remove explicitly a notion presumably entertained by his audience, as in the second instance: 'not to destroy (as your call to do away with the καταλύοντες implies that you assume) but to save'. By contrast μέντοι marks a *new* statement about a *subsequent* state of affairs as contrasting with what might have been expected on the strength of what went

---

[1] For the difference between ἀλλά and μέντοι see the next section.
[2] P. 405.
[3] Cf. C.J. Ruijgh (1971) 137: 'Contraste déséquilibré: le second membre a plus de poids que le premier (...)'.

before. The difference between the two particles, then, is not in the *degree* of the contrast between the two members opposed to one another by each of them.

10.4.   To return to Lysias, in his first speech ἀλλά is found at the beginning of a sentence only at I.28 in ἀλλ', ὦ ἄνδρες, οἶμαι καὶ ὑμᾶς εἰδέναι ὅτι οἱ μὴ τὰ δίκαια πράττοντες ... αὐτοὶ ψευδόμενοι ... ὀργὰς τοῖς ἀκούουσι κατὰ τῶν τὰ δίκαια πραττόντων παρασκευάζουσι '—however, gentlemen, I think you too are aware that unjust men cast aspersions on just men...'. Here, then, it is not a statement or suggestion which is rejected by means of ἀλλά, but more generally a conversational move, in this case a strategy of refutation which is abandoned: the speaker's previous words were not invalid, but they are to no purpose: the words of such evil-doers as our adversary are discredited from the start. This use may be compared to that in such instances as Soph. *Phil.* 11 ἀλλὰ ταῦτα μὲν τί δεῖ λέγειν; ἀκμὴ γὰρ οὐ μακρῶν ἡμῖν λόγων, Eur. *El.* 1123 παῦσαι λόγων τῶνδε. ἀλλὰ τί μ' ἐκάλεις, τέκνον, Ar. *Thesm.* 457 (νῦν οὖν ἀπάσαισιν παραινῶ καὶ λέγω τοῦτον κολάσαι τὸν ἄνδρα ...) ἀλλ' εἰς ἀγορὰν ἄπειμι· δεῖ γὰρ ἀνδράσιν πλέξαι στεφάνους..., & *Ach.* 186 ἐγὼ δ' ἔφευγον· οἱ δ' ἐδίωκον κἀβόων – οἱ δ' οὖν βοώντων· ἀλλὰ τὰς σπονδὰς φέρεις;

In each of these contexts the speaker does not replace one *statement*, but one *topic* with another—a use of ἀλλά which is often found in conjunction with a change in the audience addressed, or from argument to injunction, or more generally from words to action.

10.5.   In Lysias XII ἀλλά is found at the beginning of a sentence at five places.[1] The context at XII.20 in οὐδὲ κατὰ τὸ ἐλάχιστον μέρος τῆς οὐσίας ἐλέου παρ' αὐτῶν ἐτυγχάνομεν[2] ἀλλ' οὕτως εἰς ἡμᾶς διὰ τὰ χρήματα ἐξημάρτανον ὥσπερ ἄν κτλ. is a straightforward example of 'not A ἀλλά –A', while that at XII.50, coming just after an instance *within* the sentence representing the variety 'A, ἀλλ' οὐ[3] –A', serves to oppose (ἀλλ' οὗτος ...) what he in fact *did* do (... τὴν μὲν πόλιν ἐχθρὰν ἐνόμιζεν εἶναι) to what he *should* (χρῆν δ' αὐτόν ...) have done (ὑπὲρ τῆς ὑμετέρας σωτηρίας ταύτην τὴν προθυμίαν ἔχειν) and by implication did *not* do.

Three instances of the particle occur in XII.86-7. In 84 the speaker has called attention to the brazen insolence shown by Eratosthenes' coming

---

[1] Not counting the collocation ἀλλὰ γάρ in 83, where Hude by the application of square brackets countenances the omission of γάρ in C.

[2] The full stop printed by Hude seems unduly heavy.

[3] Or, as in this context of χρῆν and infinitive, ἀλλὰ μή –A.

to plead not guilty in front of the very witnesses, and indeed victims, of his evil doings; and ascribed this insolence to either contempt of his judges, or trust in 'others' (ἑτέροις). He urges that (85) both of these motives 'deserve to be taken care of' (ἄξιον ἐπιμεληθῆναι) and proceeds to deal with one class of associates, the accomplices (συμπράττοντες) of Eratosthenes' past actions who will try to secure his acquittal for their own interest of ἄδεια. He then (86) turns to another class, of men who will speak in Eratosthenes' favour, in the words ἀλλὰ καί τῶν συνερούντων ἄξιον θαυμάζειν πότερον ... ἢ ..., anticipating their possible line of defence: 'whether they will pose as καλοὶ κἀγαθοί and pretend their own ἀρετή outweighs his wickedness, or as virtuoso argufiers will paradoxically attempt to whitewash his actions ...', and dismisses their pleas, or his own speculations, with another ἀλλά: '... whatever they may say, none of them ever raised his voice when the issue was *your* interests, or common justice'.[1] And finally he comes to the class formed by the witnesses for the defence in (87) ἀλλὰ τοὺς μάρτυρας ἄξιον ἰδεῖν, where this second recurrence of ἄξιον proves the cohesion with what precedes, and the absence of καί with the present third member may contribute to an effect of accumulation: 'but look at his advocates too (...), look at his witnesses (...)', which is spoilt by indenting a new paragraph at this point.

11. ἀλλὰ γάρ

The collocation ἀλλὰ γάρ is not found in Lysias I, and in XII is found in two rather different contexts. The sentence which it introduces at XII.99 contains both (1) Lysias' declaration that he chooses to allow the previous subject, which is that of τὰ μέλλοντα ἔσεσθαι, to rest, and (2) what may be interpreted as his motivation of this preference, which is that he is not even able to express τὰ πραχθέντα (ὑπὸ τούτων).[2] It is possible to regard this context as exemplifying a slightly compressed form of the pattern found in fully explicit form in Eur. *Hipp.* 51

ἀλλ'—εἰσορῶ γὰρ τόνδε παῖδα Θησέως
στείχοντα, θήρας μόχθον ἐκλελοιπότα
Ἱππόλυτον —ἔξω τῶνδε βήσομαι τόπων.

---

[1] This use of ἀλλά invites comparison with that of μέντοι within the preceding oblique question here dismissed, in '... will pretend that their ἀρετή outweighs his wickedness— well, I would rather have had them as eager to save the city as those people to ruin it'. It seems clear that this μέντοι differs from the subsequent ἀλλά in marking the objection to a propositional content, while remaining within the same universe, or rather compartment, of discourse. Cf. p. 34 above.
[2] A closely similar instance is Lys. VII.9 ἀλλὰ γάρ ... περὶ μὲν τῶν προτέρον γεγενημένων πολλὰ ἔχων εἰπεῖν ἱκανὰ νομίζω τὰ εἰρημένα.

In other contexts the two elements distinguished above may have merged into a more indissoluble whole, as in Pl. *Apol.* 42 A 2 ἀλλὰ γὰρ ἤδη ὥρα ἀπιέναι.[1] At XII.40 Lysias has rhetorically encouraged his audience to ask his opponent three questions which he takes to be unanswerable: 'tell him to show (you) where they have killed as many enemies as they have killed fellow-citizens', &c. A sentence introduced by ἀλλὰ γάρ then offers two claims on the same pattern,[2] which his adversary might put up in defence: 'oh yes, they have stripped as many on the enemy side of their arms as they have of you, they have taken city walls just like the ones of their own native city they have dismantled', after which a sentence beginning with the relative connection οἵτινες serves to discredit such a plea in advance by adding to the debit side: 'men who went so far as to dismantle the fortresses around Attica' &c. Here, then, we do not have a change of subject such as in 99, but a shift from questions made up by the speaker to weaker counter-claims made up by the speaker[3] and held up for momentary consideration—only to be demolished by statements of fact which the speaker makes in his own name.[4] These two very different contexts do not obviously support any more general statements.

12. *What is called asyndeton*

Thirteen[5] out of the 128 sentences constituting Lysias I do not begin with any particle establishing their position in the context. The term 'asyndeton' which is used to refer to this situation should not be taken to imply that the one crucial feature in all these cases is the absence of a σύνδεσμος or (syntactic) 'connection' between two successive sentences.

---

[1] Alternatively one of them, in particular the first, i.e. the statement of the change of subject (or abandoning of the subject) may have been left implicit, as in Eur. *Herc.* 138 ἀλλ' εἰσορῶ γὰρ τῆσδε κοίρανον χθονὸς / Λύκον περῶντα τῶνδε δωμάτων πέλας, and by a further extension ἀλλὰ γάρ may just accompany the new statement which the previous subject was shoved aside to make room for as in Pl. *Prot.* 310 E 5 ἀλλὰ γὰρ, ὦ Σώκρατες, πάντες τὸν ἄνδρα ἐπαινοῦσιν, and *Phaedo* 95 C 9-D 1 ἀλλὰ γὰρ οὐδέν τι μᾶλλον ἦν ἀθάνατον.

[2] The series τοσούτους ... ὅσους, τοσαύτας ... ὅσας, τοιαύτην ... οἵαν is echoed in ⟨τοσαῦτα Reiske⟩ (...) ὅσα, τοιαῦτα ... οἷα.

[3] There is no need to attribute these answers to a third party, as Gernet-Bizos do in translating 'Dira-t-on qu'ils ont dépouillé' &c.

[4] Compare the two instances of the collocation in the context of Pl. *Meno* 94 C 6-E 2, where the second one dismisses the counter-bid which the first one had introduced: οὐκοῦν δῆλον ὅτι οὗτος (i.e. Thucydides) οὐκ ἄν ποτε ... ταῦτα μὲν ἐδίδαξε ..., ταῦτα δὲ οὐκ ἐδίδαξεν, εἰ διδακτὸν ἦν; ἀλλὰ γὰρ ἴσως ὁ Θουκυδίδης φαῦλος ἦν...; καὶ ... καὶ ἐδύνατο μέγα ... ὥστε εἴπερ ἦν τοῦτο διδακτόν, ἐξευρεῖν ἂν ... ἀλλὰ γάρ, ὦ ὑταῖρε Ἄνυτε, μὴ οὐκ ἦ διδακτὸν ἀρετή.

[5] Not counting I.40, where the transmitted conjunction ὅτι has been deleted by Reiske.

12.1.   In four of the in this respect unmarked sentences the speaker resumes, following interruptions of his speech by the reading of a law[1] or by a questioning of witnesses,[2] with a new vocative address.[3]

12.2.   At I.17 and 21 the speaker after quoting an interlocutor in direct speech continues his narrative without a particle in the words ταῦτα εἰποῦσα and ὡμολόγει ταῦτα ποιήσειν respectively. Also in 17 the words ταῦτά μου πάντα εἰς τὴν γνώμην εἰσῄει καὶ μεστὸς ἦν ὑποψίας round off a section beginning[4] πάντα μου εἰς τὴν γνώμην εἰσῄει καὶ μεστὸς ἦν ὑποψίας. In these three instances the relation of the sentence to the preceding context is adequately defined by the demonstrative ταῦτα.[5]

12.2.1.   In I.22 a sentence similarly beginning with a demonstrative, τούτῳ ἡλίου δεδυκότος ἰόντι ἐξ ἀγροῦ ἀπήντησα, is preceded by one likewise lacking a particle at the beginning, Σώστρατος ἦν μοι ἐπιτήδειος καὶ φίλος. This sentence in its turn follows a sort of in-between προκατασκευή consisting of a promise of proof and an announcement of the last section of the narration in the words, following a lacuna assumed by Reiske, ὡς ἐγὼ μεγάλοις ὑμῖν τεκμηρίοις ἐπιδείξω.[6] πρῶτον δὲ διηγήσασθαι βούλομαι τὰ πραχθέντα τῇ τελευταίᾳ ἡμέρᾳ. The absence of a particle at the beginning of this section, then, is comparable to the regular absence of one at the beginning of the narration as a whole;[7] and having introduced the *dramatis persona* peculiar to this section[8] in the first sentence, the speaker can refer to this person in the next sentence and mark it as its topic with a bare demonstrative.

12.3.   At I.2, 27 and 32 new sentences are opened by οὕτως as a self-contained deictic, not anticipating and referring forwards to an ὥστε.[9] Here again the relation between successive sentences is sufficiently defined by the, now adverbial, demonstrative for the speaker to dispense with additional markers in subjoining what in each case amounts to no more than an inference from, or indeed interpretation of what precedes: in 2 of the universally severe punishment of adultery, in 27 of his own ac-

---

[1] At I.29, 30, and 32.
[2] At I.43.
[3] (ὦ 29, 30) ἄνδρες, following the second person verb form ἀκούετε in 30 & 32.
[4] Ib.
[5] Just as it sometimes is by a relative. Cf. the section on relative connection, pp. 18-20 above.
[6] A colon would be sufficient punctuation.
[7] E.g. XII.4.
[8] Cf. I.39.
[9] In all three instances followed by ὦ ἄνδρες.

count of the events in the light of the law, and 32 of the letter of the law itself.

12.4.   In the instances of what is called asyndeton quoted so far, either (1) a speech which has been interrupted is continued, a situation in which the need to define any further the relation to the preceding context does not arise; or (2) a demonstrative pronoun (e.g. ταῦτα, τούτῳ) or adverb (οὕτως) at the beginning of the second sentence suffices to define this relation. At I.14 in ἐσιώπων ἐγὼ καὶ ταῦτα οὕτως ἔχειν ἡγούμην neither of these explanations of the absence of any particle applies. Here it is worth taking account of the sequel, which after an expression of the speaker's considerations in ἔδοξε δέ μοι ... ἡμέρας returns to his immediate response in ὅμως δ' οὐδ' οὕτως οὐδὲν εἰπὼν ... ᾠχόμην ἔξω σιωπῇ before proceeding to the next stage in the narrative—following that of ἐρομένου δέ μου ... ἔφασκε κτλ.—with (15) μετὰ δὲ ταῦτα ... χρόνου μεταξὺ διαγενομένου κτλ. Had Lysias written ἐσιώπων δὲ ἐγώ,[1] this would have been perceived by the audience as itself already constituting another step in the narrative, and the occurrence of δέ in ἔδοξε δέ μοι would now be taken to mark the next step, thereby somewhat obscuring the relation of contrast envisaged between words (ἔφασκε) and mien (τὸ πρόσωπον) of the speaker's wife; had he written καὶ ἐσιώπων ἐγώ,[2] this response would have been included with the stage of ἐρομένου δέ μου ... ἔφασκε κτλ. more or less as a constituent of it. As it is, the absence of a particle raises in the audience the question of the assessment of his wife's conduct as this question has occupied the speaker, and opens a paragraph enabling him to state the case in all its complexity before closing it with the verbal echo of σιωπῇ. Concurrently the demonstrative immediately after the first 'colon' or rather 'comma' in the ancient sense in καὶ ταῦτα οὕτως ἔχειν ἡγούμην, comparable to that in 21 ὡμολόγει ταῦτα ποιήσειν quoted above,[3] helps to smooth over any harshness or lack of cohesion which might otherwise have resulted.

12.5.   A number of instances of so-called asyndeton in Lysias XII can be accounted for along the lines laid down above: thus after structural incisions in XII.4 at the beginning of the narration announced in 3; at 25 in

---

[1] Or perhaps rather ἐγὼ δὲ ἐσιώπων.
[2] Or perhaps καὶ ἐγὼ ἐσιώπων.
[3] P. 41.

questioning the defendant;[1] at 48[2] and 62 after witnesses; and after references by means of some sort of demonstrative in 16 (after 15 ἐδόκει μοι ... ἐνθυμουμένῳ ὅτι ..) ταῦτα διανοηθεὶς ἔφευγον, 17 (after Πολεμάρχῳ δὲ παρήγγειλαν ... πίνειν κώνειον πρὶν τὴν αἰτίαν εἰπεῖν ...) οὕτω πολλοῦ ἐδέησε κριθῆναι καὶ ἀπολογήσασθαι, and 84 (after ὅστις ... ὄντων τῶν δικαστῶν ... αὐτῶν τῶν κακῶς πεπονθότων ἥκει ἀπολογησάμενος πρὸς αὐτοὺς τοὺς μάρτυρας τῆς τούτου πονηρίας·) τοσοῦτον ἢ ὑμῶν καταπεφρόνηκεν ἢ ἑτέροις πεπίστευκεν.

Three instances of ὥστε (unattended by a particle) opening a sentence at 37, 58, and 91 are capable of an explanation similar to that of the sentences containing demonstratives referring backwards; indeed its form of a relative rather than a demonstrative, as well as the continuity between what may be called its adverbial and conjunctional uses makes ὥστε even more apt to be used without a particle.

The complex period opening the speech features both the virtual demonstrative τοιαῦτα and an ὥστε at the asyndetic beginning of two successive clauses. The absence of a particle with τοιαῦτα (where γάρ might have been used) ensures that the audience perceives the sentence which follows not just as a foundation provided for the opening clause, but at least equally as the upbeat to an urgent denunciation. The reference of τοιαῦτα, then, is forwards to ὥστε as much as backwards: it is significant that editors have differed over the punctuation required between (ταῦτα ...) εἴργασται and ὥστε, with Hude printing a comma where Thalheim preferred a colon. A similarly ambivalent or rather double reference attaches to οὕτως at 44 in οὗτοι δὲ ... ὅ τι δέοι χειροτονεῖσθαι ... παρήγγειλον ...· οὕτως ... καὶ ὑπὸ τούτων πολιτῶν ὄντων ἐπεβουλεύεσθε ὅπως μήτ' ἀγαθὸν μηδὲν ψηφιεῖσθε κτλ.

A comparable but simpler, purely 'progressive'[3] use of τοιοῦτος is involved at 24 in τοιαύτην γὰρ γνώμην ἔχω, where the specification of this γνώμη at once follows asyndetically in ἐπὶ μὲν τῇ τούτου ὠφελίᾳ καὶ ... διαλέγεσθαι ἀσεβὲς εἶναι νομίζω, ἐπὶ δὲ τῇ τούτου βλάβῃ καὶ πρὸς αὐτὸν τοῦτον ὅσιον καὶ εὐσεβές.

An 'expressive' special use of asyndeton is that in XII.100 at the end of this as of other speeches in παύομαι κατηγορῶν· ἀκηκόατε ἑωράκατε πεπόνθατε ἔχετε· δικάζετε. The appeal to the jury to work out the rel-

---

[1] One of the questions put to him actually is introduced by a particle: ἦσθα δ' ἐν τῷ βουλευτηρίῳ ὅτε κτλ., which differs from the others in being completely independent of the question preceding it, in this case ἀπήγαγες Πολέμαρχον ἢ οὔ;

[2] Here μέν does not so much establish a connection with what precedes as with what follows in τὸ δὲ τελευταῖον κτλ.

[3] In the sense of 'facing forwards'.

evance of their own observations and experience to their final verdict is all the more impressive and effective for being left implicit.

13. *Conclusion and summary*

The above is intended to serve the understanding of the distribution, function, and meaning of a number of Greek particles which have usually been described as 'connecting' particles in the literature. The sample which has been studied to this end consists of Lysias I and XII; for these two speeches the transitions between all sentences contained in them have been scrutinized. For the demarcation of what is to count as a sentence the punctuation in the Oxford edition by Hude has here been accepted as criterial: a 'sentence' for the present purpose is any portion of text followed in his edition either by a full stop or by a colon or by a question mark. Of the particles occurring at these junctions in each of the two speeches either all instances or a representative selection have been discussed.

It is not pretended that the results of the present inquiry are valid for, and can be transferred to, texts outside the sample which they are based on; indeed it is to be expected that the use of the same particles in other types of text, e.g. in dialogue rather than continuous speech, and in texts from different periods, answers to a different description. Here further investigations are required, which should preferably be based on observation of the ways in which entire texts are articulated, rather than on isolated examples selected from a heterogeneous corpus with a view to illustrating a prematurely comprehensive hypothesis. This, however, does not imply that the present results are irrelevant to the rest of Lysias' oeuvre or to related writings, authors, and types of text.

13.1.   In both of the texts here studied the position of a sentence within its context in a large majority of instances can be established with the help of a particle marking the beginning of the sentence. In addition there are three other possibilities:

- the speech as an oral address may have been interrupted, e.g. by a hearing of witnesses or by the reading of a law, in which case the new section of text can generally do without any marker at the beginning of the first sentence;
- a correct understanding of the relation of the sequel to what precedes may be secured by other means than the use of a particle, such as a demonstrative pronoun or adverb or a 'relative connection'; or

– the speaker by deliberately dispensing with any marker aims to achieve some special effect.

13.2. The terminology which is used to refer to these alternatives, including the terms 'connexion' and 'asyndeton', is misleading. What is at stake is not the connecting (or leaving unconnected) of sentences—and a fortiori not that of 'sentence contents'—but the articulating the discourse in question and marking the relation between the successive sections within the narrower or wider context which they form part of. Such relations between what precedes and what follows may occupy any point on a scale ranging between the extremes of continuity and discontinuity, and the single word 'connexion' cannot do justice to the fact that one of the characteristics distinguishing between these particles is precisely in the definition of the range of possible values on this scale of continuity which is peculiar to each of them.[1]

13.3. It is here assumed that the particles discussed do not convey information about relations—adversative, causal, consecutive, inferential, &c. —between sentence *contents*. Such relations, whether between statements or between states of affairs in the world referred to by the text, cannot be established on the strength of these particles as such, though they may amount to an interpretation of the context as a whole. Attempts to put the results of such interpretation on the count of the 'meaning', 'sense', 'force', or 'value' of the particles in themselves are open to the following objections:

– the 'basic value' of a number of particles is given definitions of such elasticity that they fail to express what is *distinctive* for the particle defined. A typical situation is that of the concept 'opposition' coming to include such wider notions as those of 'contrast' and of 'difference';
– more than one alleged 'sense' (or related notion) is ascribed to a single particle, so that we get an 'assentient' ἀλλά[2] besides an 'adversative' ἀλλά and an ἀλλά which is said to 'break off',[3] a 'connective' as well as an 'adversative' δέ,[4] and an 'emphatic' in addition to an 'adversative' μέντοι;[5]
– particles are declared to be used 'in place of' other particles. An instructive instance is found in Denniston's treatment of δέ where, un-

---

[1] For the terminology of scale and range here employed cf. vO, 79 f. below.
[2] *GP* 16.
[3] *GP* 13-4.
[4] *GP* 162 ss.
[5] *GP* 399 ss.

der 'Particular uses of connective δέ',[1] he laconically affirms that 'it will be convenient to drop the distinction between continuative and adversative henceforward', and proceeds to discuss 'δέ for γάρ, οὖν (or δή), ἦ. When he observes that 'δέ is not infrequently used where the context admits, *or even appears to demand*,[2] γάρ (or, occasionally, οὖν or ἦ)', the proposed account has become self-refuting;

– in the numerous cases where there is an overlap between what is offered as the definition of the meaning, or the description of the use, of two or more particles, the distribution of these particles is either reduced to 'stylistic' preferences of the author in question, or left without any explanation at all.

13.4.　It should be borne in mind that the form of a text is never determined directly by the events recounted or states of affairs described in the statements making up the text, but always by the author presenting these data and placing them in some particular light for reasons of his own. The world apart from the author, if it is there, is irrelevant to the linguistic[3] interpretation of the text.

More concretely, if it is correctly stated above[4] that καί in the sequence '*a* καί *b*', unlike δέ, invites the hearer to include the *dictum* here denoted by *b* with that denoted by *a*, and so establishes a relation between *a* and *b*, this should not be taken to imply that an author is obliged by any relation existing between the elements of his argument or story independently of him to use καί in one case, that of *a* and *b* forming part of one connection, and δέ in another. If one compares e.g. Lysias I.23 ὁ δ' Ἐρατοσθένης ... εἰσέρχεται, καὶ ἡ θεράπαινα ἐπεγείρασά με εὐθὺς φράζει ὅτι ἔνδον ἐστί with Lysias III.13 ὁ δὲ ῥίψας τὸ ἱμάτιον ᾤχετο φεύγων. ἐγὼ δὲ ἡγούμενος ἐκεῖνον μὲν ἐκφεύξεσθαι ... ᾠχόμην ἀπιών, it seems legitimate to speculate that the speaker in the second context too might have chosen καί, but that it would not have served his purpose to suggest more of a connection between his departure and the supposed escape of his boyfriend—'and what did I do? I ran off in a different direction'—even apart from other possible motives concerning the articulation of the text.

Such alternative forms of presentation are highly functional, and nowhere more so than in persuasive speeches such as these by Lysias. For instance, to support a statement by means of a causal clause (introduced by διότι or ἐπεί) is to direct the attention of one's audience to the question

---

[1] *GP* 169.
[2] Italics CMJS.
[3] As distinct from e.g. an historical or philosophical interpretation.
[4] P. 11.

whether the argument does in fact support the claim, or indeed whether it is at all relevant to it; on the other hand to support one's statement with the help of a clause introduced by γάρ is to provide one's audience with a quasi self-evident explanation for what it might have failed to grasp—which may be a more effective procedure rhetorically.

It is within such a comparative framework alone that accounts of the type 'τὸ δὲ ἀντὶ τοῦ γάρ' make sense: when they are based on observation of the types of context in which certain particles are operative. Here they may throw light on the presentation adopted in a particular context without suggesting, as in the ancient grammarians and scholiasts, that we are dealing with a deviation from what is logically or linguistically required or correct and proper—what is κύριον. This is one of the reasons why the speeches of Lysias lend themselves to the treatment here proposed: the conventions of the genre make it possible to point out and explain similarities and differences between comparable contexts.

13.5. The four particles most important for the articulation of texts are at the same time the most frequent ones: δέ, γάρ, καί, and οὖν.

13.5.1. Δέ marks the beginning of a portion of text which the speaker wishes to subjoin to what precedes as a new unit. In the sequence 'a. b δέ ...' there is a *discontinuity* between a en b to the extent that the speaker does not suggest that b forms part of the same context in a narrow sense as a, as well as a *continuity* to the extent that both a and b, other things being the same, form part of a larger argumentative or narrative whole which is coherent at its own level.

13.5.1.1. The consecution of μέν and δέ may function in one of two different ways: either

- the two sections introduced by these two particles form part of one sentence which is marked as being such in its own right, or
- the section containing δέ has the status of a new, self-contained sentence, in which case the scope of any devices (e.g. οὖν or γάρ) used to mark the sentence containing μέν may extend over the sentence containing δέ.

This implies that from the point of view of the organisation of the text the combination of μέν and δέ operates at one level below that at which single δέ, οὖν or γάρ are operative.

---

[1] Compare e.g. the first sentence of Pericles' *Funeral Oration* (Thuc. II.35), where the μέν in οἱ μὲν πολλοί simply prepares the hearer for the balancing sentence (ἐμοὶ δέ ...) that is to follow.

A consequence is that single or 'solitary' μέν at the beginning of a section of text yields what is called an 'asyndeton'.[1] An example is Lysias I.43, at which point the text has been interrupted by the hearing of witnesses. Μέν does not here serve to define the contextual relation of the new sentence to the one that precedes, but to prepare the hearer for the change of subject, in the sense of topic, which will be effected in σκέψασθε δὲ κτλ.[1]

13.5.2. With 'a καί b' the hearer is invited to take in and include b in one and the same connection with what precedes—a use which καί may serve both *between* sentences and *within* sentences, between clauses or lower level constituents. The speaker may choose to do so for a variety of motives: to extend, expand, or elaborate what he has said, or make it more specific (by means of what is described as καί *explicativum*); to achieve a climax, or to suggest a connection between the facts stated ('and *at the same time*': hence 'and *so*', 'and *yet*'), &c. Thus whereas δέ makes for discontinuity, καί makes for continuity and cohesion.

13.5.2.1. Cohesion is a fortiori involved in the case of what is called 'relative connection'. Here the speaker includes and incorporates within the new sentence a constituent of the previous sentence (usually one with topic-function) together with all that he has predicated of it (usually with a different pragmatic function[2]). An example is Lysias I.36 'it is with these laws that I expect you to agree'.[3]

13.5.3. Γάρ and οὖν share the characteristic of assigning to a section of the text a different status from the preceding section, in the sense that

- γάρ marks a section as containing information supposed to be necessary towards understanding *what* has been said, or *that* it has been—or will be—said; while
- οὖν conveys that what precedes served an introductory or explanatory purpose: the speaker proceeds from preliminaries to main substance, or continues his argument or narrative after an inserted explanation or digression.

13.5.3.1. Μὲν οὖν in common with single οὖν marks a transition or return from introductory or explanatory or otherwise subsidiary matter to

---

[1] It may be speculated that, had there been no interruption of the continuous speech, Lysias might have chosen μὲν οὖν rather than μέν.

[2] For the present use of the term cf. Dik, *Functional Grammar*.

[3] P. 19 above.

the argument or story proper, but in addition marks a *conclusion* to the previous section.

13.6. With καίτοι, τοίνυν and μέντοι the speaker demands the special attention of his audience for a statement, for instance because he assumes, or pretends to assume, that this deviates from—or goes beyond—the expectations of his audience, or because it is to make a direct appeal to his audience, which may be in the sphere of volition.[1]

Of the three (1) καίτοι may be regarded as in competition, in the sense of overlapping distribution, with καί, (2) τοίνυν may be considered as competing both with δέ and with οὖν, and (3) μέντοι as an alternative, in certain conditions and with special characteristics, for δέ.

A tendency may be observed to attribute to καίτοι an 'adversative' value. This may be explained by the circumstance that one prominent motive for calling attention to what one presents as part of the same connection as that which precedes, may precisely be a contradiction or contrast, real or apparent, between the new and the preceding statement. In 'X is strong and meek as a lamb' it is possible to interpret 'and' as 'and *yet*'. To express an adversative relation, however, the speaker of Greek has other devices at his disposal, such as the adverb ὅμως; if he limits himself to using καίτοι he may be regarded as inserting an exclamation mark, and pointing a contrast is just one of several possible motives for his doing so.

With μέντοι a speaker introduces a statement that he wishes to uphold, regardless of whatever suggestion may have arisen from what precedes. It is characteristic of the particle that any tension which may be felt between the statement marked by μέντοι and the one that preceded, does not detract from the impact of this preceding statement, as it would in the case of ἀλλά. The use of μέντοι conveys that the speaker accepts full responsibility for the second *as well as* for the first claim.

13.7. For ἀλλά we find, besides a use often characterized as *adversative*, one of *breaking off*. The common factor between the two can be identified if it is accepted that in 'a ἀλλά b' the hearer is invited to replace *a* with *b*. In 'οὐκ a ἀλλά b' (or 'a ἀλλ' οὐ b') there is envisaged a *complete* substitution of *b* for *a*, in 'a ἀλλά b' a *partial* substitution is intended, for instance of *b* for a connotation, implication or suggestion contained in *a*, as in 'short but stout', 'slight but valiant', 'brief but intense' or 'poor but honest'.[2]

---

[1] Cf. vO, 153 ff. below.

[2] The term 'éliminer' applied to the case of 'οὐκ a ἀλλά b' by Ruijgh (see p. 36 above)

The common factor between expressions of the types '*a*, ἀλλά *b*' and 'οὐκ *a* ἀλλά *b*' is their rhetorical function. The effect of a presentation making use of ἀλλά appears to be to add relief to what is expressed by *b*. In expressions of the type 'not cold, no: nice and warm' this is achieved by removing an actual or possible misconception on the part of the audience and replacing it with what is allegedly the case. To say that 'he is slight but valiant' is halfway to overcome the disbelief which the bare claim that 'he is valiant' might have encountered among an audience that happened to be aware of his unwarlike physique.

In both cases the main burden seems to reside in what is here denoted by *b*. The claim that 'it is not in my nature to hate, but to love' can be reduced to one that 'it is in my nature to love' without any loss to the factual content, and similarly the qualification 'unpleasant, but necessary' is more a way of stressing the necessity than a twofold predicate (such as 'both a duty and a pleasure'), compounded of two halves of equal importance.[1]

All in all the value of ἀλλά does not appear to consist in calling attention to an adversative relation between contents of sentences, but in replacing one proposition or other notion by another one which is nearer to the heart of the speaker's concerns. It is this same value which is involved in instances of ἀλλά 'breaking off'; what is special about these is just that it is not the content of the previous statement which is replaced, but the entire subject, or even, in the case of what is somewhat misleadingly referred to as 'adhortative' ἀλλά, the very act of speaking which is 'replaced' in a turn towards action.

It is easily shown that the use of ἀλλά is primarily a matter of presentation rather than of oppositions existing in fact, by replacing ἀλλά in '*a*, ἀλλά *b*' (type 'short but stout') with καί, which can be done without running into any obstacles of a 'logical' nature. On the other hand in 'οὐκ *a* ἀλλά *b*' (type 'I do not love but hate') a relation of contradiction in fact obtains; not, however, between the two complete statements linked by ἀλλά, but between *b* and the denial of *a* or, what amounts to the same thing, between *b* and *a* divorced of the negation which in this context goes with it. This mutual exclusion obviously stands in the way of substitution of καί for ἀλλά.

---

is less felicitous to the extent that the focus is on the substitution of *b* rather than on the removal of *a*. His use of 'corriger' to characterize '*a*, ἀλλά *b*' is not open to this objection.

[1] This justifies the references of Ruijgh to a 'contraste déséquilibré'.

APPENDIX

Σύγκειται μὲν γὰρ ἐκ τριῶν ὁ λόγος. ἐκ τε τοῦ λέγοντος καὶ περὶ οὗ λέγει καὶ πρὸς ὅν, καὶ τέλος πρὸς τοῦτον ἐστι, λέγω δὲ τὸν ἀκροατήν (Arist. *Rhet.* 1358 a 37-b 2)

The aim of this appendix is to offer some considerations bearing on the value and use of (1) δή/δῆτα, μήν, ἦ, που and τοι, and (2) of some particles found in interrogative sentences, which have been neglected at the cost of our understanding of these particles. The discussion is mostly confined to Attic Greek of the fifth and fourth centuries, in particular the tragic poets, Aristophanes, Plato.[1]

Δή/δῆτα, μήν, ἦ, που and τοι all differ from the particles treated so far in primarily serving an 'interactive'[2] use rather than one of text articulation: they are among the instruments by which a speaker may direct and indeed manipulate the interaction between himself and his audience, in particular by taking into account what pragmatical information it had previously, and anticipating its possible responses. The objective is to show that a recognition of this aspect is indispensable to the understanding of the particles in question, not to suggest that a discussion of them under this aspect alone could do full justice to their uses.[3]

1. μήν *and* δή

The use of both μήν and δή is brought by Denniston under the headings 'emphatic' and 'connective'. In the case of δή the 'connection' implied is characterized as 'temporal or logical, or something between the two',[4] in that of μήν as 'adversative' and 'progressive', when it 'adds a fresh point, marks a fresh stage in the march of thought'.[5] The 'emphatic' value of δή, from which its connective force is taken to derive,[6] is characterized as

---

[1] The particles in question are distinctly rare in the *corpus Lysiacum*. For some of the reasons why see p. 58-9 below.

[2] Or 'interactional'. Cf. Caroline Kroon, 'Causal Connectors in Latin: the Discourse Function of *nam, igitur* and *ergo*', in M. Lavency & D. Longree, *Proceedings of the Vth Colloquium on Latin Linguistics*, CILL 15.1-4 (1989) 231-43.

[3] The question to what extent ἄρα belongs to the same set seems to require a wider frame of reference than is adopted for the present purpose. Cf. vO at pp. 82ff. below.

[4] P. 238; cf. (vO) infra 146.

[5] P. 336.

[6] P. 204.

follows: 'δή denotes that a thing really and truly is so: or that it is very much so',[1] after which it is stated[2] that 'it is difficult to grasp the exact difference in sense between μήν and the much commoner δή'. It will be argued here that the contribution of δή to a conversation is radically different from that of μήν: it is possible to describe δή as a primarily 'evidential' sentence particle which presents a statement as immediately evident to the senses or the understanding or as common knowledge.[3] It thus implies that speaker and hearer are in the same position with respect to this statement.[4] This makes it apt to mark *successful* interaction, and confers on it what may be called a 'socializing' function in that it brings into relief the information which is *shared* by the interlocutors. With μήν on the other hand the speaker shows himself aware that his audience may not be inclined to accept the statement, and indicates that he will nevertheless uphold it. It thus implies the possibility of a *distance* between the two.

1.1. δή

For illustration of the diversity which the use of δή shows in Plato alone the reader is referred to the discussion below.[5] Here I confine myself to a few instances exemplifying the aptness of δή to convey to the hearer the speaker's suggestion that the two of them share information, in a wider sense including opinions.

In εἰ μὲν τυγχάνει ἀληθῆ ὄντα ἃ λέγω, καλῶς δὴ ἔχει τὸ πεισθῆναι (Pl. *Phaedo* 91 B 2-3)[6] a rendering of δή by 'evidently' is materially adequate. However, the use of the particle seems to be motivated less by an urge on the part of the speaker to call attention to the evident character of the, in itself trivial, statement than by Socrates' particular interest in having his audience committed to the principle here enunciated just as he himself is committed to it.

In μόνον δὴ τὸ αὐτὸ κινοῦν ... οὔ ποτε λήγει κινούμενον (Pl. *Phdr.* 245 C 7) δή is used to mark the evident nature of a statement—evident at least in the light of what precedes—because this is to serve as the point of departure for further inferences: Socrates as it were 'cashes in' the commitment of his audience to what will provide the foundation for his next construction. The alleged common ground between speaker and hearer may

[1] Ib.
[2] P. 330.
[3] Cf. (vO) p. 141 below.
[4] Cf. (vO) p. 83 below.
[5] (vO) p. 140 ff.
[6] Cf. (vO) p. 145 below.

consist in their *attitude* with regard to the information or it may simply consist in the *availability* of the information as such. The latter possibility is involved in those contexts in which the scope of δή does not extend beyond the word or phrase (i.e. the linguistic counterpart to what in logic would be a *term*) to the clause or sentence (i.e. the counterpart to the *proposition* of logic).[1] δή here stresses that speaker and audience have the same information at their disposal. An example is οὗτος (...) δὴ ὁ Ἀπολλόδωρος τῶν ἐπιχωρίων παρῆν (Pl. *Phaedo* 59 B 6):[2] the character or behaviour (τρόπος) of Apollodorus has just been referred to (59 A 8), so the speaker can take it for granted that the audience knows who he is talking about.[3]

Another case in point is the entrance, in Aeschylus' *Persians* 159, of the Queen Atossa taking her clue from the anxiety just expressed by the chorus (εἴ τι μὴ δαίμων παλαιὸς νῦν μεθέστηκε στρατῷ) with the words ταῦτα δὴ λιποῦσ' ἱκάνω ... 'That in fact is precisely why I have come'. In Eur. *Med.* 68 too πεσσοὺς προσελθὼν ἔνθα δὴ παλαίτατοι θάσσουσι the particle conveys an appeal to shared information: 'the place where, as you know ...', as at Pl. *Phaedo* 60 A 4 τοιαῦτ' ἄττα εἶπεν, οἷα δὴ εἰώθασιν αἱ γυναῖκες: the audience is sufficiently familiar with the characterizations alluded to for these to be left implied.

1.1.1. The presence of a marked interactive component in δή is reflected in the high incidence of the particle in dialogue (tragic poets, Plato). The evidence from Aristophanes suggests that in ordinary language certain uses of δή were more frequent than others. Thus in the *Acharnians* the particle is invariably found in the second position of the sentence in a limited number of characteristic contexts: (1) in a call to action that the person addressed was prepared for, such as ἄγε/φέρε δή, λέγε δή, ἀκούετε δή, ἴτε δή, (2) following an interrogative pronoun or adjective such as ποδαπὴ δή; τί δή;[4] (3) following a deictic pronoun or adverb such as ταῦτα δή, νῦν δή, and (4) exclamative or virtually 'elative' designations of quality or quantity such as πολλὰ δή, ὅσα δή and οἷα δή. Only at *Ach.* 693 in a passage of sung verse θερμὸν ἀπομορξάμενον ἀνδρικὸν ἱδρῶτα δὴ καὶ πολύν do we find an instance of δή in a not similarly stereotyped idiomatic context.

---

[1] Cf. (vO) p. 81 below.
[2] Cf. (vO) p. 143 below.
[3] This usage is particularly frequent in Herodotus. See e.g. 1.43.2.
[4] Cf. p. 66 below.

1.2. μήν

The particle μήν seems to be at home in expressing the contrary of what the person addressed might either (1) suppose or (2) wish. This can be illustrated from Aristophanes' *Frogs*: thus for (1) compare e.g. *Ran.* 106 καὶ μὴν ἀτεχνῶς γε παμπόνηρα φαίνεται, for (2) e.g. 258 – οἰμώζετ᾽· οὐ γάρ μοι μέλει – ἀλλὰ μὴν κεκραξόμεσθά γ᾽ ὁπόσον ἡ φάρυγξ ἂν ἡμῶν χανδάνῃ δι᾽ ἡμέρας. The message may contain a threat, as at *Ran.* 285[1] in νὴ τὸν Δία καὶ μὴν αἰσθάνομαι ψόφου τινός. With the future tense especially the particle underlines a firm intention on the part of the speaker which could well impose a threat on the addressee as in five instances in the *Frogs*' ἀγών alone.[2]

Some of the contexts in which μήν figures invite comparison with typical contexts of μέντοι, e.g. *Ran.* 1036 καὶ μὴν οὐ Παντακλέα γε ἐδίδαξεν ὅμως τὸν σκαιότατιον 'surely this does not apply to Pantacles'.[3] Compare Pl. *Parm.* 153 A 1 οὐκ ἔχω λέγειν.– τόδε γε μὴν ἔχεις λέγειν, ὅτι κτλ. 'your "I can't" for one thing doesn't go for...'.

The aptitude of the particle to mark a distance between interlocutors[4] is made particularly clear in Plato's *Gorgias* at 449 C 3 in τούτου μὴν δεῖ, ὦ Γοργία· καί μοι ἐπίδειξιν αὐτοῦ τούτου ποιήσαι, τῆς βραχυλογίας, where Socrates echoes an earlier use of μήν by Gorgias (B 10) as he promised to be brief, and thereby makes it understood that Gorgias' capacity for and inclination towards prolixity are not called upon in Socrates' company. Similarly at Pl. *Tht.* 193 D 7 in ὃ ἐν τοῖς πρόσθεν οὕτως ἔλεγον καί μου τότε οὐκ ἐμάνθανες. – οὐ γὰρ οὖν. – τοῦτο μὴν ἔλεγον, ὅτι κτλ.: although Theaetetus may not have taken the point, *this* is what Socrates was claiming. Denniston's classification[5] of this instance under 'progressive' μήν, translated "Well, this is what I meant", at once posits a superfluous heading and yet fails to do justice to the peculiar contribution of μήν.

1.2.1. Denniston's assumption that (single) μήν 'is preeminently a Doric particle'[6] is severely qualified by the observation that 115 instances of it are found in Aristophanes alone.[7] The higher incidence of μήν in Plato in

---

[1] Cf. *Ran.* 288.
[2] At 907, 1119, 1198, 1249, 1263.
[3] See p. 34 above.
[4] Cf. p. 52 above.
[5] P. 337.
[6] P. 329.
[7] In Ionian the *form* of μέν does not discriminate between the *functions* of what are elsewhere μέν and μήν.

Republic books 2 to 10 and later dialogues[1] is perhaps better attributed to the conversational tone which characterizes the works in question than, with Denniston, to Plato's sojourn in Doric-speaking Sicily. The distinction drawn by Denniston[2] between the value of single μήν and that which the particle brings to its more frequent occurrence in certain collocations[3] may be feared to run into an objection against begging the question: the only methodically correct approach would seem to take its point of departure from an initial assumption that the proper value of μήν both *explains* its affinity with οὐ, with ἀλλά and with ἦ,[4] and *is preserved* in its collocations with these.

2. ἦ

ἦΗ is described by Denniston[5] as an 'affirmative', by Kühner-Gerth less aptly as a 'confirmative'[6] particle. More to the point is Ruijgh's supposition that 'at some time before Homer ἦ and οὐ served as counterparts, the one underlining the affirmative and the other the negative character of the utterance':[7] the particle is used for affirming as opposed to denying—compare Hesychius' ἦ· ἀληθῶς, ὄντως—and should be understood as a kind of opposite number to a negative. In communicating with an audience just as the need to deny a proposition expressly may be felt when there is a suspicion that the audience is disposed to assent to this proposition, so there may be good reasons for explicitly affirming what the audience may be inclined to disbelieve or to disregard, which is precisely the use of ἦ.

2.1. While the possibility of a confusion with ἤ makes it harder to estimate the frequency of ἦ,[8] it seems safe to state that the particle is uncommon in historical prose and hardly found in oratorical prose, the collocation of ἦ που[9] excepted. For Aristophanes Todd records 51 instances, for Euripides Allen-Italie list the same number in nearly twice as much plays. The highest incidence of the particle is found in Plato with over 300 instances.

---

[1] *Parm., Tht., Phdr., Polit., Phil., Laws, Seventh Letter.*
[2] GP 329.
[3] These include οὐ μήν, οὐδὲ μήν, οὐ μήν ... ἀλλά, ἀλλὰ μήν, ἦ μήν.
[4] For ἦ μήν cf. p. 56 below.
[5] P. 280.
[6] II.144.
[7] '... à une époque antérieure à Homère se faisaient pendant, l'un soulignant le caractère affirmatif, l'autre le caractère négatif de la phrase' (1971) 194.
[8] Compare Allen and Italie's *Concordance to Euripides* s.v.
[9] For which see p. 61-3 below.

This distribution is perhaps best accounted for by assuming that affirmative ἦ is a conversation idiom, rather than, with Denniston,[1] that it is 'mainly a verse idiom'.

ˏΗ is quite often seen in the company of other particles: in addition to ἤτοι, which is usually written as one word, Brandwood notes (1) ἦ ... ἄρα, (2) ἦ που ἄρα, (3) ἦ που, (4) ἦ μήν, and (5) ἦ γάρ, as well as ἦ οὖν, and ἦ καί. If it is true that ἦ balances οὐ, in the sense that it is affirmative as οὐ is negative, these collocations would seem to be accounted for by taking the part of the τοι, ἄρα, που, and μήν in them, respectively, to be to indicate what might be called the communicative 'impact' of the affirmation. Some collocations are clearly especially frequent in particular contexts, such as ἦ μήν in oaths and adjurations, e.g. Xen. *An.* VI.1.31 ὀμνύω ὑμῖν θεοὺς πάντας καὶ πάσας, ἦ μὴν ἐγώ κτλ., Pl. *Phaedo* 115 D 8 ὑμεῖς δὲ ἦ μὴν μὴ παραμενεῖν ἐγγυήσασθε ἐπειδὰν ἀποθάνω κτλ., and, with Socrates pretending to be under oath, *Apol.* 22 A 2: καὶ νὴ τὸν κύνα, ὦ ἄνδρες Ἀθηναῖοι, δεῖ γὰρ πρὸς ὑμᾶς τἀληθῆ λέγειν, ἦ μὴν ἐγὼ ἔπαθόν τι τοιοῦτον.[2]

2.2.   Motives for presenting a statement explicitly as affirming some state of affairs can be many and varied. Thus in Aristophanes' *Frogs* we have five instances of ἦ:

–   one with τοι at 33-4 οἴμοι κακοδαίμων· τί γὰρ ἐγὼ οὐκ ἐναυμά-χουν; —ἦ τἄν σε κωκύειν ἂν ἐκέλευον μακρά: here the speaker uses ἦ to enhance the threat: 'take it from me (even if it can no longer be proved) that I would have...', or negatively expressed, which does more justice to the idiom: 'don't you fancy you would have got away without a ...!';[3]

–   twice with μήν:
103-4 σὲ δὲ ταῦτ' ἀρέσκει; – μᾶλλα πλεῖν ἦ μαίνομαι. – ἦ μὴν κόβαλά γ' ἐστίν, ὡς καὶ σοὶ δοκεῖ: the assertion is directly opposed to that of the interlocutor, and
1470 μεμνημένος νυν τῶν θεῶν οὓς ὤμοσας ἦ μὴν ἀπάξειν μ' οἴκαδ' (...): Euripides cites Dionysus' promise in the form of an oath;[4] and

–   twice with που:
803: ὁ γὰρ Εὐριπίδης κατ' ἔπος βασανιεῖν φησι τὰς τραγῳδίας.—

---

[1]   *GP* 280.
[2]   Cf. Ar. *Ranae* 1470, quoted below.
[3]   And perhaps also to overcome a reluctance which may be supposed to exist on the part of his addressee to accept a disagreeable truth: 'don't flatter yourself ...'.
[4]   Cf. above.

ἦ που βαρέως οἶμαι τὸν Αἰσχύλον φέρειν: to Aeacus representing the point of view of Euripides, Xanthias opposes that of Aeschylus. The collocation ἦ που is repeated for special effect a little later at the beginning of the choral song at
814: ἦ που δεινὸν ἐριβρεμέτας χόλον ἔνδοθεν ἕξει (...).[1]

3. που

3.1. *Distribution*

On που some of Denniston's statements concerning its distribution[2] are somewhat misleading or insufficiently specific. It is true that the particle occurs only sporadically in the orators.[3] However, that 'there are few examples in Thucydides', whereas the particle 'admirably suits the easy colloquial style of Herodotus' is hardly borne out by the facts.

In Herodotus κου is found other than in a local sense in 41 instances, ten of which occur in passages of direct speech. Twenty of the remaining 31 instances may be more or less confidently[4] assigned to Powell's heading of 'approximately' e.g. 1.18.4 μεσοῦντι δέ κου τῆς ἀναβάσιος ..., or 1.119.2 ἔτεα τρία καὶ δέκα κου μάλιστα γεγονώς, contexts in which Herodotus makes it understood that his indications of time and place do not pretend to accuracy. A similar reserve seems to be involved in such contexts as 1.178.1 τῆς δὲ Ἀσσυρίης ἐστὶ μέν κου καὶ ἄλλα πολίσματα πολλά (...) and 1.184.1 τῆς δὲ Βαβυλῶνος ταύτης πολλοὶ μέν κου καὶ ἄλλοι ἐγένοντο, in which κου seems to be an acknowledgement of the lack of further specification, just as at 6.11.1 in καὶ δή κού σφι καὶ ἄλλοι ἠγορόωντο, ἐν δὲ δὴ καὶ (...) Διονύσιος.

In some places κου conveys that we are dealing with an unverifiable surmise on the part of Herodotus, as at 5.1.3 καὶ εἶπάν κου παρὰ σφίσι αὐτοῖσι... and at 7.214.2 πάντως κου τὸ ἀτρεκέστατον πυθόμενοι (...), where the presumption that his authorities were acquainted with the facts of the case is used to support Herodotus' claim that a λόγος which implies that they were not cannot be credited. An arguably similar context is 6.98.1, on a single unique earthquake on Delos unattested by any but the inhabitants, καὶ τοῦτο μέν κου τέρας ἀνθρώποισι τῶν μελλόντων ἔσεσθαι κακῶν ἔφηνε ὁ θεός, where the rare collocation of μέν—here equivalent

---

[1] For the use of ἦ που in tragedy underlying the present use see below, p. 62.
[2] P. 491.
[3] At the only place quoted by Denniston (p. 491, 494) from Lysias (VI.25) Reiske conjectured, and Hude, Thalheim, and Bizos have all adopted, πω.
[4] Cf. Sicking, Stork, & Van Ophuijsen (forthcoming) on 7.10 θ 3.

to μήν—and κου betrays a certain ambivalence: the putative earthquake at this holy spot 'cannot but' be a sign from Apollo, but whether it has really occurred is uncertain.

Two instances that are harder to assess are

6.128.2 καὶ δή κου μάλιστα τῶν μνηστήρων ἠρέσκοντο ⟨οἱ⟩ οἱ ἀπ᾽ Ἀθηνέων ἀπιγμένοι,καὶ τούτων μᾶλλον Ἱπποκλείδης where the particle may have been motivated by the absence of further specification, but may just as well convey a touch of scepticism with regard to a statement conceivably reflecting a (pro–)Athenian bias; and

7.1.2 καὶ δή κου ἐν τῇ νυκτὶ εἶδε ὄψιν τοιήνδε, ὡς λέγεται ὑπὸ Περσέων, a context which invites comparison with 6.98.1:[1] though it is possible to distrust the Persian report, the sign from above coming at this moment has a high intrinsic probability.

In Thucydides non-local uses of που are predominantly[2] found in direct speech, where they may help to define the relation between the speaker and his audience.[3] Of the contexts in which Thucydides is speaking in his own person, the most significant are those contained in statements,[4] such as II.17.3 καὶ ὡς ἕκαστος που ἐδύνατο and III.82.8 οὐ μέχρι τοῦ δικαίου καὶ τῇ πόλει ξυμφόρου προτιθέντες ἐς δὲ τὸ ἑκατέροις που αἰεὶ ἡδονὴν ἔχον ὁρίζοντες,[5] where the presence of που seems to mark the speaker's dispensing with a specification. The difference between the two historians, discounting direct speech and local που, is seen to reside mostly in the comparative frequency in Herodotus and near-absence in Thucydides of που as 'approximately', a difference which may be connected not so much with a more or less 'colloquial' style as with differing standards of accuracy in dealing with quantitative data.

In all που is most common in dialogue, particularly in that of Plato; among the dramatic poets it is proportionally much less frequent in Aeschylus than it is either in Sophocles and Euripides, or in Aristophanes and Menander. This suggests that που is properly at home in (the μίμησις of) conversation.

The virtual absence of the particle in oratorical prose is of a piece with the general rarity of 'interactive' particles in these texts, which may be an

---

[1] Quoted above.

[2] Out of a total of 40 instances listed by Von Essen (including one of δήπου in a speech at I.1.214), 11 are local. Of the remaining 28 instances of non-local single που, 19 occur in speeches.

[3] As the three instances of the particle in Nicias' speech to his despondent troops in VII.77 do.

[4] The aptness of the particle to occur in the hypothetical contexts of εἴ (τι) που with optative (4 x) and of ἤν που (1 x) is too self-evident to cast much light on the present issue.

[5] Cf. the remaining two instances at III.82.3 and VIII.99.

indication of the distance between the orator and his often large audience, but also, and more particularly,[1] of the distance between that artefact in stylised language which is the oration at least in the form in which it has been 'published', i.e. released for circulation, and all genuinely non-epideictic prose. That που in the orators is even rarer than ἦ or δή is presumably owing to its value as leaving room for difference of opinion, which is at odds with the purpose of persuasive speech.

3.2. *Value*

As to the value of που, it is by Denniston supposed to 'convey a feeling of uncertainty in the speaker', and thereby to lend itself to ironical use, 'with assumed diffidence, by a speaker who is quite sure of his ground'. It seems preferable, however, to address the issue not in terms of communication of real or pretended feelings on the part of the speaker, but of presentation and of the conversational stance adopted: with που a speaker presents his statement as a surmise whose accuracy he does not vouch for[2] so that disputing it need not impair the basis for an understanding between the two partners in the conversation.

In Plato που very often serves to introduce in a casual way what is obvious or even trivial, so as to avoid any impression of smugness or pedantry. Examples are *Gorgias* 453 E 7 (ἀποκρινούμεθά που αὐτῷ ὅτι ...), 460 B 8 (ὁ δὲ δίκαιος δίκαιά που πράττει), 464 A 1 (σῶμά που καλεῖς τι καὶ ψυχήν;), 495 C 4 (ἐπιστήμην που καλεῖς τι;), 496 A 1 (νοσεῖ που ἄνθρωπος ὀφθαλμούς...;), 504 A 3 (κοσμοῦσί που τὸ σῶμα...),[3] in all of which the interlocutor is required in the name of the λόγος to agree with uncontroversial claims. This has less to do with the "ironical bent of Plato" supposed by Denniston[4] than with Socrates' insistence on his partner voluntarily agreeing with each step, however trivial, in his ἔλεγχος, rather than being forced to do so. Some cautious reserve is in place when guessing at the opinions of one's partner's in conversation as at *Gorgias* 453 E 7 & 495 C 4; cf. *Prot.* 312 D 2; outside Plato e.g. Herodotus 3.72.1 (Otanes) οἶδάς κου, & 7.8 β 3 (Xerxes) ἐπίστασθέ κου πάντες, or when calling on the other person's memory, as at *Gorgias* 476

---

[1] Considering that this distance can hardly be greater than that between such an author as Thucydides and *his* public of *readers* in whose work the incidence of these particles is actually rather higher.

[2] Cf. LSJ s.v.: *"perhaps, I suppose"*.

[3] Cf. *Prot.* 313 D 1, 323 E 2, 349 E 8.

[4] P. 491.

E 3 in τὰ δὲ δίκαιά που καλὰ ὡμολόγηται and *Prot.* 357 E 1 in ἴστε που καὶ αὐτοί.[1]

3.2.1. In three contexts in Plato's *Gorgias* we find a more pregnant use of the particle. At the beginning of a serious attempt to bring his φίλος Polus over to his own point of view Socrates recapitulates the thesis that is crucial to it at 473 A 4 in the words εἶπον ἐγώ που ἐν τοῖς ἔμπροσθεν τὸ ἀδικεῖν τοῦ ἀδικεῖσθαι κάκιον εἶναι. Here the use of που does not appear to be motivated either by 'a feeling of uncertainty' or by irony so much as by a conscious effort on Socrates' part to ease conversational relations with Polus by not ignoring his conviction that he has effectively refuted Socrates (cf. 473 A 10 ἐξηλέχθην & B 2 ἀληθῆ γε οἰόμενος): the particle testifies to Socrates' awareness that Polus is arguing from a position different from his own.

At 503 A 6 Socrates has been saying that there are, besides politicians striving for the well-being of their fellow-citizens, others who only consider their own interest. Callicles, while he is prepared to concede this, chooses a euphemistic expression to refer to the latter kind: εἰσὶν δὲ καὶ οἵους σὺ λέγεις. Socrates is more specific: εἰ γὰρ τοῦτό ἐστι τὸ διπλοῦν, τὸ μὲν ἕτερόν που τούτου κολακεία ἂν εἴη καὶ αἰσχρὰ δημηγορία. On the face of it που here leaves room for Polus to contest this unreservedly negative qualification. In effect it is Socrates' polite way of depriving Callicles from any pretext he might have taken for contesting it; and at *Gorgias* 477 E 3 in ἀλλὰ μὴν που τό γε μεγίστη βλάβῃ ὑπερβάλλον μέγιστον ἂν κακὸν εἴη τῶν ὄντων Polus will on pain of inconsistency have to grant Socrates' claim, and so in the last resort will be forced to acknowledge ἀδικία and ψυχῆς πονηρία as the greatest of evils. In this exceptional[2] collocation of που with μήν, μήν intimates that a denial from Polus would destroy any chance of an agreement, and που together with the potential optative allows Polus to save his face while losing his stake.

3.2.2. The high incidence of που in Plato suits the kind of conversation that his dialogues aspire to be a μίμησις of, and his way of using it suits the conditions on which Socrates seeks an understanding with his partners in them: λόγος comes first, regardless of pretence or prestige. In the tragic poets a different situation applies. For some unmarked and unre-

---

[1] Pl. *Prot.* 339 C 2 οἶσθα οὖν, ἔφη, ὅτι προϊόντος τοῦ ᾄσματος λέγει που is an interesting example of a primarily local που serving in the context of a tactful reminder and thus pointing to a continuity between local and non-local uses under the interactive aspect.

[2] For Plato Brandwood records καὶ μήν που *La.* 193 C 9 and, followed by another καί, *Resp.* 381 A 6 & 486 A 1.

markable uses cf. Sophocles *OT* 769 ἀξία δέ που μαθεῖν κἀγὼ τά γ᾽ ἐν σοὶ δυσφόρως ἔχοντ᾽, ἄναξ, where the effect of using που is that Iocaste's urgent request to be informed cannot be disregarded without brusquerie, and *OC* 1587... ὡς μὲν γὰρ ἐνθένδ᾽ εἶρπε καὶ σύ που παρὼν ἔξοισθ᾽.

More often a linguistically similar application of the particle contributes to a quite different final interpretation: thus at *OT* 1115 in τῇ δ᾽ ἐπιστήμῃ σύ μου προὔχοις τάχ᾽ ἄν που, τὸν βοτῆρ᾽ ἰδὼν πάρος the idiomatic phrase referring to what the chorus is supposed to know and Oedipus is supposed not to know will prove to be tragically inappropriate. A to some extent comparable context is Soph. *Electra* 1473, where the ingenuous appeal εἴ που κατ᾽ οἶκον ἡ Κλυταιμήστρα, κάλει is answered by the gruesome display of Clytaemnestra's dead body. On the other hand, at *Ajax* 469, where the hero entertains the proposition of dying on the field of honour and rejects it in the words ἀλλ᾽ ὧδε γ᾽ Ἀτρείδας ἂν εὐφραίναιμί που, what we have is not tragic irony but gross understatement of an unpalatable truth.

3.3. ἦ που *and* δήπου

Of more or less fixed collocations of που with other particles the most frequent are ἦ που and δήπου.

3.3.1. ἦ που

Of these ἦ που is found in two typical situations. Lysias has 11 instances,[1] all of them but the two in the Epitaphios appearing in the conclusion of an enthymeme, e.g. 27.15 καίτοι εἰ τοῖς μὴ δικαίως ἐπεξιοῦσιν ὀργίζεσθε, ἦ που σφόδρα χρὴ αὐτοὺς τοὺς ἀδικοῦντας τιμωρεῖσθαι, 30.17 ἔπειτα εἰ ταῦτα νομίζεις δεινά, ἦ που νῦν σφόδρα ἐκείνους ἡγεῖ ἀδικεῖν κτλ., and 25.17 ὅστις γὰρ τότε οὐδὲν ἐξήμαρτον (...) ἦ που νῦν σφόδρα προθυμήσομαι χρηστὸς εἶναι. Denniston's observation that these occur 'in a fortiori argument'[2] cannot serve as a characterization of this use: the presence of σφόδρα contributes more to the a fortiori interpretation than that of ἦ που, as is shown by the fact that two of the other contexts, in which σφόδρα is not found, do not lend themselves to such an interpretation: cf. 6.12 καίτοι ὁπότε οὗτος παρ᾽ ἑτέρου ἠξίωσε δίκην ἀσεβείας λαβεῖν, ἦ που ἑτέρους γε παρὰ τούτου λαβεῖν δίκαιον καὶ εὐσεβές ἐστιν, and 8.11 καίτοιγε σφῶν γε αὐτῶν κατήγορουν. εἰ γὰρ ἃ μετὰ τούτων ⟨ἔπραττον⟩ ἀδικουμένῳ μοι μηδὲν ἦν δίκαιον εἰπεῖν, ἦ που κακῶς συνέπραττον.

---

[1] 2.37, 2.39, 6.12, 7.8, 8.11, 12.35, 13.57, 13.69, 25.17, 27.15, 30.17.
[2] P. 28.

Similar contexts are found among only ten instances in all of ἦ που in Plato; thus at *Gorgias* 469 B 3 when Socrates has laid it down that whoever kills unjustly is miserable and whoever kills justly may not be miserable but is not enviable either, Polus infers ἦπου ὅ γε ἀποθνήσκων ἀδίκως ἐλεινός τε καὶ ἄθλιός ἐστιν. Compare *Phaedo* 84 D 9 ἦ που χαλεπῶς ἂν τοὺς ἄλλους ἀνθρώπους πείσαιμι ὡς οὐ συμφορὰν ἡγοῦμαι τὴν παροῦσαν τύχην, ὅτε γε μηδ' ὑμᾶς δύναμαι πείθειν, and from Thucydides I.142.3 τὴν μὲν (sc. ἐπιτείχισιν) χαλεπὸν καὶ ἐν εἰρήνῃ πόλιν ἀντίπαλον κατασκευάσασθαι, ἦ που δὴ ἐν πολεμίᾳ τε καὶ οὐχ ἧσσον ἐκείνοις ἡμῶν ἀντιτετειχισμένων, VI.37.2 and V.100, all in speeches, and from Aristophanes *Thesm.* 63 ἦ που νέος γ' ὢν ἦσθ' ὑβριστής, ὦ γέρον.[1] In such contexsts ἦ που may be viewed as a bid to confer on a statement the maximum impact short of causing irritation and provoking contradiciton.

The other principal use is best illustrated from Aristophanes:

Plut. 698: προσιόντος γὰρ αὐτοῦ μέγα πάνυ ἀπέπαρδον· (...) – ἦ πού σε διὰ τοῦτ' εὐθὺς ἐβδελύττετο 'that must be the reason why he at once felt a loathing for you'; *Lys.* 1089: ἦ που πρὸς ὄρθρον σπασμὸς ὑμᾶς λαμβάνει 'it seems as if you men are troubled at day-rise by convulsions', where the speaker presents by means of ἦ που as an innocent surmise a statement of observed fact which is painful to the person addressed. In both contexts the speaker is not really in doubt, and to present his statement as only arguable when no alternative is available to the addressee is to rub it in.

In the tragic poets ἦ που is not used by Aeschylus except at *Prom.* 521 ἦ πού τι σεμνόν ἐστιν ὃ ξυναμπέχεις, and is found twice[2] in Euripides in the context of a supposition with regard to the thoughts of the addressee; at *Heraclid.* 55 ἦ που καθῆσθαι τήνδ' ἕδραν καλὴν δοκεῖς and *Bacch.* 939 ἦ πού με τῶν σῶν πρῶτον ἡγήσῃ φίλων. In such contexts που is standard[3] and ἦ adds a tone of threat: the speaker will see to it that the addressee is proved wrong.

In Sophocles too the collocation is infrequent.[4] Typical contexts are *Ajax* 1008 ἦ πού με Τελαμὼν δέξαιτ' ἂν εὐπρόσωπος, 382 ἦ που πολὺν γέλωθ' ὑφ' ἡδονῆς ἄγεις, 622 ἦ που παλαιᾷ μὲν σύντροφος ἀμέρᾳ (...) μάτηρ (...) γόον (...) ἥσει, 1229 ἦ που τραφεὶς ἂν μητρὸς εὐγενοῦς ἄπο | ὑψήλ' ἐφώνεις, all of them suppositions, the certainty of which is brought

---

[1] Here according to Denniston 282 'the *a fortiori* relationship is implied'.

[2] *Hel.* 1465 που bears a local interpretation.

[3] Cf. p. 59 above.

[4] In some instances it may be disputed whether ἤ που or ἦ που should be read: cf. Ellendt-Genthe s.v.

into relief by the speaker's seemingly calling them in question in a pathetic (622) or taunting way.

In Plato a tone of irony may be sometimes suspected, as at *Resp.* 450 D 5 in ἦ που βουλόμενός με παραθαρρύνειν λέγεις; where D 8 (τοὐναντίον ποιεῖς) shows that the desired effect is not achieved, and at *Gorgias* 448 A 3 in ἦ που ἄρα ῥᾳδίως ἀποκρινῇ, ὦ Γοργία: his ease in answering will land Gorgias in difficulty. But irony is not an inherent feature of the collocation, as witness *Ly.* 207 D 5 ἦ που, ἦν δ᾽ ἐγώ, ὦ Λύσι, σφόδρα φιλεῖ σε ὁ πατὴρ καὶ ἡ μήτηρ; and *Polit.* 285 D 8 ἦ που τὸν τῆς ὑφαντικῆς γε λόγον αὐτῆς ταύτης ἕνεκα θηρεύειν οὐδεὶς ἂν ἐθελήσειεν νοῦν ἔχων.

3.3.2. δήπου

With rererence to δήπου Denniston's assessment of the distribution[1] 'rare in tragedy,[2] frequent in comedy[3] and prose (though in Thucydides only in viii 87.4: 87.5)' is more adequate for the verse than for prose. In Lysias δήπου is found in one context of οὐ δήπου and ten of οὐ γὰρ δήπου.[4] In Plato Brandwood lists 161 instances, which with those classed separately of γὰρ δήπου (41 x), γε δήπου (9 x), δὲ δήπου (10 x), καὶ δήπου (3 x), μὲν δήπου (1 x), μὲν οὖν δήπου (1 x), οὔκουν δήπου (1 x), οὖν δήπου (1 x) adds up to 228. It seems a fair account of these data to say that δήπου in the here considered authors is more than marginally present only in dialogues aspiring to a species of realism, and is really frequent only in Plato.[5]

3.3.2.1. Semantically there is some tension between the two components of δήπου: the dictum is offered as being self-evident, yet it is at the same time implicitly acknowledged that its self-evidence is only surmised and might be called in doubt. In such an instance as Sophocles *OT* 1041 τῶν Λαΐου δήπου τις ὠνομάζετο there seems to be genuine hesitation on the part of the speaker. In Ar. *Nub.* 369 αὗται δήπου Socrates' use of δήπου seems to be elicited by Strepsiades' naive simplicity: 'if it isn't Zeus who causes rain, who is it?' 'Why, the clouds of course! who else?' Compare Pl. *Prot.* 313 C 6-7 τρέφεται δέ, ὦ Σώκρατες, ψυχὴ τίνι; – μαθήμασιν δήπου, ἦν δ᾽ ἐγώ 'Why, with μαθήματα of course!' In the fairly numer-

---

[1] P. 267.

[2] I.e. not in Aeschylus except at *Prom.* 1064 and not in Euripides. For Sophocles Ellendt-Genthe refer to *Ant.* 381, *Trach.* 418, and *OT* 1042.

[3] There are 26 instances listed in Todd.

[4] Not counting Sauppe's conjecture at XII.87, or that of Denniston (p. 268: οὔκουν δήπου) at XXIX.4

[5] Herodotus, whether he as a non-Attic writer was meant to be comprehended under Denniston's heading of 'prose' or not, does not in fact have *δήκου, though he has καὶ δή κου (e.g. 9.113.1: 'and naturally as might have been expected').

ous instances of the type of *Phaedo* 68 C 7 πάντως δήπου, ἔφη the collocation seems apt to avoid committing oneself too strongly to what is apparently the obvious answer: 'Quite so, I should say'.

The fine shades of δήπου as employed in questions can be seen in the following examples: Soph. *Trach*. 418 τὴν αἰχμάλωτον, ἣν ἔπεμψας ἐς δόμους, κάτοισθα δήπου: 'I presume you know'; Ar. *Av*. 179 οὐχ οὗτος οὖν δήπου 'στὶν ὀρνίθων πόλος; 'isn't this, then... ' & *Eccl*. 327 τίς ἔστιν; οὐ δήπου Βλέπυρος ὁ γειτνιῶν; 'it seems I have to take it that this is Blepyrus', and Plato, *Prot*. 309 C 2 οὐ γὰρ δήπου τινὶ καλλίονι ἐνέτυχες ἄλλῳ ἔν γε τῇδε τῇ πόλει 'for we may safely exclude the possibility of your having met—in this town—with any more handsome than Alcibiades, with its 'echo' in D 1 σοφωτάτῳ μὲν οὖν δήπου τῶν γε νῦν, εἴ σοι δοκεῖ σοφώτατος εἶναι Πρωταγόρας 'surely the wisest man in our generation, I dare say—if in your opinion the wisest man is Protagoras'.

4. τοι

The generally accepted etymological connection of τοι with the second person dative pronoun accounts for the extent to which justice has been done to the interactive aspect of this particle, e.g. by Denniston:[1] 'Its primary function is to bring home to the comprehension of the person addressed a truth of which he is ignorant, or temporarily oblivious: to establish in fact, a close rapport between the mind of the speaker and the mind of another person. As a natural corollary, τοι implies, strictly speaking, an audience (...) of one'. The only objection to such a description may be a slight overemphasis of cognitive content at the cost of motives of commanding attention to what might be a special concern to, or might not be expected by, the hearer—which explained the presence of τοι in the compound particles καίτοι, μέντοι and τοίνυν discussed above.[2]

Cases in point are Eur. *Bacch*. 1118 ἐγώ τοι, μῆτερ, εἰμί, παῖς σέθεν | Πενθεύς and Pl. *Ly*. 211 C 5 πάρεστι δέ τοι αὐτός οὐχ ὁρᾷς; each of which is concerned with calling attention to what the person addressed seems to ignore.

5. *Question and answer*

An extensive treatment of the use of particles in questions is beyond our present scope. What follows may illustrate how the value of the particles discussed above enters into the interplay of question and answer.

---

[1] P. 537.
[2] P. 28 ff.

A paraphrase of Plato's *Gorgias* 468 E 10-470 A 8 is meant to bring out how some of the particles found here (δέ, οὖν) serve to cement the cohesion of the conversation, while others (δή, ἦ, που &c.) help to define the basis for an understanding between the partners.

Our section begins with Polus' noting that Socrates does not crave the prerogative of acting as he pleases within the community he forms part of. Socrates at 468 E 10 requires a specification: does Polus refer to acting δικαίως or ἀδίκως? Polus in turn asks if this distinction is relevant: is not a man who can act at his own pleasure enviable in any case? Neither of these questions features a particle, which may be read as an indication that converstional relations are so far unmarked. When Socrates calls on Polus to stop saying things which are taboo (εὐφήμει[1]) the counter-question at 469 A 3 is τί δή; The particle may be understood as conveying the questioner's assumption that his interlocutor is aware of the reason for asking the question and inability to imagine what was wrong with what he has said.

Socrates' reply is just as if Polus' question had merely been 'why?': 'because one should not envy but pity a man who is not enviable'. For anyone who, like Polus, is not familiar with the principles from which Socrates starts this reply is less than illuminating. Polus therefore asks (469 A 6) τί δέ; which is a natural way of asking a question aiming at a more complete answer: Polus does not see that Socrates' answer is in fact complete, and explains: surely the men he refers to are not miserable? But this is precisely what Socrates took for granted: 469 A 8 πῶς γὰρ οὔ;—a rhetorical question, marked by γάρ as an explanation of what Polus failed to grasp before, but has now understood to the point of being able to guess at the point Socrates is making, which he marks by οὖν at 469 A 9-10 in the words 'He οὖν who kills whom he wishes and does so justly is miserable and pitiful?'. Socrates at 469 A 11 denies this in οὐκ ἔμοιγε, but goes on to reject with οὐδέ an illegitimate inference which Polus might be tempted to make: οὐδὲ μέντοι ζηλωτός. From Socrates' rejecting the qualification ἄθλιος Polus must not conclude to the contrary. But Polus thinks he can convict Socrates of an inconsistency: hasn't he just said that he thinks such a man miserable? Socrates' reply is to say that that particular term (γε 469 B 1) should be reserved for anyone who kills unjustly, and (δέ 469 B 2) that he that kills justly is ἀζήλωτος.

Polus now tries a different approach: there is no denying (ἦ 469 B 3) that a man who comes to an undeserved bad end is miserable.The που

---

[1] The choice of a present imperative conveys Polus' view that Socrates is now in fact saying such things. Cf. my 'The Distribution of Aorist and Present Tense Stem Forms in Greek, Especially in the Imperative', *Glotta* LXIX, 1991, 160-1.

subjoined to this prevents an impression of uncalled for verbal aggres-
siveness and implies that Polus expects Socrates to agree. But Socrates'
reply is (469 B 5-6) that it is more miserable to kill unjustly or to die a
deserved (δικαίως) death. Polus' response at 469 B 7 in πῶς δῆτα, ὦ
Σώκρατες is a last effort to preserve a basis for understanding, in which
δῆτα, a strong variant of δή, conveys a 'you can see why I have to ask'.
Socrates, however, pretends he does not see why and replies just as if
Polus had been asking for a simple explanation: 'In the sense, I mean, that
committing injustice is (τυγχάνει ...) the greatest of evils'. Polus wants
to get this clear: 469 B 10 ἢ γὰρ τοῦτο μέγιστον; οὐ τὸ ἀδικεῖσθαι μεῖζον; 'Is this to be explained (γάρ) by your sincere conviction that committing injustice is indeed (ἢ), and suffering injustice is not (οὐ) the worse
of the two evils?' Socrates' unqualified affirmative answer allows Polus
to infer that on this supposition (ἄρα)[1] Socrates would prefer being a
victim to being a perpetrator of injustice. Socrates at 469 C 1-2 confirms
that, though preference hardly comes into it, he would indeed in the absence of an alternative choose to ἀδικεῖσθαι rather than to ἀδικεῖν. Polus
again takes him up on this (469 C 3): 'Socrates does not ἄρα wish to be a
tyrant?' When Socrates qualifies his agreement by the preliminary re-
quirement of a correct definition of being a tyrant Polus with ἀλλά at 469
C 5 does away with these refinements: τυραννεῖν for him is still the freedom to kill, banish and generally act at one's pleasure. The conversation
thus seems to have been abortive, with Polus holding the same views he
held before. It is only now that Socrates shows any interest in serving the
basis for communication at 469 C 8 in ἐμοῦ δή λέγοντος ἐπιλαβοῦ,[2]
appealing to an earlier (467 C 1-2) agreement to this procedure: 'Well
then, here I begin with my λέγειν, and do you ...'. He starts with an
example: when a man owes his sense of power to the possession of a
knife, is this Polus' idea of μέγα δύνασθαι? The reply, as expected, is a
categorical no: οὐ δῆτα οὕτω γε (470 A 1). But Socrates in addition requires a motivation (470 A 1-2): ἔχεις οὖν εἰπεῖν δι' ὅτι μέμφῃ τὴν τοιαύτην δύναμιν; Polus by fixing on the sentence meaning and ignoring
the utterance meaning of Socrates' question trespasses tantalizingly
against Grice's 'principle of cooperativeness':[3] (470 A 3) ἔγωγε 'Yes I
do'. Now it is Socrates' turn to be perplexed: 470 A 4 τί δή; λέγε. 'What?
You will have to tell me. Now?'

---

[1] For this and following use of ἄρα see vO below 102 f.
[2] Thus Dodds, adopting the deletion of τῷ λόγῳ (or, secondarily, τοῦ λόγου) by Hir-
schig.
[3] Cf. *e.g.* G. LEECH, *Principles of Pragmatics*, London & New York 1983.

PART TWO

OYN, APA, ΔH, TOINYN:
THE LINGUISTIC ARTICULATION OF ARGUMENTS
IN PLATO'S *PHAEDO*

J.M. VAN OPHUIJSEN

ACKNOWLEDGMENTS

The ideas contained in the following pages were first developed in a some-times critical *Auseinandersetzung* with those laid down by Des Places, by Denniston, by the late Mrs. M.L. Sicking-Meyjes in a number of surveys of Greek particle usage intended for the use of students of Classics at Leiden University, and by Professor C.M.J. Sicking. They took shape under the supervision of Professor Sicking as Head of the Department of Greek at Leiden, who read and helpfully commented on successive drafts. The author has been uncommonly fortunate in the readers who have, not in any official capacity, taken interest in his work in progress. I have greatly profited from detailed annotations by my first teacher of Greek, H. Chr. Albertz of The Hague, and by Professor C.J. Ruijgh of the University of Amsterdam even before submitting this study for publication in the series in which by his consent it now appears. Ms Caroline Kroon of the University of Amsterdam offered pertinent criticisms as commentator to the oral presentation of an earlier version. Professor A.A. Long of the University of California at Berkeley very kindly found time to improve the wording of the *pars generalis*, and showed the need to state more fully and explicitly my views on ἄρα in particular; the result was scrutinized by my senior colleague in the Leiden Department of Greek, Dr. P. Stork, who in addition assisted in processing the copy. A few conversations with Dr. Egbert J. Bakker and with Dr. Peter Stork were most stimulating in different ways. I call on the indulgence of these dedicated Greek and Latin scholars for all the imperfections that remain.

JMvO

CHAPTER ONE

AIMS, LIMITATIONS, DISTINCTIONS, CAUTIONS

1.   Ancient Greek has four particles which regularly appear in the conclusions of arguments. All four of them have long been credited with, *inter alia*, a 'connective' force, and more specifically with a 'logical' or an 'inferential' value, in spite of the fact that their use is by no means limited to such contexts.

Given such a plurality of devices with an overlapping distribution, two obvious questions arise:

(1) In similar contexts, why should one particle have been chosen rather than another? In other words, which subordinate differences provide a *raison d'être* for the presence of several particles competing for what appears to be the same role? And

(2) For each particle, what is the relationship between its use in conclusions and its uses in other contexts?

One impediment to solving and indeed to addressing these problems is a tendency towards generalization which is both premature and insufficiently rigorous. On the one hand uses of particles are not infrequently lumped together for no better reason than the accident of admitting translation by the same phatic word in one of the modern languages, each of them, German not excluded, far poorer in, and far less dependent on, this class of words than Greek; where this superficially comparative approach fails to yield a plausible equivalent, the Greek expression is often characterized with the help of the hardly more illuminating notion of emphasis or of other prosodic features of modern languages.

On the other hand, the general or basic values which come to be ascribed to particles in this way are far too diverse, as well as too diffuse and indistinctive, to make it possible to define the contribution of a particle to a context, and to clarify how in a given instance of particle usage the final interpretation is the sum, or a product, of this contribution and a number of other signs in the context.

Another impediment has been the comparative neglect, in the study of Greek as of other languages, of connections above the level of the single sentence with the wider context, whether this consists of the larger utterance of the same speaker or, e.g., of those of his partner in a dialogue or of his or her opposite number in a play.

Thirdly and in connection with this, attention has inevitably been largely confined to the semantic contribution of particles to that part of the
content of a sentence which does not get lost in paraphrase, and even
where this limitation has been overcome the value of particles has still
been assumed to rest on emotional attitudes[1] evinced, whether consciously
and deliberately or not, by the speaker alone; the conception of an utterance as an attempt to act on, to influence or even manipulate the person
spoken to has not often been applied systematically to the description of
Greek particles.

The present study is an attempt to outline the contribution made by
each of these particles in Platonic dialogue, not just to the semantics of
the sentence but to the organization of a complete utterance, and indeed to
the conversation as a whole. Although it is hoped that the result may be
relevant to the study of pragmatics, its primary objective is to further the
study of Greek and the understanding of Plato's dialectic. As for the latter, it is worth finding out whether Plato had four words meaning *ergo* or
'therefore' at his disposal, or just one, or none at all. The question becomes even more interesting in a diachronic perspective, if we (1) accept
that Plato's dialogues offer some of the most life-like evocations of Attic
speech that we have, (2) grant the claim of EUCKEN[2] that the four particles
concerned have become interchangeable in Aristotle, and (3) try to trace
in Plato's writings the development of the formalized art of inference out
of informal everyday public debate. As to the knowledge of Greek, the
expected profit is of a critical rather than a heuristic nature: without pretending to better the intuitions of connoisseurs of the language, the descriptive apparatus used in accounting for these could well be developed
in such a way as to enable us to eliminate more strictly and authoritatively
numerous untenable readings, both in the sense of textual variants and of
proposed interpretations. And beside the advancement of pure scholarship, it is reasonable to hope for a benefit to the teaching and learning of
Greek which might be proportional to the neglect that the subject of particle usage has suffered from.

2. I presuppose that it is not merely legitimate but also advisable to inquire into the role of a particle by giving a comparative analysis of a
number of particles whose distribution overlaps, i.e. which may occur in
similar contexts and may be said to compete. Such groups of particles are
not mutually exclusive and, while some classifications are more obvious
than others, it is probably safest to assume, until further notice, that they

---

[1] 'moods of emotion' *GP* p. xxxviii s. with note.
[2] P. 41, cited by Denniston p. 238.

are not objective natural classes but may to a considerable extent be constituted *ad hoc* according to arbitrary criteria varying with the purpose of
the investigation. Thus we may in what follows discuss δή in relation to
οὖν, ἄρα, and τοίνυν without feeling the need to take δέ, generally considered to be a weakened form of δή, into account; conversely it would be
possible with equal justification to discuss the relations between δή and
δέ without so much as mentioning οὖν, ἄρα, and τοίνυν. Similarly ἄρα
and δή might fruitfully be contrasted with ἦ and μήν, whereas a comparison with these two would not perhaps throw as much light on τοίνυν, let
alone οὖν. The most adequate treatment of the use of a particle will be a
unified account of its place in these various relationships.

It will be noted that the criterion for including the present four particles is not linguistic in any strict sense; it is based on the common and
long-standing recognition that all four of them are found in inferences as
identified not by any formal means but merely in view of their content.
This need not worry us so long as we are able to agree on what is to count
as an inference in practice, but it does mean that our inquiry cannot any
more than earlier ones on Greek particle usage aspire to the status of
formal linguistics. I submit that this restricts its use for students of Greek
less severely than its value for theory. The understanding of a language,
or a stage of a language, for which we have nothing but written records
will always be more dependent on the interpretation of texts than would
please an expert in spoken languages or a student of general linguistics. In
Greek, where so much has been achieved in the interpretation of the texts
at a time when the application of the modern science of linguistics to the
language is in its infant stage, the most promising approach would seem
to be the eclectic one of trying to impose more rigorous standards of clarity and consistency on traditional learning rather than to supersede it.

3. The informal nature of the characteristic which binds our four particles to each other has unfortunately promoted a tendency to define their
common denominator in rather diverse terms: on the one hand in terms of
cause and *effect*, where a 'consecutive' value is attributed to them; on the
other hand of *premise* and *consequence*, in which case a 'logical' or 'inferential' value is ascribed to them, as by ancient grammarians who speak
of a σύνδεσμος συλλογιστικός. The term 'conclusion' invoked above
conceals another troublesome ambiguity in that it may denote, in addition
to logical consequences, any other statement by which we may round off
some stretch of speech, such as a summary. The first lack of discrimina-
tion has tempted scholars to derive the value of the particles in question
from an older temporal value according to the old logical formula *post*

hoc ergo propter hoc: thus DES PLACES[1] on all four particles. Such an explanation seems plausible enough as long as we are discussing sequences of events in time: 'It grew dark and we lost our way', but it does not self-evidently extend to the relationship of logical consequence: in an Aristotelian syllogism the premises, though in a sense 'prior' to the conclusion, are not true at an earlier time than it, so that the continuum of *post hoc* and *propter hoc* and 'anything between the two' which DENNISTON twice appeals to[2] is not obviously applicable. So for each particle we have three questions: is it correctly credited with (*a*) a temporal, and (*b*) an inferential value, and if the answer to both of these is affirmative, (*c*) is this ambivalence explicable by the use of the particle with reference to those situations in which it does make sense to posit such a continuity.

The chief authority on Greek particle usage is Denniston, but for three of the four particles which will occupy us the connective use in question is abundantly documented from Plato by Des Places, to whom Denniston pays homage on the first page of his preface and from whom he freely draws. We have noted in passing that neither of these scholars takes great pains to differentiate between the particles in question. That Des Places does not do so is explained by his statement[3] that extending his inquiry to other particles, though it would have contributed to Platonic lexicography, would not have increased the number of types of argument encountered: his interest was in the largely identical contexts in which his three 'particules de liaison' figure rather than in the particles themselves. Denniston too, though his interests were different, seems to have been more struck by the resemblance between the particles, as appears from such statements as 'τοίνυν, like δή and οὖν, combines the notions of inference and pure progression'[4] and '... (in Plato) we find ἄρα used practically as a variant for οὖν and δή...'.[5] Where he does tentatively distinguish between them the difference he sees is one of degree: thus the sentence last quoted continues 'though even in Plato ἄρα perhaps conveys a slightly less formal and more conversational connexion than those particles'; similarly, on τοίνυν, 'its logical force is for the most part not very strong, rather weaker, on the whole, than that of οὖν, which comes nearest to it in meaning';[6] and between οὖν and δή, equated by implication in the remarks on ἄρα just quoted, a similar difference of degree is supposed to

---

[1] P. 3.
[2] *GP* 237 on δή, 425 on οὖν.
[3] P. ii.
[4] P. 239.
[5] P. 41.
[6] P. 568.

obtain: 'δή here' [i.e. in its connective use] 'like οὖν, expresses *post hoc* and *propter hoc*, and anything between the two, tending on the whole to denote a less strictly logical sequence than οὖν'.[1] Such expressions as 'practically', 'perhaps', 'slightly', 'for the most part', 'rather', and (twice) 'on the whole' show more than the usual scholarly reserve, and detract a little from the usefulness of these statements. The need for them makes one suspect that the occurrence of all these words in similar contexts is not sufficient to account for their individual value, and in particular that we should beware of taking it for granted that (1) *occurring in* an inference equals *marking* an inference, or that (2) within such a role all possible variation would be difference of degree.

With this lack of distinctions the derivation of the logical force in question from a basic meaning ascribed to each particle could hardly fail to be problematic. In Des Places the problem is transferred wholesale to these basic meanings, which are themselves too indefinite to have any great explanatory power: οὖν 'dit correspondance entre une énonciation et la réalité (...) la réalité peut (...) être *antérieure à* l'énonciation, étant elle-même une affirmation (...) dont il peut même tirer une conclusion (...)';[2] on the other hand ἄρα 'semble témoigner d'une évolution *analogue à* celle de οὖν et être passé d'une valeur purement temporelle (...) à des emplois logiques (...)',[3] and τοίνυν (p. 285) 'par son origine, *comme* οὖν, serait une particule affirmative *ou* temporelle (...)'.[4] Denniston is more discriminating on the subject of basic meanings for his particles,[5] but his accounts of those three (excluding τοίνυν) in which the alleged original meaning is non-connective seem to imply that what may be called 'connectivization' is a secondary process which tends to superimpose a meaning of its own on the original sense of a particle, one important form of this specifically connective sense being the logical variety. Thus on ἄρα: '(...) in Aristotle the particle has been completely devitalized, and is a pure connective'.[6] Here, then, whatever explanatory force the basic meaning might have had has been lost.

What follows rests on different presuppositions: (1) the fact that a particle regularly occurs in a conclusion does not imply that it marks a conclusion as such; (2) the fact that different particles regularly occur in conclusions imposes an obligation to look for a different use for, or con-

---

[1] P. 237.
[2] P. 3; italics JMvO.
[3] P. 229; italics JMvO.
[4] P. 285; italics JMvO.
[5] Pp. 32 s. ἄρα, 203 s. δή, 415-7 οὖν, & 568 s. τοίνυν.
[6] P. 41.

76   CHAPTER ONE

tribution from, each of them; (3) the most promising way to define these
different uses in similar contexts is to compare the contribution of each of
these particles to different contexts, preferably in the same corpus, in
which they are not competing.

4.   The quest for distinctions between our four particles will be found to
involve a fair amount of more detailed interpretation and analysis of the
arguments than the standard reference works on particles can accommodate; in particular it has proved necessary to relate the instances discussed
to much wider contexts[1] than are usually taken into consideration. The
sample covered in this way consists, besides the examples quoted for logical and similar uses by Des Places and Denniston, of the single occurrences of all four particles in declarative utterances in Plato's *Phaedo*. It
has been assumed that the role of particles in genuine interrogation, as
opposed to leading questions, and in injunctions or 'directive' sentences
marked by imperative or adhortative subjunctive, as well as that of collocations of particles, is more fruitfully discussed on the basis of a supposition with regard to the way the single particles function in statements,
though exceptions have been made as the argument seemed to require,
especially in the case of τοίνυν, the least frequent of the four, and the one
whose use in 'directive' utterances is particularly characteristic. On this
severely limited material basis a hypothesis with regard to the distinct
character of each of them has been built.

5.   While we do not for our present purpose need to provide a definition
of the class of particles as a whole, it may be useful to review some of the
subclasses they have been divided into. In the transmitted text of the grammar ascribed to Dionysius Thrax[2] ἄρα and τοίνυν are listed as συλλο-
γιστικοί, but οὖν and δή as παραπληρωματικοὶ σύνδεσμοι or 'expletive
conjunctions'. Though Denniston, as we have seen, regards οὖν as more
'syllogistic' than both ἄρα and τοίνυν, the classification as 'syllogistic'
is the ultimate source of the approach here criticized; we shall find it more
pertinent to ἄρα than to either τοίνυν or οὖν. As to the classification as
'expletive', the only positive suggestion to be derived from it is that these
particles were presumably in their distribution less restricted to special
contexts, and this will be confirmed below to the extent that οὖν and δή,

---

[1] It should be noted that the demarcation of contexts to be quoted is always and necessarily to some extent arbitrary and tendentious, so that even with ample quotations it is
advisable to consult a complete text and to regard the extracts as implicit interpretations.

[2] 20.7-8 / p. 95-100 Uhlig. Questions of authenticity and of interpolation need not
detain us in the present connection.

as well as being more common, turn out to be more versatile than the other pair with regard to the types of speech act they are appropriate to.

Dionysius' name of σύνδεσμοι 'conjunctions' for the genus comprehending these species is worth pondering, for while it is well known that this very ancient term of grammar denotes much more than the class of items now usually called particles, it ought at the same time to connote less than the sum of the uses these items may be put to, if we are to go by the terminology of modern authors: in particular the phrase 'particules de liaison' in Des Places' subtitle, and Denniston's distinction[1] between a connective and an adverbial sense in the historical evolution of various particles, both imply that there is more to these words than is covered by the concept of connection.

However, this later usage is itself problematic. Des Places seems to take for granted not only, as we have seen, the transition from succession to consequence, but also, and even more surprisingly, an allegedly prior transition from affirmation to succession, both of which are for this purpose regarded[2] as realizations of a correspondence between statement and fact, varying only according to whether this fact is present or anterior, in which latter case it too is, or may be, a statement. The attribution of such versatility to one item, as we have seen, offers no help in distinguishing this item from its competitors; it has the additional drawback of leaving the account hermetically sealed off from any risk of being falsified.

The use of the term 'connective' in *GP* is not open to quite the same criticism, inasmuch as the transition to being used as a connective is here not the automatic development of one inherent value common to all these words, but it is ambiguous between syntactic, semantic and pragmatic criteria. In these fields much that is relevant to our subject has been achieved since Denniston's time. A distinction between *coordinators* and *connectors* has been applied to a number of Greek particles by SLINGS[3] and by SICKING.[4] Criteria for distinguishing coordinators had been devised by DIK;[5] connectors were defined by PINKSTER.[6] Briefly, the *distinction* may be said to be that between items marking a *syntactic* relation between *sentences*, and items marking not a syntactic but *only* a *semantic* relation between *contents* of sentences. Confusion is easy because one item may well perform both functions; in such cases, if it is agreed that

---

[1] *GP* p. xliii.
[2] P. 3; above p. 74.
[3] Slings 1980.
[4] Sicking 1986.
[5] Dik (1968) 34-41
[6] Pinkster 1972.

we should refrain as long as we can from assigning one word to two different word classes,[1] it seems best to follow Pinkster in taking the syntactic form as criterial and defining connectors negatively: 'those words which establish various semantic relations between paratactic sentences, are not coordinators, and can be shown not to be adverbs either'.[2]

If we follow Slings' suggestion[3] of applying to Greek the *juxtaposition* criterion devised by Dik for distinguishing coordinators from *i.a.* 'adverbial connecting particles',[4] the result is that, for Plato at least, οὖν, ἄρα, and δή are all ruled out as potential coordinators by the fact that they are found next to ἀλλά and δέ, whose coordinator status, in these juxtapositions at least, is presumably unassailable.[5]

An interesting consequence of this procedure would be that a considerable number of Greek sentences, and among them the majority of those quoted in the following pages, become syntactically asyndetic as lacking an explicit coordinating device, whereas we have been brought up to regard asyndeton as something normally avoided in Greek.[6] By itself this is not a valid argument against denying coordinator status to these particles as used in Plato, since the notion that asyndeton is avoided is bound up with the traditional sense of the term asyndeton, and its truth depends on this sense: if we take it as meaning that most Greek sentences feature one of the devices subsumed by ancient grammarians under the label of σύνδεσμοι, then it is indeed true, but its truth has no implications for the question whether coordination as we may choose to define it now is usually made explicit in ancient Greek.[7]

Although τοίνυν is not ruled out as a potential coordinator by the same test, we are now no longer bound to regard it as one just because it is found at the beginning of a sentence in the absence of other coordinators.

If οὖν, ἄρα, and δή at least cannot count as coordinators, could they be admitted as connectors? If Pinkster's criteria for distinguishing connectors from adverbs are applied to them, the same collocation with ἀλλά and δέ which ruled them out as coordinators will now exclude them from the class of connectors according to the criterion of 'occurrence in the second member of a coordination pattern',[8] but if we follow another sug-

---

[1] It must be granted that it is sometimes unavoidable to do so, as the case of so-called adverbial καί shows.

[2] Pinkster (1972) 154.

[3] Slings (1980) 105 n. 4.

[4] Dik (1968) 34.

[5] Slings (1980) 104 n. 2, 105 n. 4.

[6] Cf. *GP* xliii ss.

[7] More on asyndeton above, (Sicking) p. 40-4.

[8] Pinkster (1972) 161.

gestion made by Slings[1] to the effect that this 'coordination test', which was devised by Pinkster for application to Latin, may have to be dropped for Greek, they might still be connectors. At this point the first question to be considered seems to be: what alternatives offer themselves?

Two more classes of particles, besides coordinators and connectors, are distinguished by Sicking. The first of these consists of 'sentence particles' in the terms of Dik, since they bear on the sentence in which they occur in its entirety.[2] Their contribution to this sentence is to 'establish a basis for the communication between speaker and hearer',[3] more specifically, to lay down terms for debating the statement one is making, i.e. to indicate conditions for, and possible consequences of, doing so for relations between speaker and addressee:[4] they define the 'communicative relationship'[5] which the speaker is trying to maintain. The more uncontroversial representatives of this class are ἦ, μήν, solitary μέν, and που; a little apart from these we find ἄρα, δή, and οὖν tentatively classified as being primarily sentence particles, but showing some traits of connectors, and thereby approaching the status of connectors—in conclusions more than in other contexts, and οὖν more so than the other two.[6]

The remaining division in Sicking's classification, exemplified by γε and adverbial καί, contains particles which are said to mark the *scope* of a statement.[7]

6. This account has two important implications:

(1) If particles may share in the characteristics of morre than one class, then subclasses of particles are not in practice watertight compartments. It might be more profitable to represent them as forming a sliding scale, on which different particles occupy different places; and
(2) individual instances of one and the same particle may approximate to one or another type in varying degrees, i.e. may occupy different places on this scale.[8]

---

[1] Cf. p. 77 above.
[2] Sicking (1986) 132.
[3] Id. 125.
[4] Id. 138.
[5] Id. 137.
[6] Most of these particles are reconsidered by Sicking above, esp. p. 25-7 (οὖν) and *Appendix*, pp. 51-64.
[7] Id. 125.
[8] That this variation may be ascertained between individual instances of a particle, and not just between different particles, is implied by Sicking (1986) 134 in the last paragraph under 8.1.

We are thus carried back from the more taxonomic ways of 19th and 20th
century positivist scholarship, to a highly relevant insight expressed over
four hundred years ago by DEVARIUS in one of the earliest treatments of
the Greek particles:[1] a word may acquire, in addition to its own meaning
(*significatio*), some other force (*vis et qualitas*) from the discourse it forms
part of (*ex modo sermonis*);[2] for instance, it may in a single sentence
signify affirmation, but in a series of sentences be used to signify logical
steps.[3] Such an attempt to understand the occurrence of a particle in function of its context seems a more sensitive approach than the derivational
histories of the value of particles cited above. The danger inherent in it is
that it might tend to blur the distinction between the value contributed to
the context by the particle as such, and the final interpretation of the utterance as a whole; this happens all the more easily since many occurrences
of particles are so unsurprising as to seem relatively insignificant. Given
that all continuous discourse, whether in monologue or in dialogue form,
will naturally show a considerable amount of coherence, it is presumably
wise to appeal to the notions of connection and connectivity only sparingly in definitions of the values of particles, and wherever it is unavoidable to do so—i.e. whenever connections cannot plausibly be explained
without taking the particle into account—to attempt to specify what type
of connection is involved.

7.   It will now be suggested that some of the criteria constituting classes
in existing classifications of particles are better treated as variables which
could be set up as co-ordinates in the comparative description of a particle. One of these, which obviously cuts across the classes distinguished
above, is that of the *range* or *scope* of a particle as defined by the amount
of context which is involved in its uses and in the interpretation of these;
this could be applied at the level of the instances of a particle, and subsequently at that of the particle in general as compared with its competitors.
It may be convenient to reserve the term 'scope' for the stretch of context
relevant to an individual occurrence, and to use 'range' for the extent
defined by the maximum and minimum scope of a given particle. The
values which these may assume will, I suggest, extend at one end well
beyond a sequence of two sentences, and at the other end below the sentence down to a single word. To anticipate: we shall find both ἄρα and δή
bearing on a main clause or a sentence as a whole, but also ἄρα used with

---

[1] Devarius (1588), referred to by Schenkeveld (1988).

[2] *praeter propriam significationem aliam quandam vim, & qualitatem ex modo sermonis
acquirant* Devarius (1588) 4.

[3] Devarius' example is ἦπου.

a scope limited to one subordinate clause, and δή bringing into relief just one referring expression. The implications of this scope for the interpretation are not negligible: at their lower limit δή is much farther from qualifying a sentence than ἄρα is, since the dependent clause containing ἄρα, even if it is not asserted, still contains a proposition in the sense of a description of a conceivable state of affairs, whereas the nominal phrase accompanied by δή is not a bearer of truth or falsity. This divergence between them could perhaps be made to throw light on their use in contexts in which they are both at home. At the other end of the scale we find ἄρα used in winding up a long stretch of argument, οὖν at the return from an extensive digression, and τοίνυν introducing a complex proposal. Here it may be worth asking whether the relevant scope extends mainly forwards or backwards, and whether we find indications which justify a distinction between a scope covering a continuous stretch of text and one bridging a section; and here again our findings may prove applicable to contexts within the middle range common to several of the particles.

It would seem, then, that this notion of scope, though it is evidently applicable in the description of so-called connectors and sentence particles, cannot serve to distinguish between these classes, i.e. that the criterion constituting them is not whether a particle bears on one sentence or establishes a relation between two sentences; and this is in accordance with the fact that another characteristic which is quite independent of their scope is by Sicking ascribed to them as being common to them. It might be supposed that his fourth class, containing γε and καί, of what we may provisionally refer to as 'extent-defining' particles, provides a different case, since the range of these is evidently restricted to components below the level of the sentence. On closer inspection, however, it seems more accurate to state that these mark a component of a clause as limiting or extending the reference of the clause as a whole: thus they establish, or at least highlight, a relationship, and in a sense could be said to involve two scopes. Such an account would be capable of being extended to non-adverbial καί, which could be said to differ from e.g. δέ and τε in establishing a relation between the new clause or other item introduced and that which preceded it, rather than allowing the addition to pass as a matter of course.[1]

The characteristic role assigned to sentence particles by Sicking, of establishing the basis for communication, or the conditions and consequences of a dispute, seems highly relevant to τοίνυν, which does not figure in his survey, as well as to ἄρα and to δή. I think it is much less

---

[1] On καί cf. above (Sicking) p. 14 ff.

relevant to οὖν, without implying that οὖν is to that extent more of a connector in any current sense of the term. To chart the different use of each of the other three in such a conversational strategy comparatively I propose that we should distinguish two more variables, those of

(1) the ostensible commitment of the speaker to the statement he is making, and
(2) the agreement which the speaker presupposes on the part of, or admits to expecting from, the addressee.

Plotting ἄρα and δή along these new co-ordinates, one may arrive at the following modified restatement of Sicking's account:

δή presumes that the addressee—who is supposed to have the same relevant information at his disposal as the speaker—is ready and willing to commit himself to what is being stated;[1] given that it is natural, in making a statement, to look for assent, the point of adding δή is to hint that the addressee is actually bound to subscribe to the statement as much as the speaker is.

With ἄρα the speaker adopts the different, yet related stratagem of suggesting that he is not himself any more committed to his statement than the addressee can be supposed to be. I do not believe that of itself ἄρα *expresses* surprise;[2] rather, it serves the pretence that both partners have dismissed all personal considerations and are simply 'following the λόγος where it leads'. This is not to deny its appropriateness to contexts in which a speaker is supposed to be, or supposes his interlocutor will be, surprised.

These two particles have in common that the speaker implies that his partner and himself are equally and similarly placed with a view to accepting or rejecting the proposition in question. This shared characteristic sets them apart from τοίνυν, which in its more typical uses does not presuppose that the interlocutors are in the same position on this score, but openly admits to the speaker's own commitment as well as to his awareness that the addressee may not be inclined to share this, and sollicits his adhesion or compliance. A consequence of these characteristics is that while ἄρα and δή envisage an intersubjective reality and truth, τοίνυν, which preserves in its first component the pronoun of the second person, appeals *ad hominem*. To offer a laboured paraphrase,

---

[1] Cf. Sicking (1986) 137.
[2] As Denniston p. xxxix & 35 and Sicking (1986) p. 133 & 137 suppose.

'p δή'	= 'p, as we both can see',
'p ἄρα'	= 'we cannot but conclude that p', and
'p τοίνυν'	= 'now you take it from me that p';

schematically, along the co-ordinates set up above:

degree of personal *commitment*	avowed by *speaker*	presupposed in *addressee*
ἄρα	low	low
δή	high	high
τοίνυν	high	low

It is no cause for surprise that the theoretical possibility of a low degree of committal shown on the part of the speaker combined with a high degree implicitly ascribed to the addressee is not realized in the form of a separate device belonging to the same system. The effect would be that of casting doubt on a statement. A way to achieve this by the means we are discussing is to use δή ironically. Another particle which may be used to this effect is που, but this, too, has other uses, in which it might perhaps fruitfully be compared to ἦ and μήν.[1]

Between ἄρα and δή the choice is largely a matter of tact and tactics: it depends on the speaker's estimate of the hearer's accessibility to a proposition, which reflects his general assessment of his interlocutor and, more interestingly, in one conversation with the same interlocutor will vary with the significance of the proposition as defined by its unexpectedness; thirdly, it may perhaps sometimes be noted as a symptom of whether the speaker himself is more of an εἴρων or of an ἀλάζων. With neither of these particles does the speaker give warning that the addressee is not supposed to contradict him; with ἄρα he ostensibly leaves the field open, but with δή he at least intimates that he does not expect to be contradicted: he does not schedule a breathing space for it, as it were. τοίνυν is more peremptory; the speaker declares himself, and should be expected to do all he can to hold his ground if he is opposed.

If this analysis is correct, the comparative frequency of these three particles may be accounted for. It is generally conducive to relations with your partner in a conversation, as elsewhere, to pass over any differences between the two of you in information, awareness of its implications, and willingness to have it corrected and added to or to act on it as it is; therefore phatic words tending to confirm that this is so will rarely come amiss.

---

[1] On these, and on δήπου, cf. above (Sicking), *Appendix* pp. 52 f., 63 f.

By contrast a less pacific conversational device like τοίνυν, to be effective, should be used more sparingly. Between ἄρα and δή the order of
frequency is presumably determined by the general preponderance of uncontroversial and even redundant statements—even in disputes, if only as
ἔνδοξα premises—over unpredictable new ones. The motives for using
τοίνυν are, in proportion to its low frequency, comparatively varied: its
distribution overlaps with that of δή when it reinforces a point which is
not any longer in dispute but on which a quite explicit agreement is required if the debate is to move beyond it, and with that of ἄρα at a new
step in an argument, but it has a use peculiar to itself in contradicting a
statement by substituting another statement for it, and it has a marked
affinity with expressions of will and contexts of disposition to a course of
action.

8.   So far we have considered ἄρα, δή, and τοίνυν almost entirely within
the confines of the sentence or clause in which they occur. While it is not
claimed that this is sufficient for an adequate description of their use, in
my view the fact that it is possible to do so at all divides these three from
οὖν, which, I submit, cannot profitably be discussed in terms of a contribution to a single sentence, nor, by implication, in terms of commitment
to a statement. The minimum scope of οὖν seems to cross the line between *two* statements. Does it therefore make sense to pronounce οὖν a
connector rather than a sentence particle? Not, I think, in the accepted
sense of 'connector' as denoting a word establishing a relationship between the *meaning* of two sentences. By using οὖν a speaker does not
intimate that the truth of his present statement should be granted on the
strength of his preceding statement; he is imposing an arbitrary relationship on his statements, indicating that what went before need occupy his
listeners only in so far as it may assist them in grasping what follows. He
is marking a move from what is subservient to what this was intended to
serve, from background to foreground. He is merely articulating his discourse by imposing a structure of his own device on it, with no objective
validity claimed or subjective adhesion required.

In frequency οὖν among the four particles here discussed takes second place after δή. While the range of the two, in the sense defined above,
seems to differ appreciably at both ends, that of δή extending much farther downwards and that of οὖν farther upwards, there is still a considerable overlap in the incidence of the two, which is not restricted to particular types of speech act. Thus in questions, where ἄρα is at home, and
τοίνυν is significantly absent, and in directive utterances, where τοίνυν is
often employed, but ἄρα is not, both οὖν and δή are just as common as

they are in assertions. In these, one of the contexts in which they compete is at the transition from one section of a conversation to another, as marked for instance by a change of participants or by the end of a monologue. In view of their frequency it would be vain to look for a distinctive contribution from each particle in every single instance; it is more realistic to postulate a basic meaning which can be seen to be operative in a number of 'prototypical'[1] instances, and which is not obviously incompatible with the application of the particle in a number of 'peripheral' instances where it overlaps with peripheral uses of other particles. Thus in the situation just mentioned of 'This (δή/οὖν) having been said by X, Y replied ...' it might be suggested that δή, from marking what is plain to see, has come to be used in any repetition or recapitulation of earlier information, while οὖν, from marking a turn towards the more topical, has come to mark successive steps in a narration. It might be inferred from this that, in spite of their identical position in the sentence, in these situations δή should have come in, so to speak, via the absolute genitive adjunct and 'face backwards', whereas οὖν could be said to relate to the new information contained in the main clause which follows and face forwards, even though we might sometimes lack contextual indications confirming that this distinction corresponds to a difference in the intention of a speaker.

9.   In the last section but one an attempt was made to paraphrase the contribution of δή, ἄρα, and τοίνυν to a statement. The paraphrase offered for δή, '..., as we both can see', comes nearest to being a qualification of the content of the sentence; it is a small step from this to 'as we all can see', 'as anyone can see', 'evidently', δηλονότι: i.e. to a sentence adverb. I suggest that the pragmatic value of δή lends itself most easily to becoming semanticized. But this does not exhaust its versatility: its appropriateness to information shared by the participants in an act of communication makes it apt to accompany anaphoric expressions, e.g. when marking someone or something mentioned earlier for the role of topic in what follows—a use which seems relevant to its derivative δέ—and more generally any information which is redundant as far as its news value is concerned, but for that very reason is suitable as a discourse marker or means towards ordering and spacing one's larger utterances.

ἄρα 'we cannot but conclude that p' is more intricately bound up with its context and situation. As to verbal context, when ἄρα is used in an argument it follows from the absence both of any pretence to objective truth and of any claim on the commitment of the addressee, that the only

---

[1] For this concept, and its opposite 'peripheral', cf. Bakker (1988) 14-7.

grounds for accepting the new statement are in those previously agreed
to. This is what has made it possible to assimilate ἄρα to a connector
'therefore'. Even in such contexts its lack of insistence might be thought
to make it resemble the conditional statement '*if* (hypothesis) *then* (consequence)' more than the inference schema '(assertion) *therefore* (assertion)'; yet an important difference from both is seen in non-dialectic contexts: that the grounds for accepting the ἄρα-statement do not necessarily
take the form of a proposition, but may consist in, e.g., a sense perception
not yet expressed in words: in other words, it may be situational rather
than contextual. The attribution of a connotation of 'surprise' to it may be
seen as an attempt to represent semantically its contribution especially to
non-argumentative contexts; this attempt, however, is successful only in a
minority of cases. The common denominator in as well as outside arguments seems to be that ἄρα establishes an informal truth-function, i.e.
makes the truth of a statement conditional on some data outside it. What
these data are, and in particular what truth value they in their turn may lay
claim to, is not prejudged; and this is precisely what makes the particle
apt to help a statement carry conviction in a conversation purporting to
aim at ὁμολογία between intellectual equals.

In the case of τοίνυν the paraphrase 'now you take it from me that *p*'
is intended to bring out the fact that no addition at all is made to the
propositional content of the sentence; in other words, the contribution of
the particle remains firmly within the field of pragmatics.

With οὖν the possibility of paraphrase appears to break down. In the
case of a return from a side-issue to the main line of the larger utterance
'however this may be' would seem adequate, which is a far cry from
anything like *propter hoc*; the common ground between these uses is that
what went before should from now on be considered in its bearing on
some other proposition. This is a matter neither of semantics nor of pragmatics understood as the study of the use of language in context, but of
discourse organization. This subject was seen to be relevant to one aspect
of the use of δή; I doubt whether it affects the use of ἄρα much; I submit
that is involved in that of τοίνυν in continuous speech—marginal as far
as Plato is concerned—and would claim that it is quite central to an understanding of οὖν.

10.   On these hypotheses we should have two particles (δή, ἄρα) which
direct the attention to the content of the utterance and two (τοίνυν, οὖν)
which are in some way more concerned with the act of uttering it. This
division cuts across the main division along the parameter of scope, where
we have two particles whose distinctive potential may to a considerable

extent be realized and interpreted within the limits of one sentence (τοίνυν somewhat less than δή), as against two which by themselves implicitly refer to a wider context (ἄρα and even more clearly οὖν). Schematically:

bearing primarily on	content	act
sentence	δή	τοίνυν
context	ἄρα	οὖν

In those contexts in which these four particles have been noted to compete, these distinctions may be said to work out as follows:

- οὖν regards only the intentions a *speaker* has with his successive (part-) utterances
- δή focuses on the *proposition*, which is represented as speaking for itself;
- ἄρα ties the acceptance of the proposition to an assumption in the *context*;
- τοίνυν leaves the merits of the proposition aside to concentrate on the *addressee's* stipulated agreement or compliance with it.

11. It remains to consider some implications of our descriptive apparatus for classification. It is worth recalling the consequence derived from Sicking's account, that classes are not in this connection mutually exclusive divisions, but more like types to which particles may be assimilated by abstracting from differences both between different particles and between different uses of one particle. We have been occupied in analysing, for two such classes, some of the characteristics which constitute these types. It must be confessed that the two classes as such have disappeared in this process, since the variables by which we have tried to represent these characteristics, when applied across the boundaries between these classes, do not to a significant degree appear to be correlated: there is no connection, e.g., between a limited scope and a high degree of commitment.

As far as Greek is concerned, it was the original definition of the class of sentence particles which first showed an awareness of, and did justice to, the need to look for a pragmatic motivation for the use of a particle in cases where neither a syntactic one, such as accounts for coordinators, nor a semantic one, such as they are offered for uncontroversial connectors, was forthcoming. This important insight should not blind us to the possibility that a linguistic sign performs a function simultaneously in more than one of the fields which we identify as syntax, semantics, and pragmatics. If this possibility should be allowed, it would open a prospect of differentiating between observable uses of a particle according to which function is predominant. Thus if one of our set of particles is juxtaposed with an acknowledged coordinator it is unmotivated syntactically, so we feel bound to look for a semantic and/or a pragmatic motivation; similarly if δή is found in a statement which is anything but obvious, its most semanticized value applies only in a non-straightforward way: its pragmatic tenor of presupposing agreement is as it were exploited in stealing assent.

Under these circumstances it seems sensible to be as open-minded and undogmatic as possible, and to adopt a deliberately eclectic approach which involves applying any co-ordinates of the kind exemplified which might be relevant, without prejudging the question of their relations to each other or to systematic sub-groupings of particles.

12.   The following chapters focus on certain more or less formally recognizable uses of particles, and it might be felt that these have been somewhat over-exposed at the cost of others. These chapters should be understood in the light of the preceding one, which I hope has lent some substance to a conviction that the continuity between these uses is more conspicuous than the differences between them. At the same time, any attempt to account for the use of a particle in terms sufficiently explicit to distinguish it from that of other particles stands in danger of lapsing into over-interpretation. To an objection on this score it is tempting to retort that any exaggeration is preferable to the facile cribs one is usually put off with. But there is a very real problem, which is that the perspective which would enable us to discriminate between the more significant instances of a particle and those in which it has faded into a kind of verbal padding, should elude us. This κριτική, which is related to, but not the same thing as, the linguistic distinction between 'prototypical' and 'peripheral'[1] uses of a particle, is perhaps best served by the philologist's skill of responsible interpretation of texts. It is hoped that any distortions contained in the paraphrases offered below may at least help to define the room for worthwhile disagreement.

---

[1] Cf. above, p. 85.

CHAPTER TWO

OYN

1. General

In οὖν the logical force is apparently so vital that it could be allotted a disappointingly cavalier treatment in Denniston's *Greek Particles*[1] in the bland statement that 'the inferential use of οὖν is too common to need illustration'. Here, then, we must look to Des Places for enlightenment.

A glance at the table of contents of his *Études* shows that it deals with each of its three 'particules de liaison' as far as possible along parallel lines, and this impression is confirmed by the schematic summaries attached to each section.[2] Thus one finds, when trying to focus on the arguably logical and inferential uses of οὖν, that two general categories,[3] and five of the six species which promise to be most fertile in this connection,[4] turn up again in the classification of ἄρα or of τοίνυν—four of them in both.

This similarity of treatment has the advantage of providing an opportunity for a comparative study of the particles concerned: nothing could be more helpful towards assessing the difference in value between them than an investigation of what, other things being equal, is contributed by each of them to similar contexts such as 'conclusions drawn from a reply'.[5]

But if Des Places offers his readers this opportunity, it must be confessed that he himself largely fails to make use of it. His logic-inspired classification, rather than providing the basis for an explanation of the value of these particles, is made to take the place of such an explanation. Actually there are indications that the case of οὖν is more desperate than the other two: while it may be of some use to establish that all three are used both in *deduction*, in the conclusion of a syllogism,[6] and in *induction*, in the statement of a law,[7] it is downright confusing to be told that

---

[1] P. 426.

[2] Cf. especially pp. 83-4, 276-7, & 306-7.

[3] II & IV; out of four.

[4] II.1-4 = pp. 11-47, & IV.1-2 = pp. 67-72.

[5] 'marque une conclusion tirée de la réponse de l'interlocuteur' Des Places 15 (οὖν), 240 (ἄρα), 289 (τοίνυν).

[6] Pp. 11, 231, 286.

[7] Pp. 14, 239, 289.

οὖν, alone of the three, is used both *with* a 'notion of consequence'[1] in the conclusion, and *without* this notion in the minor premiss of a syllogism; or that, like τοίνυν, it is used both *with* this notion in the statement of a law, and *without* it in adducing a fact in view of or in support of a law.[2]

What is clearly required is an account which relates such almost diametrically opposed applications of the particle to an underlying value relevant to both opposites, and not just to these fairly specialized and technical uses, but to the common occurrence of the particle in non-argumentative prose and verse as well. We shall begin our quest for such a basic notion in the *Phaedo*.

2. *Distinctive uses in* Phaedo

Two fairly typical situations, to some extent overlapping, may provide a clue to the basic function of οὖν. They share the characteristic of a *shift of focus*.

2.1. *With verbal repetition; not preceded by* γάρ

59 E 8
>   ... ἐκέλευεν ἡμᾶς εἰσιέναι. εἰσιόντες οὖν κατελαμβάνομεν τὸν μὲν Σ. ...

116 A 4
>   ... ἡμᾶς δ' ἐκέλευε περιμένειν. περιεμένομεν οὖν ...

118 A 5
>   ... ἡμῖν ἐπεδείκνυτο ὅτι ψύχοιτο ... καὶ εἶπεν ὅτι ἐπειδὰν πρὸς τῇ καρδίᾳ
>   γένηται αὐτῷ, τότε οἰχήσεται. Ἤδη οὖν σχεδόν τι αὐτοῦ ἦν τὰ περὶ τὸ
>   ἦτρον ψυχόμενα ...

If we had to form an opinion on the basis of 59 E 8 and 116 A 4 alone, it might be conceived that οὖν expresses consequence: 'we were invited in' (or: '– were told to wait'), '*so* we went in' (or: '– waited'). But this interpretation will not do for 118 A 5; the most that we can say that applies to all three is that we have been *prepared* for the information contained in the sentence with οὖν by that preceding it. This also fits a context lacking verbal repetition but otherwise very similar:

60 A 3
>   ... κατελαμβάνομεν τὸν μὲν Σωκράτη, τὴν δὲ Ξανθίππην ... ὡς οὖν εἶδεν
>   ἡμᾶς ἡ Ξ., ἀνηυφήμησέ τε καὶ ...

---

[1] 'Idée de conséquence' Des Places 11.
[2] 'L'énoncé d'une loi' Des Places 14, 'un fait particulier en vue ou à l'appui d'une loi' 70; for τοίνυν cf. 289 & 302 respectively.

That we caught sight of her does not imply that she noticed us, but it is at least not surpising that she did.

Elsewhere a wider context suggests that there is a little more to the use of οὖν:

58 B 1, 4

> (How did it come about that such a long time elapsed between his condemnation and his execution? – It happened that the ship bound for Delos had just been rigged. – What are you talking about? –)

> τοῦτ' ἔστι τὸ πλοῖον ... ἐν ᾧ οὖν 'Απόλλωνι ηὔξαντο ... εἰ σωθεῖεν ... θεωρίαν ἀπάξειν ... ἐπειδὰν οὖν ἄρξωνται τῆς θεωρίας, νόμος ἐστὶν ... μηδένα ἀποκτεινύναι.

Evidently there can be no question of consequences in the case of the first οὖν, since the vow *precedes* their deliverance. Yet οὖν does not just underline the recurring reference to σῴζειν and to θεωρίαι and thereby strengthen the continuity between the sentences; more specifically it seems to signpost the road back to the question which occasioned the detour, that about the delay:

> 'Now I mention their safe arrival because they had made this vow to send an embassy, and I mention the embassy because this is what prevented the execution.'

οὖν indicates, then, that what follows comes nearer to the *point* than what precedes; that what precedes owes its *relevance* to what follows.

The context of

98 D 2

> ... (C 3) ὥσπερ ἂν εἴ τις ... ἐπιχειρήσας λέγειν τὰς αἰτίας ἑκάστων ὧν πράττω, λέγοι πρῶτον μὲν ὅτι διὰ ταῦτα νῦν ἐνθάδε κάθημαι, ὅτι σύγκειταί μου τὸ σῶμα ἐξ ὀστῶν καὶ νεύρων, καὶ τὰ μὲν ὀστᾶ ἐστιν ..., τὰ δὲ νεῦρα οἷα ..., περιαμπέχοντα τὰ ὀστᾶ ... · αἰωρουμένων οὖν τῶν ὀστῶν ἐν ταῖς αὐτῶν συμβολαῖς χαλῶντα καὶ συντείνοντα τὰ νεῦρα κάμπτεσθαί που ποιεῖ οἷόν τ' εἶναι ἐμὲ νῦν τὰ μέλη, καὶ διὰ ταύτην τὴν αἰτίαν συγκαμφθεὶς ἐνθάδε κάθημαι ·

likewise has οὖν coming to the point announced: questioned about the αἰτίαι why Socrates is acting as he is, the imaginary respondent launches into five lines of description of what Socrates' body is composed of, and only after these presuppositions, with οὖν comes to his explanation of how these components make Socrates capable of physical action or, as the case may be, rest, and thereby account for his present seated position.

At 69 E 3 (prepared for by D 7, ταῦτ' οὖν ἐγώ, ..., ἀπολογοῦμαι ...)

> εἴ τι οὖν ὑμῖν πιθανώτερός εἰμι ἐν τῇ ἀπολογίᾳ ἢ τοῖς 'Αθηναίων δικασταῖς, εὖ ἂν ἔχοι,

οὖν winds up a discussion begun as many as six Stephanus pages earlier in

63 B 4

> φέρε δή, ..., πειραθῶ πιθανώτερον πρὸς ὑμᾶς ἀπολογήσασθαι ἢ πρὸς τοὺς δικαστάς:

the verbal reminiscences are unmistakable.

A more complex but very telling case of οὖν focusing on the issue is found at 83 B 5. The relevant context is from 82 C 2 to 83 E 6: 82 C 2 τού-των ἕνεκα ... οἱ ὀρθῶς φιλόσοφοι ἀπέχονται τῶν κατὰ τὸ σῶμα ἐπιθυ-μιῶν ἁπασῶν. This abstinence is first provided with a positive motivation:

82 D 5

> ἡγούμενοι οὐ δεῖν ἐναντία τῇ φιλοσοφίᾳ πράττειν καὶ τῇ ἐκείνης λύσει ... τρέπονται ᾗ ἐκείνη ὑφηγεῖται

which is at once explained:

82 D 9

> γιγνώσκουσι γάρ, ..., οἱ φιλομαθεῖς ὅτι παραλαβοῦσα αὐτῶν τὴν ψυχὴν ἡ φιλοσοφία ἀτεχνῶς διαδεδεμένην ἐν τῷ σώματι ... (83 A 3) λύειν ἐπι-χειρεῖ.

This process of λύειν is expatiated on for nine lines, summarized in the following statement:

83 B 5

> ταύτῃ οὖν τῇ λύσει οὐκ οἰομένη δεῖν ἐναντιοῦσθαι ἡ τοῦ ... ὡς ἀληθῶς φιλοσόφου ψυχὴ οὕτως ἀπέχεται τῶν ἡδονῶν τε καὶ ἐπιθυμιῶν ... λογι-ζομένη ὅτι ...

which provides the transition to the negative half of the argument specify-ing how the ἐπιθυμίαι stand in the way of the λύσις aimed at, summa-rized in its turn at

83 E 5-6

> τούτων τοίνυν ἕνεκα... οἱ δικαίως φιλομαθεῖς κόσμιοί εἰσι ...

Clearly, as at 58 B 1 and 4 and at 98 D 2,[1] οὖν does not mark a conclusion so much as a step or a turn or return in the direction of what we were heading for: by means of οὖν the preceding description is brought to bear on what was to be proved.

Within the compass of our last example we find the same focusing proc-ess on a smaller scale at

---

[1] P. 91 above.

83 A 1

Ἐγὼ ἐρῶ (...) γιγνώσκουσι γάρ (...) οἱ φιλομαθεῖς ὅτι παραλαβοῦσα
αὐτῶν τὴν ψυχὴν ἡ φιλοσοφία ἀτεχνῶς διαδεδεμένην ἐν τῷ σώματι...
(there follow five lines detailing the condition of the soul) ... – ὅπερ οὖν
λέγω, γιγνώσκουσιν οἱ φιλομαθεῖς ὅτι οὕτω παραλαβοῦσα ἡ φιλοσοφία
ἔχουσαν αὐτῶν τὴν ψυχὴν ... λύειν ἐπιχειρεῖ...

οὖν leads back to the issue, which was not the dismal condition of the
unredeemed soul, but the power of philosophy to redeem her.

At 86 C 2, finally, οὖν is found in a context admittedly too diffuse to
offer much help in isolating the role of a particle, yet in which I submit
that the facts relevant to the use of οὖν are few and simple: there is a
parenthesis in which it is mentioned that we (B 6-9)

ὑπολαμβάνομεν ... ψυχὴν ... εἶναι ... ἁρμονίαν

followed by a conditional and a main clause

εἰ οὖν τυγχάνει ἡ ψυχὴ οὖσα ἁρμονία τις, δῆλον ὅτι ... τὴν μὲν ψυχὴν
ἀνάγκη εὐθὺς ὑπάρχει ἀπολωλέναι κτλ.

The particle directs us to the relevance of the parenthesis: the conception
of the soul there outlined may or may not be accurate, but if it should be
accurate, then the consequences for the continued subsistence of our souls
after death, which is what we have been concerned with all along, are as
follows. Had Plato's Simmias wished to stress not the relevance of his
conception but the fact that it may or may not be true, he would have
chosen ἄρα; δή would have carried the suggestion that it is in fact true.[1]

It should be noted that in these cases of οὖν with verbal repetition the
shift of focus is *away* from the constituent repeated, which may have had
focus function at its first occurrence but is now reduced to topic status,
thus making room for a new focus constituent.

2.2. *Preceded by* γάρ (Phaedo)

Not seldom a sentence containing οὖν is preceded by one that is explicitly
marked as subsidiary by the use of γάρ. Whereas in general the context
relevant to the understanding of οὖν includes at least the preceding sentence, in the present species it extends backwards at least as far as the
sentence preceding that which contains γάρ, so that we have at least three
sentences to take into account: one (*a*) calling for some kind of explanation in the widest sense of the word, one (*b*) supplying this explanation,
and one (*c*) resuming the subject which called for the explanation.

---

[1] Cf. Chh. 3 & 4 below.

2.2.1. *With verbal repetition*

The most transparant examples of this situation overlap with that identified by verbal repetition:

59 E 2

> (*a*) τότε πρφαίτερον συνελέγημεν· (*b*) τῇ γὰρ προτεραίᾳ ... ἐπυθόμεθα ὅτι τὸ πλοῖον ... ἀφιγμένον εἴη. (*c*) παρηγγείλαμεν οὖν ἀλλήλοις ἥκειν ὡς πρφαίτατα εἰς τὸ εἰωθός. καὶ ἥκομεν καὶ ...

Here only (*a*) and (*c*) share a lexical element. More typically (*c*) will combine words from (*b*) with words from (*a*):

109 C 3

> (περὶ γῆς (108 D 2) ... πέπεισμαι (109 A 7) ...) (*a*) πάμμεγά τι εἶναι αὐτό, καὶ ἡμᾶς οἰκεῖν ἐν σμικρῷ τινι μορίῳ ... (*b*) εἶναι γὰρ πανταχῇ περὶ τὴν γῆν πολλὰ κοῖλα ... (*c*) ἡμᾶς οὖν οἰκοῦντας ἐν τοῖς κοίλοις αὐτῆς λεληθέναι ...

98 B 1

> (97 D 6 ηὑρηκέναι ᾤμην διδάσκαλον τῆς αἰτίας περὶ τῶν ὄντων ..., καί μοι ... ἐπεκδιηγήσεσθαι τὴν αἰτίαν ... λέγοντα τὸ ἄμεινον ...· ...) (*a*) περὶ ἡλίου ... παρεσκευάσμην ὡσαύτως πευσόμενος ... καὶ τῶν ἄλλων ἄστρων, ..., πῇ ποτε ταῦτ' ἄμεινόν ἐστιν ἕκαστον ... πάσχειν ἃ πάσχει. (*b*) οὐ γὰρ ἄν ποτε αὐτὸν ᾤμην ... ἄλλην τινὰ αὐτοῖς αἰτίαν ἐπενεγκεῖν ἢ ὅτι βέλτιστον ... (*c*) ἑκάστῳ οὖν αὐτῶν ἀποδιδόντα τὴν αἰτίαν ... τὸ ἑκάστῳ βέλτιστον ᾤμην ... ἐπεκδιηγήσεσθαι ...

In 109 BC the chief new contribution of the γάρ sentence are the κοῖλα, in 98 A the *novum* is the small step from ἄμεινον to βέλτιστον.

59 D 4

> (*a*) ἀεὶ γὰρ δὴ ... εἰώθεμεν φοιτᾶν ... συλλεγόμενοι ἕωθεν εἰς τὸ δικαστήριον ...· (*b*) πλησίον γὰρ ἦν τοῦ δεσμωτηρίου. (*c*) περιεμένομεν οὖν ἑκάστοτε ἕως ἀνοιχθείη τὸ δεσμωτήριον ..., (*d*) ἀνεῴγετο γὰρ οὐ πρῴ

is somewhat complicated by the fact that the data adduced in explanation have been distributed over two sentences, one preceding and the other following that which contains οὖν: *a*, *b* γάρ, *c* οὖν, *d* γάρ.

The pattern may be obscured by expansions:

92 E 2

> (C 8 ὅρα πότερον αἱρῇ τῶν λόγων, τὴν μάθησιν ἀνάμνησιν εἶναι ἢ ψυχὴν ἁρμονίαν;) – (*a*) πολὺ μᾶλλον ... ἐκεῖνον... (*b*) ὅδε μὲν γάρ μοι γέγονεν ... μετὰ εἰκότος τινὸς ... ὁ δὲ περὶ τῆς ἀναμνήσεως καὶ μαθήσεως λόγος ... δι' ὑποθέσεως ἀξίας ἀποδέξασθαι εἴρηται.... ἐγὼ δὲ ταύτην ... ἀποδέδεγμαι. (*c*) ἀνάγκη οὖν μοι ... διὰ ταῦτα μήτε ἐμαυτοῦ μήτε ἄλλου ἀποδέχεσθαι λέγοντος ὡς ψυχή ἐστιν ἁρμονία ...

Here (c) is a negative version of (a), and (b) virtually implies both of them. διὰ ταῦτα makes it clear that οὖν is not equivalent to 'therefore'.[1] Simmias' rejection of 'harmony' is more topical than his acceptance of 'recollection', because it is the 'harmony' hypothesis which will continue to occupy the participants in the dialogue for some time.

The verbal correspondences may be only approximate. At 95 B 1

(a) τουτονὶ γοῦν τὸν λόγον τὸν πρὸς τὴν ἁρμονίαν θαυμαστῶς μοι εἶπες ὡς παρὰ δόξαν. (b) Σιμμίου γὰρ λέγοντος ὅτε ἠπόρει, πάνυ ἐθαύμαζον εἴ τι ἕξει τις χρήσασθαι τῷ λόγῳ αὐτοῦ· (c) πάνυ οὖν μοι ἀτόπως ἔδοξεν εὐθὺς τὴν πρώτην ἔφοδον οὐ δέξασθαι τοῦ σοῦ λόγου

each of the three members shares, in addition to λόγος which is found in all three, one lexical element with each of the other two:

(a) θαυμαστῶς ... ὡς παρὰ δόξαν
(b) πάνυ ἐθαύμαζον
(c) πάνυ ... ἀτόπως ἔδοξεν

At 64 A 6

(a) (63 E 9) φαίνεται εἰκότως ἀνὴρ τῷ ὄντι ἐν φιλοσοφίᾳ διατρίψας τὸν βίον θαρρεῖν μέλλων ἀποθανεῖσθαι ... πῶς ἂν οὖν δὴ τοῦθ' οὕτως ἔχοι ... πειράσομαι φράσαι. (b) κινδυνεύουσι γὰρ ὅσοι τυγχάνουσιν ὀρθῶς ἁπτόμενοι φιλοσοφίας λεληθέναι τοὺς ἄλλους ὅτι οὐδὲν ἄλλο αὐτοὶ ἐπιτηδεύουσιν ἢ ἀποθνῄσκειν τε καὶ τεθνάναι. (c) εἰ οὖν τοῦτο ἀληθές, ἄτοπον δήπου ἂν εἴη προθυμεῖσθαι μὲν ἐν παντὶ τῷ βίῳ μηδὲν ἄλλο ἢ τοῦτο, ἥκοντος δὲ δὴ αὐτοῦ ἀγανακτεῖν ὃ πάλαι προυθυμοῦντό τε καὶ ἐπετήδευον.

ἐπιτηδεύειν is common to (b) and (c); τῷ ὄντι ἐν φιλοσοφίᾳ διατρίψας τὸν βίον in (a) is resumed both by ὀρθῶς ἁπτόμενοι φιλοσοφίας in (b) and by ἐν παντὶ τῷ βίῳ in (c); and εἰκότως ... θαρρεῖν and μέλλων ἀποθανεῖσθαι in (a) are equivalent to ἄτοπον ... ἀγανακτεῖν and ἥκοντος ... αὐτοῦ respectively in (c). Once more, οὖν indicates the relevance of the preceding sentence to, and takes us back to, what this sentence was meant to throw light upon.

2.2.2. *Without verbal reminiscences*

While lexical recurrences help to identify this function of οὖν, they are not a necessary condition of it.

---

[1] Cf. p. 149 below on διὰ ταῦτα δή.

89 B 2

(a) ὡς εὖ ἡμᾶς ... προύτρεψεν ... (b) ἔτυχον γὰρ ἐν δεξιᾷ αὐτοῦ καθ-
ήμενος ... (c) καταψήσας οὖν μου τὴν κεφαλὴν ... ἔφη ... ἔγωγ' ἄν, εἰ σὺ
εἴην, ἔνορκον ἂν ποιησαίμην ... μὴ πρότερον κομήσειν πρὶν ἂν νικήσω...

The relating of Socrates' pep talk requires that Phaedo should explain
how they were seated; with οὖν we are told in what way these positions
mattered.

At 61 C 4

οἷον παρακελεύῃ ... Εὐήνῳ. πολλὰ γὰρ ἤδη ἐντετύχηκα τῷ ἀνδρί· σχεδὸν οὖν ἐξ ὧν ἐγὼ ᾔσθημαι οὐδ' ὁπωστιοῦν σοι ... πείσεται.

the explanation is of an exclamation: the point of Simias' reference to his
frequent encounters with Evenus is brought out in the οὖν sentence, and
particularly in the phrase ἐξ ὧν ἐγὼ ᾔσθημαι: 'I am qualified to judge;
now I can tell you...'

At 108 D 3

πῶς ταῦτα ... λέγεις ...; περὶ γάρ τοι γῆς καὶ αὐτὸς πολλὰ δὴ ἀκήκοα, οὐ
μέντοι ταῦτα ἃ σὲ πείθει· ἡδέως οὖν ἂν ἀκούσαιμι.

the explanation is of a question. A minor irregularity is that the first half
of the γάρ sentence is only a foil for the second half, which contains the
actual explanation.

At 96 A 1

οὐ φαῦλον πρᾶγμα ... ζητεῖς· ὅλως γὰρ δεῖ περὶ γενέσεως καὶ φθορᾶς
τὴν αἰτίαν διαπραγματεύεσθαι. ἐγὼ οὖν σοι δίειμι περὶ αὐτῶν, ἐὰν βούλῃ, τά γε ἐμὰ πάθη ...

the γάρ sentence has specified just how big a πρᾶγμα Cebes is after. The
οὖν sentence proceeds from these comments to what Socrates for his part
can do about it.

2.3. *In arguments* (Des Places)

If we try to remedy the lack of instances exemplifying the 'inferential
use' of οὖν as a 'connecting particle' in *Greek Particles*[1] by drawing
upon Des Places, the first place to look for them is in section II, 'οὖν avec
ideé de conséquence', under (1), 'οὖν introduit la conclusion d'un syllo-
gisme ou d'un enthymème'.[2] One example:[3]

---

[1] P. 425-6.
[2] P. 11.
[3] P. 13.

Resp. 353 B 6

οὐκοῦν καὶ ἀρετὴ δοκεῖ σοι εἶναι ἑκάστῳ ᾧπερ καὶ ἔργον τι προστέτακται; ... ὀφθαλμῶν ... ἔστι τι ἔργον; ... ἆρ' οὖν καὶ ἀρετὴ ὀφθαλμῶν ἔστιν;

This in itself is, just like 59 E 8 and 116 A 4 quoted above,[1] compatible with the notion that οὖν expresses consequence. Another example, at

Euthyd. 300 A 4

– Πότερον ... ὁρῶσιν ... οἱ ... ἄνθρωποι τὰ δυνατὰ ὁρᾶν ἢ τὰ ἀδύνατα;
– Τὰ δυνατά ...
– Οὐκοῦν καὶ σύ ...; – Κἀγώ.
– Ὁρᾷς οὖν τὰ ἡμέτερα ἱμάτια; – Ναί.
– Δυνατὰ οὖν ὁρᾶν ἐστὶν ταῦτα.

is similar in argumentative structure, yet casts doubt on this interpretation by the sheer fact of containing an instance of the particle both in the conclusion and in the minor premiss, as it is put in Des Places.[2] Our hypothesis of οὖν leading to the point, on the other hand, is obviously compatible with both occurrences, and so it is with *Resp.* 353 B 6: we have been discussing ἔργα from 352 D 8-9 onwards and are now proceeding to ἀρεταί. The general principle having been given (ἑκάστῳ ᾧπερ B 3) we shall apply it to *eyes*; we begin with their ἔργον, but only as a stepping-stone: it is their ἀρετή which concerns us now.

Our alternative interpretation receives additional support from other passages cited in Des Places[3] under οὖν introducung a minor premiss,[4] in which inversion of major and minor premiss or other logical informalities make it clear that the habitat of οὖν is not the minor premiss in any technical sense of logic, but simply the *second* of two premisses, or more generally the *last* premiss before a 'conclusion' or ἄρα sentence: thus *La.* 192 D 4, *Crat.* 403 C 5, *Resp.* 451 E 3, *Parm.* 161 D 6, *Tht.* 160 D 1.

Resp. 552 D 8 & E 1

δῆλον ... ἐν πόλει οὗ ἂν ἴδῃς πτωχούς, ὅτι εἰσί που ἐν τούτῳ τῷ τόπῳ ... κακῶν δημιουργοί. ... τί οὖν; ἐν ταῖς ὀλιγαρχουμέναις πόλεσι πτωχοὺς οὐχ ὁρᾷς ἐνόντας; ...μὴ οὖν οἰόμεθα ... καὶ κακούργους πολλοὺς ἐν αὐταῖς εἶναι ...;

like 353 B 6 quoted above, require a wider context than they are given in Des Places.[5] The subject is oligarchy; we have been confronted with a

---

[1] P. 90.
[2] P. 13.
[3] P. 68-9.
[4] P. 67.
[5] P. 70.

statement applying to other constitutions as well (ἐν πόλει D 3). The first οὖν question takes us back to the topic of oligarchy and the second duly applies the general statement to this particular constitution.

The use of οὖν in *in*ductive arguments is not sufficiently different to warrant Des Places' separate heading:[1]

Phd. 71 A 9

(70 E 4) τοῦτο οὖν σκεψώμεθα, ἆρα ἀναγκαῖον ὅσοις ἔστι τι ἐναντίον, μηδαμόθεν ἄλλοθεν αὐτὸ γίγνεσθαι ἢ ἐκ τοῦ αὐτῷ ἐναντίου. οἷον ...

five pairs of opposites are examined; after that

– ἱκανῶς οὖν ... ἔχομεν τοῦτο, ὅτι πάντα οὕτως γίγνεται, ἐξ ἐναντίων τὰ ἐναντία πράγματα; – Πάνυ γε.

That 'οὖν amène l'énoncé d'une loi' (Des Places) is true but it is not the whole truth: we began with a general question, the intervening examples were given for the sake of it, and with οὖν we now return to the original question to answer it.

2.4. *Remaining uses of* οὖν *in* Phaedo

A limited number if instances of οὖν in the *Phaedo* resist classification by any external criterion.

60 C 5 resembles the examples quoted under 2.2.1 above[2] in containing a repetition of the verb ἐπακολουθεῖν, it differs from them in marking the application of a general statement, rather than involving a shift of focus: (Socrates' leg is hurting. He reflects on pleasure and pain:)

διὰ ταῦτα, ᾧ ἂν τὸ ἕτερον παραγένηται, ἐπακολουθεῖ ὕστερον καὶ τὸ ἕτερον. Ὥσπερ οὖν καὶ αὐτῷ μοι ἔοικεν· ἐπειδὴ ... ἦν ... τὸ ἀλγεινόν, ἥκειν δὴ φαίνεται ἐπακολουθοῦν τὸ ἡδύ.

With οὖν Socrates returns to his own case, which occasioned his reflections.

112 C 1

(A 7) ἡ δὲ αἰτία ἐστὶν τοῦ ἐκρεῖν τε ... τὰ ῥεύματα, ὅτι ... αἰωρεῖται δὴ καὶ κυμαίνει ..., καὶ ὁ ἀὴρ καὶ τὸ πνεῦμα ... ταὐτὸν ποιεῖ· συνέπεται γὰρ αὐτῷ καὶ ... (4 lines) ... εἰσιὸν καὶ ἐξιόν. ὅταν τε οὖν ὑποχωρήσῃ τὸ ὕδωρ ...· ὅταν τε αὖ ...

---

[1] Pp. 14-5.
[2] P. 94.

likewise marks a particularization, like

97 C 6

> ... ἀκούσας ... τινός ... ἀναγιγνώσκοντος, καὶ λέγοντος ὡς ἄρα νοῦς
> ἐστιν ὁ διακοσμῶν τε καὶ πάντων αἴτιος, ταύτη δὴ τῇ αἰτίᾳ ἥσθην τε ...
> καὶ ἡγησάμην ... τόν γε νοῦν κοσμοῦντα ... ἕκαστον τιθέναι ταύτη ὅπη
> ἂν βέλτιστα ἔχη· εἰ οὖν τις βούλοιτο τὴν αἰτίαν εὑρεῖν περὶ ἑκάστου
> ὅπη ... ἔστι, τοῦτο δεῖν περὶ αὐτοῦ εὑρεῖν, ὅπη βέλτιστον αὐτῷ ἐστιν ...
> εἶναι ...

At 80 C 2

> (B 8) ἆρ᾽ οὐχὶ σώματι μὲν ταχὺ διαλύεσθαι προσήκει, ψυχῇ δὲ αὖ τὸ
> παράπαν ἀδιαλύτῳ εἶναι ἢ ἐγγύς τι τούτου; – Πῶς γὰρ οὔ; – Ἐννοεῖς
> οὖν ... τὸ σῶμα ... συχνὸν ἐπιμένει χρόνον ... · ἔνια δὲ μέρη τοῦ σώματος
> ... ὡς ἔπος εἰπεῖν ἀθάνατά ἐστιν· ἢ οὔ; – Ναί. – Ἡ δὲ ψυχὴ ἄρα ... εὐθὺς
> ... ἀπόλωλεν ...; πολλοῦ γε δεῖ,

a comparative statement about body and soul is on the point of being
exploited for an a fortiori argument, similar to that at

86 A 3

> (85 E 3) καὶ περὶ ἁρμονίας ἄν τις καὶ λύρας τε καὶ χορδῶν τὸν αὐτὸν
> τοῦτον λόγον εἴποι, ὡς ἡ μὲν ἁρμονία ... θεῖόν ἐστιν ..., αὐτὴ δ᾽ ἡ λύρα
> καὶ αἱ χορδαὶ ... τοῦ θνητοῦ συγγενῆ. ἐπειδὰν οὖν ἢ κατάξη τις τὴν
> λύραν ἢ διατέμη καὶ διαρρήξη τὰς χορδάς, εἴ τις διισχυρίζοιτο τῷ αὐτῷ
> λόγῳ ὥσπερ σύ, ὡς ἀνάγκη ἔτι εἶναι τὴν ἁρμονίαν ἐκείνην καὶ μὴ ἀπο-
> λωλέναι—οὐδεμία γὰρ μηχανὴ ἂν εἴη τὴν μὲν λύραν ἔτι εἶναι ...; τὴν
> δὲ ἁρμονίαν ἀπολωλέναι ... προτέραν τοῦ θνητοῦ ἀπολομένην

where the clause depending on ὡς does not yet give the λόγος announced,
but just the presuppositions; the actual argument occupies the intermina-
ble period which runs from ἐπειδάν οὖν, past the instance of οὖν at 86 C
2 quoted above, to the apodosis beginning ὅρα οὖν πρὸς τοῦτον τὸν λόγον
τί φήσομεν at D 1-2.

At 70 C 2

> (...;) (B 6) ἢ περὶ αὐτῶν τούτων βούλει διαμυθολογῶμεν, ...; – Ἐγὼ γοῦν,
> ἔφη ὁ Κέβης, ἡδέως ἂν ἀκούσαιμι ἥντινα δόξαν ἔχεις περὶ αὐτῶν. – Οὔκ-
> ουν γ᾽ ἂν οἶμαι, ἦ δ᾽ ὃς ὁ Σ., εἰπεῖν τινα νῦν ἀκούσαντα, οὐδ᾽ εἰ κωμῳ-
> δοποιὸς εἴη, ὡς ἀδολεσχῶ καὶ οὐ περὶ προσηκόντων τοὺς λόγους ποιοῦ-
> μαι. εἰ οὖν δοκεῖ, χρὴ διασκοπεῖσθαι. Σκεψώμεθα δὲ ...

οὖν again marks an application: 'Tonight I'm talking about fitting subjects; here comes one of them'. οὖν belongs to the compound sentence as

a whole. ἄρα would yield 'if it's your wish, as you say it is', δή 'if it's your wish, as it obviously is'.

At six places in the *Phaedo* (60 C 8, 62 E 8, 84 C 1, 86 D 5, 88 C 1, 95 E 7) οὖν after a stretch of dialogue opens a stretch of narration. Akin to these, but with a sentence intervening which describes a slight change in the outward appearance of the scene, we have (61 C 10-D 3):

'... οὐ γάρ φασι θεμιτὸν εἶναι.' Καὶ ἅμα λέγων ταῦτα καθῆκε τὰ σκέλη ἐπὶ τὴν γῆν, καὶ καθεζόμενος οὕτως ἤδη τὰ λοιπὰ διελέγετο. Ἤρετο οὖν αὐτὸν ὁ Κέβης· 'Πῶς τοῦτο λέγεις, ὦ Σ., ...'

Seven instances of οὖν form part of injunctions, six of them accompanying an imperative and one (70 E 4) an adhortative subjunctive. With all seven the speaker has been going on for some time: from two lines and a half (77 E 6) to a page. This contrasts sharply with τοίνυν found with an imperative five times and with an adhortative once, with all six instances at the beginning of the utterance.[1] οὖν immediately precedes or follows the verb in four of the seven cases;[2] two adjuncts intervene at 61 B 7; an independent clause containing γάρ is inserted at

116 C 8
νῦν οὖν, οἶσθα γὰρ ἃ ἦλθον ἀγγέλλων, χαῖρέ τε καὶ πειρῶ ...

Somewhat more complicated rhetorically is

60 D 5
περὶ γάρ ... τῶν ποιημάτων ... καὶ ἄλλοι τινές με ἤδη ἤροντο, ἀτὰρ καὶ Εὔηνος πρῴην, ὅτι ποτὲ .... εἰ οὖν τί σοι μέλει τοῦ ἔχειν ἐμὲ Εὐήνῳ ἀποκρίνασθαι ὅταν με αὖθις ἐρωτᾷ — εὖ οἶδα γὰρ ὅτι ἐρήσεται — εἰπὲ τί χρὴ λέγειν.

But the purport is not in doubt: coming between two γάρ sentences conveying the necessary background information, οὖν points forward to the directive which this information is relevant to.

---

[1] Cf. p. 153 below.
[2] 70 E 4, 77 E 6, 86 D 1, 115 D 6.

CHAPTER THREE

APA

0. *General*

ἄρα, like οὖν, is credited by Denniston with a logical force. More precisely, its use as a 'logical connective particle'[1] is classed as a particular
variety of a secondary use in which, in one description, the particle 'denotes ... the interest or surprise occasioned by enlightenment or disillu-
sionment';[2] in another description it 'marks realization or enlightenment'.[3]
In Plato, the reader is told,[4] 'we find ἄρα used practically as a variant for
οὖν and δή, though *even*[5] in Plato ἄρα perhaps conveys a slightly less
formal and more conversational connexion than those particles'. Four examples are offered, which will be discussed below.[6] I wish to submit,
however, that ἄρα is, in Plato at least, not less but more apt than οὖν and
δή to be used in cases of strictly formal connexion. To this end we shall
consider (1) Denniston's examples of logical connective ἄρα, and (2) a
special use in arguments which is ascribed to the particle by Des Places. If
my reading of these carries conviction, it still has to be conceded that a
number of uses of the particle in Plato cannot be accounted for by its
appropriateness to logical connections. I shall review (3) the instances
from the *Phaedo* and propose an account of these which for some of them
is rather different both from that given of the uses in contexts of inference, and from existing explanations. In spite of this I wish to maintain
that all these uses are related and bear a 'family resemblance'. To support
this claim an excursus into (4) uses of the ἄρα family outside Plato is
required. In particular two older prose authors, one Attic and one non-
Attic, are explored.

---

[1] *GP* p. 40.
[2] Ib. 35.
[3] Ib. 40.
[4] Ib. 41.
[5] Italics JMvO.
[6] P. 102.

1. *In arguments*

We shall first inquire whether justice is done in *GP*[1] to the examples quoted in it of logical connective ἄρα:

Charm. 161 A 6

... (160 E 4) εἶναι ὅπερ αἰδὼς ἡ σωφροσύνη ... (E 13) οὐ μόνον οὖν ἄρα καλόν, ἀλλὰ καὶ ἀγαθόν ἐστιν. – Ἔμοιγε δοκεῖ. – Τί οὖν; ... Ὁμήρῳ οὐ πιστεύεις καλῶς λέγειν λέγοντι ὅτι 'αἰδὼς δ' οὐκ ἀγαθή ...;' – Ἔγωγ', ... – Ἔστιν ἄρα, ὡς ἔοικεν, αἰδὼς οὐκ ἀγαθὸν καὶ ἀγαθόν.

'Modesty, if this is so, is good.' – 'In my opinion it is.' – 'Don't you agree with Homer when he declares that "Modesty is not good ..."?' – 'Yes I do.' – '(*If this is so, then it turns out*) modesty is both good and not good, as it appears.'

Charm. 171 B 4

(171 A 3) ... γνώσεται ὁ σώφρων τὸν ἰατρόν ... (A 8) ... ἡ ἰατρικὴ δὴ ἑτέρα εἶναι τῶν ἄλλων ὡρίσθη τῷ τοῦ ὑγιεινοῦ εἶναι καὶ νοσώδους ἐπι-στήμη (...) οὐκοῦν ἐν τούτοις ἀναγκαῖον σκοπεῖν τὸν βουλόμενον ἰατρι-κὴν σκοπεῖν ἐν οἷς ποτ' ἔστιν (...) ἐν τοῖς ὑγιεινοῖς ἄρα καὶ νοσώδεσιν ἐπισκέψεται τὸν ἰατρόν, ᾗ ἰατρικός ἐστιν, ὁ ὀρθῶς σκοπούμενος

'Medicine is the knowledge of what is wholesome and what unwholesome; it must be studied in the objects in which it resides; (*it turns out*) it will correctly be inspected, (*if this is so*), in things wholesome and unwhole-some'.

In the terms of dialectical debate these are, *pace* Denniston,[2] perfectly formal arguments. I submit that the contribution of ἄρα to these is to convey that the present statement has to be accepted on the strength of the preceding ones as soon as these are granted; that its persuasiveness ap-pears from the preceding σημεῖα. We shall find out how far this hypo-thesis takes us.

The same analysis applies to a deontic context at

La. 186 A 3

Εἴ τις ἄρα ἡμῶν τεχνικός ..., καὶ ὅτῳ διδάσκαλοι ἀγαθοί ..., τοῦτο σκεπ-τέον. – ... οὔπω ἑώρακας ἄνευ διδασκάλων τεχνικωτέρους γεγονότας ...; – ... οἷς γε ... οὐκ ἂν ἐθέλοις πιστεῦσαι ... εἰ μή τί ... ἔργον ἔχοιεν ἐπιδεῖξαι ... – ... ἀληθῆ ... – Καὶ ἡμᾶς ἄρα δεῖ ... ἐπιδεῖξαι ... διδασ-κάλους ... · ἢ εἴ τις ... ἑαυτῷ διδάσκαλον ... οὔ φησι γεγονέναι, ἀλλ' οὖν ἔργα ... ἔχειν ... ἐπιδεῖξαι ...

'The question is which of us is competent and has had good teachers.' –

---

[1] P. 41.
[2] *GP* 41, above p. 102.

'But you know some men have achieved superior competence without the benefit of good instruction.' – 'True, but you would not trust them on their word if they failed to produce a number of specimens in proof of their competence.' – 'Granted.' – 'We too, *it turns out if this is so*, have to produce either good teachers, or at least good pupils.'

The injunction is expressed by means of an indicative form of δεῖν; with an imperative or adhortative subjunctive τοίνυν rather than ἄρα tends to be used.[1]

One Platonic example of logical connective ἄρα in *GP²* remains:

Ly. 220 D 8

(219 C 7 – D 2) ἐκεῖνο ὅ ἐστιν πρῶτον φίλον, οὗ ἕνεκα καὶ τὰ ἄλλα φαμὲν πάντα φίλα εἶναι ... (220 B 6-7) μὴ φίλου τινὸς ἕνεκα τὸ φίλον φίλον εἶναι ... τὸ ἀγαθόν ἐστιν φίλον ... φιλεῖται τἀγαθὸν διὰ τὸ κακόν ... Τὸ ἄρα φίλον ἡμῖν ἐκεῖνο, εἰς ὃ ἐτελεύτα πάντα τὰ ἄλλα—ἕνεκα ἑτέρου φίλου φίλα ἔφαμεν εἶναι ἐκεῖνα—οὐδὲν τούτοις ἔοικεν.

'Things dear to us are so on account of one prime thing that is dear to us *not* on account of some other thing dear to us; the good is dear to us on account of the bad; this dear thing, *it turns out if this is so*, to which all the others can be reduced is not at all like them.'

A related form of argument likewise featuring ἄρα appears in the *Phaedo*:

74 C 4

λίθοι ... ἴσοι ... ἐνίοτε ... τῷ μὲν ἴσα φαίνεται , τῷ δ' οὔ; – Πάνυ μὲν οὖν. – ... αὐτὰ τὰ ἴσα ἔστιν ὅτε ἄνισά σοι ἐφάνη ...; – Οὐδεπώποτε ... – Οὐ ταὐτὸν ἄρα ἐστίν ... ταῦτά τε τὰ ἴσα καὶ αὐτὸ τὸ ἴσον

'equal things seem equal to one man but unequal to another; what is equal itself can never seem unequal; equal things and the equal itself, *it turns out if this is so*, are not the same thing.

These contexts, then, do not involve a notably *informal* connexion; but it may well be that they involve one that is characterized as *nothing but* a connexion: that the statement containing ἄρα is not asserted but remains expressly hypothetical. This possibility will prove relevant to certain uses of the particle in very different, non-argumentative contexts.

2. *Long term* ἄρα?

At 71 E 2[3] we find ἄρα in the conclusion of a fairly long stretch of argument. This use is called attention to in Des Places, where a separate

---

[1] Cf. p. 153 ff. below.
[2] P. 41.
[3] P. 111.

section[1] is devoted to ἄρα indicating 'une conclusion tirée de l'ensemble du raisonnement précédent'[2] and used to note 'les grandes étapes de l'argumentation'. I shall review Des Places' examples from the *Phaedo*, and suggest that, while the particle is indeed appropriate not only to connections with the proposition contained in the preceding sentence but with wider contexts as well,[3] this aptitude is integral to the force ἄρα as maintaining consistency and coherence of perspective, and so does not call for a separate heading to account for such contexts.

In 75 C 4 we have a simple and straightforward deduction:

(75 B 10) οὐκοῦν ... γενόμενοι εὐθὺς ... τὰς ... αἰσθήσεις εἴχομεν; – πάνυ γε. – ἔδει δέ γε, φαμέν, πρὸ τούτων τὴν τοῦ ἴσου ἐπιστήμην εἰληφέναι; – ναί. – πρὶν γενέσθαι ἄρα ὡς ἔοικεν ἀνάγκη ἡμῖν αὐτὴν εἰληφέναι.

'We got our senses at birth, (...), the knowledge of equal before our senses: ... (if this is so) *it turns out that* (we necessarily got that) before birth'.

72 A 4 is different only in that the conclusion is not asserted outright, but placed under the sentence operator 'it was agreed that'[4] and thus presupposed:

(71 E 9) ... ἢ ἀνάγκη ἀποδοῦναι τῷ ἀποθνήσκειν ἐναντίαν τινὰ γένεσιν; – Πάντως που. – Τίνα ταύτην; – τὸ ἀναβιώσκεσθαι. – Οὐκοῦν ... ἐκ τῶν τεθνεώτων ἂν εἴη γένεσις εἰς τοὺς ζῶντας αὕτη ...; – Πάνυ γε. – Ὁμολογεῖται ἄρα ἡμῖν καὶ ταύτῃ τοὺς ζῶντας ἐκ τῶν τεθνεώτων γεγονέναι ...

'There must be a process of becoming to balance that of dying; this is *being revived*, a coming-to-be from among the dead to the living. Along these lines too, if this is so, we are agreed that the living have come to be from among the dead.'

If A is real and equals B, then B is real.

104 E 1 is slightly more complicated:

... ἃ ἂν ἡ τῶν τριῶν ἰδέα κατάσχῃ, ἀνάγκη αὐτοῖς οὐ μόνον τρισὶν εἶναι ἀλλὰ καὶ περιττοῖς ... Ἐπὶ τὸ τοιοῦτον δὴ ... ἡ ἐναντία ἰδέα ἐκείνῃ ... ἢ ἂν τοῦτο ἀπεργάζηται οὐδέποτ' ἂν ἔλθοι ... Εἰργάζετο δέ γε ἡ περιττή; ... Ἐναντία δὲ ταύτῃ ἡ τοῦ ἀρτίου; ... Ἐπὶ τὰ τρία ἄρα ἡ τοῦ ἀρτίου ἰδέα οὐδέποτε ἥξει.

---

[1] P. 246-9. Actually Des Places does not bring 71 E 2 under this heading, though on his own terms he might have done so.

[2] P. 246.

[3] This characteristic will be found relevant to uses classed as 'anticipatory' below at p. 110ff.

[4] The relatively impersonal passive voice sits well on the particle as I understand it (P. Stork).

'What comes under the Form Three is necessarily odd; the Form contrary to that which produces it can have no dealings with it; this is the Form Even, the contrary of Odd; if this is so, the Form Even can have no dealings with Three'.

This involves two substitutions, 'Odd' for 'the Form which produces it' and 'Even' for 'the Form contrary to that'.

79 B 16 presupposes, as though this were self-evident, that what *is* (e.g. unseen) is *similar to* the (e.g. unseen):

(79 B 4) ... ὁμοιότερον ... τὸ σῶμα ... τῷ ὁρατῷ.

... (ψυχὴ) ἀιδές ...

Ὁμοιότερον ἄρα ψυχὴ σώματός ἐστιν τῷ ἀιδεῖ, τὸ δὲ τῷ ὁρατῷ. – Πᾶσα ἀνάγκη ...

'Body is more like the visible (sc. than it is like the unseen); soul is unseen; if this is so, soul is more like the unseen than body, and body more like the visible (sc. than soul)': i.e.

if		A	is more similar	to C	than	to non-C
	and	B	is more similar	to non-C	than	to C

then		A	is more similar	to C	than	B is
	and	B	is more similar	to non-C	than	A is.

In 102 C 10 ἄρα introduces an inference of a more inductive complexion:

(102 B 5) ... εἶναι ἐν τῷ Σιμμίᾳ ἀμφότερα, καὶ μέγεθος καὶ σμικρότητα ... (B 8) τὸν Σιμμίαν ὑπερέχειν Σωκράτους ... τῷ μεγέθει ὃ τυγχάνει ἔχων ... (C 4) ὅτι σμικρότητα ἔχει ὁ Σωκράτης πρὸς τὸ ἐκείνου μέγεθος; – ... – ... (C 6) ὑπὸ Φαίδωνος ὑπερέχεσθαι ... ὅτι μέγεθος ἔχει ὁ Φαίδων πρὸς τὴν Σιμμίου σμικρότητα; – ... – οὕτως ἄρα ὁ Σιμμίας ἐπωνυμίαν ἔχει σμικρός τε καὶ μέγας εἶναι ... τοῦ μὲν τῷ μεγέθει ὑπερέχειν τὴν σμικρότητα ὑπέχων, τῷ δὲ τὸ μέγεθος τῆς σμικρότητος παρέχων ὑπερέχον.

'Simmias is taller than Socrates by his own height, and by Socrates' comparative shortness; he is smaller than Phaedo by Phaedo's comparative tallness; if this is so, then this is how Simmias comes to be called both short and tall, by supplying his shortness to the greater height of the one, and his own greater height to the shortness of the other.'

Close kin to 75 C 4[1] are 74 E 9

(74 E 2) ... ἀναγκαῖόν που τὸν τοῦτο ἐννοοῦντα τυχεῖν προειδότα ἐκεῖνο ᾧ φησιν αὐτὸ προσεοικέναι ...; – Ἀνάγκη. – ... τὸ τοιοῦτον πεπόνθαμεν ... περί τε τὰ ἴσα καὶ αὐτὸ τὸ ἴσον; – Παντάπασί γε. – Ἀναγ-

---

[1] P. 104 above.

καῖον ἄρα ἡμᾶς προειδέναι τὸ ἴσον πρὸ ... τοῦ χρόνου ὅτε τὸ πρῶτον ἰδόντες τὰ ἴσα ...[1]

and 75 B 4:

(75 A 5) Ἀλλὰ μὴν καὶ τόδε ὁμολογοῦμεν, μὴ ἄλλοθεν αὐτὸ ... δυνατὸν εἶναι ἐννοῆσαι ἀλλ' ... ἔκ τινος ... τῶν αἰσθήσεων ...
Πρὸ τοῦ ἄρα ἄρξασθαι ἡμᾶς ... αἰσθάνεσθαι τυχεῖν ἔδει εἰληφότας ἐπιστήμην αὐτοῦ τοῦ ἴσου ὅτι ἔστιν

'To recognize that a thing is trying to resemble some other thing, you need to know this other thing first. This applies to 'equal things' and 'the equal itself'. It is necessary, if this is so, that we should have known the equal itself before we first became aware of equal things. Now this awareness is yielded by the senses. Before we began to perceive, *if this is so* (and *it would follow*), we must have acquired a knowledge of the equal itself.'

Another syllogistic context for ἄρα is that of 105 E 6:

(105 E 2) ὃ ... ἂν θάνατον μὴ δέχεται τί καλοῦμεν;
– Ἀθάνατον.
– Οὐκοῦν ψυχὴ οὐ δέχεται θάνατον;
– Οὔ.
– Ἀθάνατος ἄρα ψυχή.

'That which does not admit death is immortal; soul does not admit death; soul, if this is so, is immortal'.

Needless to say, ἄρα is equally appropiate to arguments lending themselves to a very different logical analysis, e.g., in the terms of propositional logic, at 94 E 8:

(C 3) ... ὡμολογήσαμεν ... μήποτ' ἂν αὐτήν, ἁρμονίαν γε οὖσαν, ἐναντία ᾄδειν ... – ... (C 8) ... νῦν οὐ πᾶν τοὐναντίον ἡμῖν φαίνεται ἐργαζομένη ... (E 2) ἆρ' οἴει αὐτὸν ταῦτα ποιῆσαι διανοούμενον ὡς ἁρμονίας αὐτῆς οὔσης καὶ οἵας ἄγεσθαι ... ἀλλ' οὐχ οἵας ἄγειν ... καὶ οὔσης αὐτῆς πολὺ θειοτέρου τινὸς πράγματος ἢ καθ' ἁρμονίαν; – (E 7) ... ἔμοιγε δοκεῖ. – οὐκ ἄρα ... ἡμῖν οὐδαμῇ καλῶς ἔχει ψυχὴν ἁρμονίαν τινὰ φάναι εἶναι ...

'If soul is harmony, she will harmonize; but she doesn't; soul, *if this is so* (and *it would follow*), is not harmony'.

From the same context we have a proof *e contrario* in 94 A 8:

(93 E 8) εἴπερ ἡ μὲν κακία ἀναρμοστία, ἡ δὲ ἀρετὴ ἁρμονία εἴη ... (94 A 1) κατὰ τὸν ὀρθὸν λόγον κακίας οὐδεμία ψυχὴ μεθέξει, εἴπερ ἁρμονία ἐστίν· ἁρμονία γὰρ δήπου ... ἀναρμοστίας οὔποτ' ἂν μετάσχοι. – οὐ

---

[1] Note the recurrence of ἀναγκαῖον (E 2 & 9, ἀνάγκη E 5) and of προειδέναι (E 3 προειδότα & 9, cf. πρὸ ... αἰσθάνεσθαι 75 B 4-5).

μέντοι. – οὐδέ γε δήπου ψυχή ... κακίας. – πῶς γὰρ ἔκ γε τῶν προειρημένων; – ἐκ τούτου ἄρα τοῦ λόγου ἡμῖν πᾶσαι ψυχαὶ ... ἀγαθαὶ ἔσονται.

'If soul is harmony, it will not partake of evil; on this definition, it turns out
(and *if this is so, it would follow*), all souls will be good'.

Des Places assigns this occurrence of ἄρα to a subspecies of his 'conclusion ... de l'ensemble ...'[1] in which the 'conclusion générale' is underlined
by expressions like ἐκ τούτου τοῦ λόγου. But it is a priori preferable to
distinguish the contribution of ἄρα from that made by the prepositional
expression. This does not just echo the immediately preceding ἔκ γε τῶν
προειρημένων; it also resumes κατὰ τὸν ὀρθὸν λόγον from 94 A 1, where
translators[2] have not heeded Burnet's note "'according to the right account
of the matter', 'to put the matter correctly.' If the soul is a ἁρμονία, ...'".

67 E 4 is a return to 64 A 4 ss.:

κινδυνεύουσι ... ὅσοι τυγχάνουσιν ὀρθῶς ἁπτόμενοι φιλοσοφίας λεληθέναι τοὺς ἄλλους ὅτι ... ἐπιτηδεύουσιν ... ἀποθνῄσκειν τε καὶ τεθνάναι. Εἰ οὖν τοῦτο ἀληθές, ἄτοπον δήπου ἂν εἴη προθυμεῖσθαι μὲν ἐν
παντὶ τῷ βίῳ ... τοῦτο, ἥκοντος δὲ δὴ αὐτοῦ ἀγανακτεῖν ὃ πάλαι προ-
εθυμεῖτο ...

'It looks as though true philosophers are always preparing themselves for
death; *if so*, it would be absurd for them to fret when it comes'

67 E 4

(67 D 4) Οὐκοῦν ... θάνατος ὀνομάζεται λύσις καὶ χωρισμὸς ψυχῆς ἀπὸ
σώματος; – Παντάπασί γε. – Λύειν δέ γε αὐτήν ... προθυμοῦνται ἀεὶ
μάλιστα καὶ μόνοι οἱ φιλοσοφοῦντες ὀρθῶς, καὶ τὸ μελέτημα αὐτὸ τοῦτό
ἐστιν φιλοσόφων, λύσις καὶ χωρισμὸς ψυχῆς ἀπὸ σώματος; – Φαίνεται.
– Οὐκοῦν, ὅπερ ἐν ἀρχῇ ἔλεγον, γελοῖον ἂν εἴη ἄνδρα παρασκευάζονθ'
ἑαυτὸν ἐν τῷ βίῳ ὅτι ἐγγυτάτω ὄντα τοῦ τεθνάναι οὕτω ζῆν, κἄπειθ'
ἥκοντος αὐτῷ τούτου ἀγανακτεῖν; – Γελοῖον ... – Τῷ ὄντι[3] ἄρα ... οἱ
ὀρθῶς φιλοσοφοῦντες ἀποθνῄσκειν μελετῶσι ...

'Death equals release of soul from body; this release is what true philosophers apply themselves to; naturally, as I have said before, they do so all the
way; true philosophers, *if this is so* (and *it would follow*), actually do apply
themselves to dying'.

This use of ἄρα is clearly bound up with a 'grande étape',[4] even though a
use of the particle might have found sufficient motivation within the limits of second quotation alone. A more extreme example of the same situa-

---

[1] P. 246.
[2] E.g. Robin, Hackforth, Gallop.
[3] Cf. λεληθέναι at 64 A 5 just quoted (P. Stork).
[4] Des Places 246.

tion is found at 106 E 9, where the sentence introduced by ἄρα settles a question raised as long ago as 70 C 4-5:[1]

σκεψώμεθα ... εἴτ' ἄρα ἐν Ἅιδου εἰσὶν αἱ ψυχαὶ τελευτησάντων τῶν ἀνθρώπων εἴτε καὶ οὔ.

This had first been investigated *ex hypothesi*: if the living arise from the dead, our souls must go to Hades (70 C 8–D 1). This supposition is proved: life and death are contraries and arise out of each other (71 D 6-13):

Ἐκ τῶν τεθνεώτων ἄρα ... τὰ ζῶντά τε καὶ οἱ ζῶντες γίγνονται; – Φαίνεται ... – Εἰσὶν ἄρα αἱ ψυχαὶ ἡμῶν ἐν Ἅιδου,

with two quite clear-cut inferential uses of ἄρα at 71 D 14 & E 2. Towards 106, however, things have become considerably more involved. The final solution, which begins in 105 C, may be analysed as follows:

(*a*)	(105 C-D)	soul brings life
	(E 4)	ψυχὴ οὐ δέχεται θάνατον
	(E 6)	ἀθάνατον ἄρα ψυχή
(*b*)	(106 A-B)	what is immortal withdraws unscathed from what is opposed to it.
(*c*)	(C-D)	what is immortal is indestructible

+ (*a*) yields

(*d*)	(E 2-3)	... ψυχὴ ..., εἰ ἀθάνατος τυγχάνει οὖσα, καὶ ἀνώλεθρος ἂν εἴη;

(*b*) + (*c*) yields

(*e*)	(E 5-7)	... Ἐπιόντος ἄρα θανάτου ... τὸ δ᾽ ἀθάνατον σῶν καὶ ἀδιάφθορον οἴχεται ἀπιόν

+ (*a*) yields

(*f*)	(E 9-107 A 1)	... Παντὸς μᾶλλον ἄρα ... ψυχὴ ἀθάνατον καὶ ἀνώλεθρον, καὶ τῷ ὄντι ἔσονται ἡμῶν αἱ ψυχαὶ ἐν Ἅιδου.

'soul is indestructible (*a* + *c* > *d*); at the approach, if this is so, of death, man's immortal part withdraws unscathed (+ *b* > *e*); soul, if this is so, is immortal and indestructible in the highest degree, and our souls *will* subsist in Hades'.

Again what is needed to justify the two steps (*e*) and (*f*) marked by ἄρα is given in the last one or two pages; yet it makes sense to relate the use of the particle to a larger stretch of argument. It should be noted,

---

[1] Cf. p. 110-11 below.

however, that an aptitude to relate to a more comprehensive whole may with equal justice be ascribed e.g. to οὖν; the distinctive feature of each has to be found elsewhere. I submit that the instances of ἄρα to which Des Places has called our attention do not so much mark the argument as such, as the fact that the status of successive statements continues to be the same, i.e. a new statement forms part of the same universe of discourse as the preceding one. The hearer or reader is directed to continue to apply the same point of view or perspective in the fairly strict sense not of holding an opinion but of, on a small scale, entertaining a proposition, and on a larger scale adopting a possible world. This formula is intended to provide *a* link, which may or may not be an, or even the, *historical* link, between an ἄρα by which the speaker periodically calls on the hearer's willingness to suspend disbelief in his story, and the ἄρα by which, in more sophisticated contexts, the speaker confronts the hearer with the consequences of accepting (1) particular premises (2) the general coherence of truth and the world at large.

3. *Distinctive uses in* Phaedo

The next step is to review some distinctive uses of the particle in the *Phaedo* which may help to substantiate the supposed link: uses which can*not* be accounted for by the aptitude of ἄρα to be used in cases of strictly formal connexion.

3.1. *Dissociative and intensional*

A proposition may be entertained without being asserted outright. If it is enlarged upon in the next sentence, ἄρα does little more than recall that the new statement is still hypothetical; the speaker, though he does not express disbelief, yet disclaims responsibility[1] for its referring to fact, and precisely to that extent *dissociates* himself from it:

97 A 3, 4

(96 E 7) ... οὐκ ἀποδέχομαι ἐμαυτοῦ οὐδὲ ὡς ἐπειδὰν ἑνί τις προσθῇ ἕν, ... δύο ἐγένετο· θαυμάζω γὰρ εἰ ὅτε μὲν ἑκάτερον αὐτῶν χωρὶς ἀλλήλων ἦν, ἓν ἄρα ἑκάτερον ἦν ..., ἐπεὶ δ' ἐπλησίασαν ἀλλήλοις, αὕτη ἄρα αἰτία αὐτοῖς ἐγένετο τοῦ δύο γενέσθαι, ἡ σύνοδος ...

111 E 5

ταῦτα δὲ πάντα κινεῖν ἄνω καὶ κάτω ὥσπερ αἰώραν τινὰ ἐνοῦσαν ἐν τῇ γῇ· ἔστι δὲ ἄρα αὕτη ἡ αἰώρα διὰ φύσιν τοιάνδε τινά.

'... and this fluctuation is supposed to *be* there owing to ...'

---

[1] Cf. *GP* p. 38.

The same use is involved in a question in the form of a dependent clause at

78 B 5

> ... μοι δοκεῖς (77 D 5) ... δεδιέναι ... μὴ ... ὁ ἄνεμος αὐτὴν ... διασκεδάννυσιν ...
> Οὐκοῦν τοιόνδε τι ... δεῖ ἡμᾶς ἀνερέσθαι ἑαυτούς, τῷ ποίῳ τινὶ ἄρα προσήκει τοῦτο ... τὸ διασκεδάννυσθαι ...
>
> '... what sort of thing this dispersal is supposed to belong to ...'

A natural extension of this use of ἄρα, the transition to which may be observed in 111 E 5 above, is that in reproducing or relating statements. We may call this 'intensional', as bearing on the content of embedded propositions. In independent sentences we have, from the same context, after a period marked as containing reported speech by an introductory λέγεται (107 D 6):

107 E 5

> ἔστι δὲ ἄρα ἡ πορεία ...

and later

112 E 5

> Τὰ μὲν οὖν δὴ ἄλλα πολλά τε καὶ μεγάλα καὶ παντοδαπὰ ῥεύματά ἐστι· τυγχάνει δ' ἄρα ὄντα ἐν τούτοις τοῖς πολλοῖς τέτταρ' ἄττα ῥεύματα, ὧν τὸ μὲν ... Ὠκεανός ..., τούτου δὲ καταντικρὺ ... Ἀχέρων, ... (B 5) Πυριφλεγέθοντα ... (C 8) Κωκυτός.
>
> '... but it happens, as we are told, that among these many there are four ...'

But the most unmistakable examples are those found in dependent clauses:

97 C 1-2

> Ἀλλ' ἀκούσας μέν ποτε ἐκ βιβλίου τινός, ὡς ἔφη, Ἀναξαγόρου ἀναγιγνώσκοντος, καὶ λέγοντος ὡς ἄρα νοῦς ἐστιν ὁ διακοσμῶν τε καὶ πάντων αἴτιος, ταύτῃ δὴ τῇ αἰτίᾳ ἥσθην ...
>
> '... and declaring that, as Anaxagoras had it ...', '... that, according to Anaxagoras' book, ...'

and that preceding 107 E 5 quoted above:

107 D 6

> λέγεται δὲ οὕτως, ὡς ἄρα ...

3.2. Anticipatory

70 C 4

> σκεψώμεθα δὲ αὐτὸ τῇδέ πῃ, εἴτ' ἄρα ἐν Ἅιδου εἰσὶν αἱ ψυχαὶ τελευτησάντων τῶν ἀνθρώπων εἴτε καὶ οὔ.

'... whether it will turn out that ...'.

I submit that ἄρα here does not relate to what has been said before, but *anticipates* the phrasing of the outcome of the inquiry in

71 E 2

Εἰσὶν ἄρα, ἔφη, αἱ ψυχαὶ ἡμῶν ἐν ᾍδου.

'Our souls, it turns out, do subsist in Hades'.

This is more than just the implication of the preceding leading question

71 D 15

Ἐκ τῶν τεθνεώτων ἄρα, ὦ Κέβης, τὰ ζῶντά τε καὶ οἱ ζῶντες γίγνονται;[1]

it is a summing up of the entire investigation from 70 C 4 onwards, including the παλαιὸς λόγος expounded in 70 C 5 – D 4.

Two more instances of anticipatory ἄρα in questions depending on a directive espression (imperative or adhortative subjunctive) differ from 70 C 4 in lacking a *precise* reference to what follows, but are at one with it in looking forward to a moment when the outcome, whether the interlocutor agrees and whether he has been talking sense respectively, will be clear beyond doubt:

103 C 10

... σκέψαι ... εἰ ἄρα συνομολογήσεις.

95 B 8

... πειρώμεθα εἰ ἄρα τι λέγεις

'... whether you will turn out to ...'

More fundamentally different are cases of εἰ ἄρα where εἰ is equivalent to 'in case' or 'if' rather than to 'whether':

60 E 3

... ἐποίησα ταῦτα ... ἐνυπνίων τινῶν ἀποπειρώμενος τί λέγοι, καὶ ἀφοσιούμενος εἰ ἄρα πολλάκις ταύτην τὴν μουσικήν μοι ἐπιτάττοι ποιεῖν. ἦν γὰρ δὴ ἄττα τοιάδε· πολλάκις μοι φοιτῶν τὸ αὐτὸ ἐνύπνιον ... ἄλλοτ' ἐν ἄλλῃ ὄψει φαινόμενον, τὰ αὐτὰ δὲ λέγον, Ὦ Σώκρατες, ἔφη, μουσικὴν ποίει ...

'... in an attempt to find out what they meant, and discharging my religious duty in case it *turned out* that this was the music they repeatedly told me to practice ...'

The ἀποπειρᾶσθαι and the ἀφοσιοῦσθαι are one operation: the discharge of a duty *in case* at the same time supplies an answer to the question

---

[1] In which, incidentally, ἄρα does mark such an immediate inference.

whether, because if Socrates has understood his dreams correctly and obeyed them they will cease to come to him. This no longer applies to the second instance:

61 A 6

νῦν δ' ἐπειδὴ ... ἡ τοῦ θεοῦ ἑορτὴ διεκώλυέ με ἀποθνήισκειν, ἔδοξε χρῆναι, εἰ ἄρα πολλάκις μοι προστάττοι τὸ ἐνύπνιον ταύτην τὴν δημώδη
μουσικὴν ποιεῖν, μὴ ἀπειθῆσαι αὐτῷ ἀλλὰ ποιεῖν

'... if it turned out that what the dream was telling me again and again to do
was to practice music in the vulgar acceptation ...':

not 'if perhaps': any reserve there may be is in the εἰ; nor does ἄρα of itself *express* reluctance, scepticism, or surprise. Socrates simply takes his final interpretation of his dreams, as pointing to the common notion of music, to be indicated by their previous recurrence.

In 64 C 10

Σκέψαι ... ἐὰν ἄρα ... συνδοκῇ

ἄρα, I submit, looks forward to the moment of revelation:

'... in case you will turn out to agree ...'.

I submit that the 'inferential' use and the uses referred to above as 'dissociative', 'intensional', and 'anticipatory' could be united under a denominator of 'provisional or conditional adoption of a point of view', whether in the more strict sense of a perspective or in the looser sense of a proposition entertained.

3.3. *Remaining instances of* ἄρα *in* Phaedo

3.3.1. *Further quasi-connective uses*

Most of the remaining occurrences of ἄρα in the *Phaedo* are found, like those under 1. and that under 2. above,[1] in contexts of advancing step by step, where a statement is presented as acceptable on the strength of the preceding one. 76 C supplies four of them, the first two in questions but with the same function.

(76 A 9) 'Were we born possessing knowledge, or do we recollect afterwards the knowledge we have acquired before? A man possessing knowledge is able to give an account, yet few or none are in fact able to do so,' –

(C1) Οὐκ ἄρα δοκοῦσί σοι ἐπίστασθαί γε ...;

---

[1] P. 102 and 103ff.

'*If this is so*, you don't think they have actual knowledge?'
– 'By no means' –

(C4) Ἀναμιμνήσκονται ἄρα ἅ ποτε ἔμαθον;

'They recollect, *if this is so*, what they once learned?'
– Necessarily.'–

Πότε λαβοῦσαι αἱ ψυχαὶ ἡμῶν τὴν ἐπιστήμην αὐτῶν; οὐ γὰρ δὴ ἀφ' οὗ γε ἄνθρωποι γεγόναμεν.

'When did our souls acquire the relevant knowledge?
Not, evidently (δή), after we were born as men.'
– 'Indeed not!' –

(C 9) Πρότερον ἄρα. 'Before, *it appears*' – 'Yes."

(C 11) Ἦσαν ἄρα ... αἱ ψυχαὶ καὶ πρότερον ...

'Our souls, if this is so, existed even before ...'

The contrast with δή at C 7 is revealing: that (1) our souls did not acquire their knowledge in our lifetime is presented as obvious by itself; that (2) they have done this before is presented as emerging as soon as (1) is granted.
Similarly 93 A 6, 8

(A 3) 'Do you think a harmony ought to be different or act or be acted upon differently from its component parts?' – 'By no means.'– (A 6-8) Οὐκ ἄρα ἡγεῖσθαί γε προσήκει ἁρμονίαν τούτων ... ἀλλ' ἔπεσθαι. – Συνεδόκει. – Πολλοῦ ἄρα δεῖ ... ἐναντιωθῆναι τοῖς αὑτῆς μέρεσιν.

'It ought not, *if this is granted*, to lead but to follow them ... it is, *if this is granted*, far from opposing its own parts'.

Akin to these in spelling out the implications of a term is

68 D 11

... φόβῳ μειζόνων κακῶν ὑπομένουσιν ... οἱ ἀνδρεῖοι τὸν θάνατον ...; – Ἔστι ... – Τῷ δεδιέναι ἄρα ... ἀνδρεῖοί εἰσι ...

'Brave men face death for fear of greater evils; they are brave, if this is so, from being scared'.

103 E 2

ἕτερόν τι πυρὸς τὸ θερμὸν ... τὸ πῦρ γε ... προσιόντος τοῦ ψυχροῦ αὐτῷ ... οὐ ... ποτὲ τολμήσειν δεξάμενον τὴν ψυχρότητα ἔτι εἶναι ὅπερ ἦν, πῦρ καὶ ψυχρόν ... Ἔστιν ἄρα ... περὶ ἔνια τῶν τοιούτων, ὥστε μὴ μόνον αὐτὸ τὸ εἶδος ἀξιοῦσθαι τοῦ αὐτοῦ ὀνόματος εἰς τὸν ἀεὶ χρόνον, ἀλλὰ καὶ ἄλλο τι ὃ ἔστι μὲν οὐκ ἐκεῖνο, ἔχει δὲ τὴν ἐκείνου μορφὴν ἀεί, ὅταν-περ ᾖ.

'Heat is not fire, yet fire (like heat) is incompatible with cold; some things, if this is so, while not being the Form itself, yet contain its features and have a claim to its name at any time'.

104 C 7

... (B 7) φαίνεται οὐ μόνον ἐκεῖνα τὰ ἐναντία ἄλληλα οὐ δεχόμενα, ἀλλὰ καὶ ὅσα οὐκ ὄντ' ἀλλήλοις ἐναντία ἔχει ἀεὶ τἀναντία ... (etc.; there follows an instance) οὐκ ἄρα μόνον τὰ εἴδη τὰ ἐναντία οὐχ ὑπομένει ἐπιόντα ἄλληλα, ἀλλὰ καὶ ἄλλ' ἄττα τὰ ἐναντία οὐχ ὑπομένει ἐπιόντα.

'It seems that it is not just these opposites which are incompatible with each other, but also those things which, while not themselves opposites, invariably comprise opposites (...). It is not, *if this is so*, just the opposite Forms which cannot stand the opposites' approach'.

A minor complication occurs in the context of ἄρα with verbs of saying or thinking.

At 103 C 7

... (B 2) τότε μὲν γὰρ ἐλέγετο ..., νῦν δέ, ὅτι αὐτὸ τὸ ἐναντίον ἑαυτῷ ἐναντίον οὐκ ἄν ποτε γένοιτο ... Ἆρα μή που ... καὶ σέ τι τούτων ἐτάραξεν ὧν ὅδε εἶπεν; – Οὐδ' αὖ ... οὕτως ἔχω· καίτοι οὔτι λέγω ὡς οὐ πολλά με ταράττει. – Συνωμολογήκαμεν ἄρα ... μηδέποτε ἐναντίον ἑαυτῷ τὸ ἐναντίον ἔσεσθαι. – Παντάπασιν ...

it is natural to take the particle with συνωμολογήκαμεν—'conclusion tirée de la réponse de l'interlocuteur'[1]—rather than with the dependent infinitive clause, which adds nothing new—though this in itself would not be an insurmountable objection against the application of ἄρα, cf. 102 C 10.[2]

At 100 E 5, on the other hand,

... (D 9) τούτου ἐχόμενος ἡγοῦμαι οὐκ ἄν ποτε πεσεῖν, ἀλλ' ἀσφαλὲς εἶναι καὶ ἐμοὶ καὶ ὁτῳοῦν ἄλλῳ ἀποκρίνασθαι ὅτι τῷ καλῷ τὰ καλὰ [...] καλά· ἢ οὐ καὶ σοὶ δοκεῖ; – δοκεῖ. – καὶ μεγέθει ἄρα τὰ μεγάλα μεγάλα ...

the acceptability of the statement marked by ἄρα is sufficiently motivated by the preceding embedded proposition:

(E 2) ... τῷ καλῷ τὰ καλὰ [γίγνεται] καλά ...
(E 5) καὶ μεγέθει ἄρα τὰ μεγάλα μεγάλα καὶ τὰ μείζω μείζω, ...;
– ναί. – ...

Immediately afterwards, however, at 100 E 8

– ναί – οὐδὲ σὺ ἄρ' ἂν ἀποδέχοιο εἴ τίς τινα φαίη ἕτερον ἑτέρου τῇ κεφαλῇ μείζω εἶναι ... ἀλλὰ διαμαρτύροιο ἂν ὅτι σὺ μὲν οὐδὲν ἄλλο

---

[1] Des Places 240.
[2] P. 105 above.

λέγεις ἢ ὅτι τὸ μεῖζον πᾶν ἕτερον ἑτέρου οὐδενὶ ἄλλῳ μεῖζόν ἐστιν ἢ μεγέθει ...

it is more plausible, though admittedly it makes little difference to the final interpretation, to relate ἄρα to the finite verb forms of the surrounding main clauses:

> '*I* think it safe to answer ... don't you?' – 'I do.'
> – '*You*, it appears, would not agree with ... either: no, you would testify to your conviction that what is larger is so by largeness ...'.

Just as at 103 C 7 quoted above,[1] the dependent clause contains nothing new: the emphasis is on Cebes' assent. Had Plato's Socrates chosen to elicit this by an appeal in the form of an imperative or (adhortative or prohibitive) subjunctive, the particle used might very likely have been τοίνυν.[2]

3.3.2. *Other contexts*

Twice in the *Phaedo* ἄρα is found in rhetorical questions representing the conclusion of an εἰκός-argument:

at 68 A 7

> ... ἀνθρωπίνων μὲν παιδικῶν ... ἀποθανόντων πολλοὶ δὴ ἑκόντες ἠθέλησαν εἰς Ἅιδου μετελθεῖν ... φρονήσεως δὲ ἄρα τις τῷ ὄντι ἐρῶν ... ἀγανακτήσει ... ἀποθνήσκων ...;[3]
> 'Many men have followed their human loves into death; will a lover of insight grieve at dying?', i.e. 'a lover of insight, *if this is so*, will not ...'

Note δή with a repeated (πολλοί A 4) empirical fact (aorist ἠθέλησαν A 5) presented as though unquestionable, as opposed to ἄρα with what needs to be argued.

At 80 D 5, too,

> ἔνια ... μέρη τοῦ σώματος ... ὡς ἔπος εἰπεῖν ἀθάνατά ἐστιν· ἢ οὔ; – ναί. – ἡ δὲ ψυχὴ ἄρα ... εὐθὺς ... ἀπόλωλεν ...;
> 'Bones are as good as immortal, but the soul is gone at once?'. i.e. 'the soul, *if this is so*, is not ...'.

the intended conclusion is presented as being inescapable as soon as the premiss is granted.

---

[1] P. 114.
[2] Cf. 153 below.
[3] For the sequel see below.

An argument a fortiori with ἄρα in a dependent clause is found at 87 C 4:

... (B 4) ὥσπερ ἄν τις ... λέγοι ... ὅτι οὐκ ἀπόλωλεν ὁ ἄνθρωπος ἀλλ' ἔστι που σῶς, τεκμήριον δὲ παρέχοιτο θοἰμάτιον ... ὅτι ἐστὶ σῶν καὶ οὐκ ἀπόλωλεν, καὶ εἴ τις ἀπιστοίη αὐτῷ, ἀνερωτῴη πότερον πολυχρονιώτερόν ἐστι ... ἀποκριναμένου δὴ ὅτι ... τὸ τοῦ ἀνθρώπου (γένος), οἴοιτο ἀποδεδεῖχθαι ὅτι παντὸς ἄρα μᾶλλον ὅ γε ἄνθρωπος σῶς ἐστιν, ἐπειδὴ τό γε ὀλιγοχρονιώτερον οὐκ ἀπόλωλεν.

'... if he thought he had proved that the man, if this is granted, is preserved, at all events, seeing that what is less permanent is still there'.

68 B 9 shows ἄρα in a question, like 68 A 7 and 80 D 5, and in a clause depending on ὅτι, just as at 87 C 4:

... (A 7) φρονήσεως δὲ ἄρα τις τῷ ὄντι ἐρῶν ... ἀγανακτήσει τε ἀποθνῄσκων ...; ... οὐ πολλὴ ἂν ἀλογία εἴη εἰ φοβοῖτο τὸν θάνατον ὁ τοιοῦτος; – πολλὴ μέντοι ... – οὐκοῦν ἱκανόν σοι τεκμήριον ... τοῦτο ἀνδρός, ὃν ἂν ἴδῃς ἀγανακτοῦντα μέλλοντα ἀποθανεῖσθαι, ὅτι οὐκ ἄρ' ἦν φιλόσοφος ἀλλά τις φιλοσώματος;

'it would be absurd for a lover of insight to fear death; isn't this a sure sign of a man whom you see grieving at the approach of death, that he was not *in that case, as it turned out*, a lover of wisdom ...?'

The laborious reproduction of the syntax is meant to bring out how ἄρα is motivated *both* by the general rule deduced first *and* by the particular observation interpreted in terms of it.

All the remaining instances of ἄρα in independent questions in the *Phaedo* can be explained along the lines laid down above. They are all of the type which takes 'yes' or 'no' for an answer, submitting for confirmation or denial a suggestion based on the preceding statement or formula of assent:

58 A 1
τῶν δὲ ἄλλων οὐδὲν εἶχεν φράζειν. – οὐδὲ τὰ περὶ τῆς δίκης ἄρα ἐπύθεσθε ...;

71 D 14
ἐξ οὖν τοῦ ζῶντος τί τὸ γιγνόμενον; – τὸ τεθνηκός ... – τί δέ ... ἐκ τοῦ τεθνεῶτος; – ... τὸ ζῶν. – ἐκ τῶν τεθνεώτων ἄρα ... τὰ ζῶντα ... γίγνονται; – φαίνεται.

76 C 1-4
πότερον ... αἱρῇ ...; ἐπισταμένους ἡμᾶς γεγονέναι, ἢ ἀναμιμνῄσκεσθαι ... ἀνὴρ ἐπιστάμενος ... ἔχοι ἂν δοῦναι λόγον ... – ... φοβοῦμαι μὴ αὔριον τηνικάδε οὐκέτι ᾖ ἀνθρώπων οὐδεὶς ἀξίως οἷός τε τοῦτο ποιῆσαι. – οὐκ ἄρα δοκοῦσί σοι ἐπίστασθαι ... πάντες αὐτά; – οὐδαμῶς. – ἀναμιμνῄσκονται ἄρα ...;

79 B 14

τί οὖν περὶ ψυχῆς λέγομεν; ὁρατὸν ἢ ἀόρατον εἶναι; – οὐχ ὁρατόν. – ἀιδὲς ἄρα; – ναί.

For 100 E 5 see above.[1]

105 D 3

ᾧ ἂν τί ἐγγένηται σώματι ζῶν ἔσται; – ᾧ ἂν ψυχή, ἔφη. – οὐκοῦν ἀεὶ τοῦτο οὕτως ἔχει; – πῶς γὰρ οὐχί; ἦ δ' ὅς. – ψυχὴ ἄρα ὅτι ἂν αὐτὴ κατάσχῃ, ἀεὶ ἥκει ἐπ' ἐκεῖνο φέρουσα ζωήν; – ἥκει μέντοι, ἔφη.

One peculiarly interesting occurence remains, at 76 C 14:

πότε λαβοῦσαι ... τὴν ἐπιστήμην ...; οὐ γὰρ δὴ ἀφ' οὗ ... · πρότερον ἄρα ... ἦσαν ἄρα ... καὶ πρότερον ...
– Εἰ μὴ ἄρα ἅμα γιγνόμενοι λαμβάνομεν ...

'Unless it *turns out* that we acquired it at the moment of birth'.

I think this is to some extent an echo of Socrates' preceding ἄρα's. But it is not entirely otiose: if we press it, it yields something like 'unless the conclusion should be ...'.

4. *Outside Plato*

4.1. *Lysias*

In the Corpus Lysiacum ἄρα is decidedly rare, with less than one instance[2] in every four speeches. One reason given above[3] for the rarity of δή and που in the orators is also pertinent to ἄρα: that it allows a wider scope for disagreement than is generally desirable in a plea. This a priori consideration seems to be confirmed by the observation that it is precisely the common Platonic use of the particle in offering a proposition for approval on the strength of previous information, which is lacking in Lysias: here most of the instances we have serve to tie the validity of the clause in which they are contained with some item of information in the context *without* stipulating for the approval of this clause in its own right.[4] To most of them a paraphrase 'on (this, his, mine, our) hypothesis' could be applied:[5] thus at 3.30

---

[1] P. 114.

[2] Eight instances in 35 speeches, including one in that on Eros in Plato's *Phaedrus* which is there ascribed to Lysias.

[3] (Sicking) p. 59.

[4] At 10.22, to be quoted presently, the particle is found in a leading question; this, then, is an instance of that rare phenomenon, the exception confirming a rule.

[5] At 8.(11-)12 in καὶ ἐγὼ μὲν ᾤμην φιλοσοφοῦντας αὐτοὺς περὶ τὸ πράγματος ἀντι

(28) λέγει δ' ὡς ἡμεῖς ἤλθομεν ... ἐγὼ ⟨δ'⟩ ἡγοῦμαι ... ῥᾴδιον εἶναι γνῶ-
ναι ὅτι ψεύδεται ... (29) τῷ γὰρ ἂν δόξειε πιστὸν ὡς ἐγὼ (προνοηθεὶς καὶ
ἐπιβουλεύων) ἦλθον ἐπὶ τὴν Σίμωνος οἰκίαν μεθ' ἡμέραν, μετὰ τοῦ μει-
ρακίου, τοσούτων ἀνθρώπων παρ' αὐτῷ συνειλεγμένων, εἰ μὴ εἰς τοῦτο
μανίας ἀφικόμην ὥστε ἐπιθυμεῖν εἷς ὢν πολλοῖς μάχεσθαι, ἄλλως τε
καὶ εἰδὼς ὅτι ἀσμένως ἄν με εἶδεν ἐπὶ ταῖς θύραις ταῖς αὐτοῦ, ὃς καὶ ἐπὶ
τὴν ἐμὴν οἰκίαν φοιτῶν εἰσῄει βίᾳ, καὶ (οὔτε τῆς ἀδελφῆς οὔτε τῶν ἀδελ-
φιδῶν φροντίσας ζητεῖν με ἐτόλμα, καὶ ἐξευρὼν οὗ δειπνῶν ἐτύγχανον,
ἐκκαλέσας) ἔτυπτέ με. (30) καὶ τότε μὲν ἄρα, ἵνα μὴ περιβόητος εἴην,
ἡσυχίαν ἦγον, συμφορὰν ἐμαυτοῦ νομίζων τὴν τούτου πονηρίαν· ἐπειδὴ
δὲ χρόνος διεγένετο, πάλιν, ὡς οὗτός φησιν, ἐπεθύμησα περιβόητος γενέσθαι; (31) καὶ εἰ μὲν ἦν παρὰ τούτῳ τὸ μειράκιον εἶχεν ἄν τινα λόγον
τὸ ψεῦδος αὐτῷ ὡς ἐγὼ διὰ τὴν ἐπιθυμίαν ἠναγκαζόμην ἀνοητότερόν τι
ποιεῖν τῶν εἰκότων· νῦν δὲ ... (32) ὥστε τῷ ὑμῶν πιστὸν ὡς ἐγὼ (πρότερον
μὲν ἐξέπλευσα ἐκ τῆς πόλεως ἔχων τὸ μειράκιον, ἵνα μὴ τούτῳ μαχοίμην,
ἐπειδὴ δὲ ἀφικόμην πάλιν ἦγον αὐτὸν ἐπὶ τὴν οἰκίαν τὴν Σίμωνος, οὗ
πλεῖστα ἔμελλον πράγματα ἕξειν ...)

'on his hypothesis', i.e. 'if Simon were speaking the truth, it is implied that
...', 'if ..., then ...'; and at the same time, 'you are asked to believe ...'.

I take it that the scope of the particle is just the clause from καὶ τότε μέν
to πονηρίαν. In the next clause the same dissociation is effected by stronger and more fully lexical means in ὡς οὗτός φησιν. The wider context of
course does stipulate for approval by the audience.

The *ex hypothesi* has a less precise reference to a sort of common
denominator between the versions put forward by each side at 3.40 in

... (37) ... δεινὸν εἰ περὶ τούτων ἐγὼ δόξω προνοηθῆναι περὶ ὧν οὗτοι
τυγχάνουσιν οὕτω δεινὰ καὶ παράνομα πεποιηκότες. (38) τί δ' ἄν ... εἰ
τἀναντία ..., εἰ ... ἐγὼ ..., ὅπου νῦν τούτου ταῦτα πεποιηκότος ...; τὸ δὲ
μέγιστον ... (39) ὁ γὰρ ἀδικηθεὶς καὶ ἐπιβουλευθεὶς ὑπ' ἐμοῦ, ὥς φησιν,
οὐκ ἐτόλμησε τεττάρων ἐτῶν ἐπισκήψασθαι εἰς ὑμᾶς. καὶ οἱ μὲν ἄλλοι,
ὅταν ἐρῶσι καὶ ἀποστερῶνται ὧν ἐπιθυμοῦσι καὶ συγκοπῶσιν, ὀργιζό-
μενοι παραχρῆμα τιμωρεῖσθαι ζητοῦσιν, οὗτος δὲ χρόνοις ὕστερον. (40)
ὅτι μὲν οὖν, ὦ βουλή, οὐδενὸς αἴτιός εἰμι τῶν γεγενημένων, ἱκανῶς ἀποδεδεῖχθαι νομίζω· οὕτω δὲ διάκειμαι πρὸς τὰς ἐκ τῶν τοιούτων πραγμάτων διαφοράς, ὥστε καὶ ἄλλα πολλὰ ὑβρισμένος ὑπὸ Σίμωνος καὶ
καταγεὶς τὴν κεφαλὴν ὑπ' αὐτοῦ οὐκ ἐτόλμησα αὐτῷ ἐπισκήψασθαι,
ἡγούμενος δεινὸν εἶναι, εἰ ἄρα περὶ παίδων ἐφιλονικήσαμεν ἡμεῖς πρὸς
ἀλλήλους, τούτου ἕνεκα ἐξελάσαι τινὰς ζητῆσαι ἐκ τῆς πατρίδος.

λέγειν τὸν ἐναντίον λόγον, (12) οἱ δ' ἄρα οὐκ ἀντέλεγον the antithesis of οἱ to ἐγώ and of
δέ to μέν enables the hearer to take the point that in the event 'as it turned out' the speaker's
surmise was disproved. Here the particle preserves much of the old use in which the teller
appeals to the listener to continue to follow him: in this case, to share his wonder (at a fact
that is not disputed; contrast 3.30, to be quoted presently, where if there is wonder, it
should serve to discredit the allegation). Cf. Herodotus 1.77.4, quoted below at p. 127.

'if, *then*, we had been quarreling over a lover-boy ...', 'given that ...', 'it being presupposed that ...'. This much at least seems undeniable;

and to 'as implied' in the familiar context of a conditional clause at 30.7 in

Ἴσως δέ, ὦ ἄνδρες δικασταί, ἐπειδὰν περὶ αὐτοῦ μηδὲν δύνηται ἀπο-
λογεῖσθαι, ἐμὲ διαβάλλειν πειράσεται. τότε δὲ περὶ τῶν ἐμῶν τούτῳ ἀξιῶ
πιστεύειν ὑμᾶς, ὁπόταν ἀπολογίας ἐμοὶ δοθείσης μὴ δύνωμαι ψευδό-
μενον αὐτὸν ἐξελέγξαι. ἐὰν δ' ἄρα ἐπιχειρῇ λέγειν ἅπερ ἐν τῇ βουλῇ, ὡς
ἐγὼ τῶν τετρακοσίων ἐγενόμην, ἐνθυμεῖσθε ὅτι ὑπὸ τῶν τοιαῦτα λεγόν-
των ἐκ τῶν τετρακοσίων πλεῖν ἢ χίλιοι γενήσονται· καὶ γὰρ τοὺς ἔτι
παῖδας ὄντας ἐν ἐκείνῳ τῷ χρόνῳ καὶ τοὺς ἀποδημοῦντας οἱ διαβάλλειν
βουλόμενοι ταῦτα λοιδοροῦσιν. (8) ἐγὼ δὲ οὕτω πολλοῦ ἐδέησα τῶν τετρακοσίων γενέσθαι, ὥστε οὐδὲ τῶν πεντακισχιλίων κατελέγην.

'He may, for want of a defence, try to blacken me. Well, believe his words the moment you find me incapable of refuting them. So if he proposes to make the same claims he made in the βουλή, about my belonging to the Four hundred, consider that on his reckoning the Four hundred will end up numbering more than one thousand'.

The particle introduces the hypothesis as an illustration of the character assassination the speaker foresees, and as an instance to which the rule he has just given for dealing with such calumnies should be applied—as the audience can see.

A similar context is *Eroticus* (35 at (*Phdr.*) 233 C 6)

(232 B 5) ...εἴ σοι δέος παρέστηκεν ἡγουμένῳ χαλεπὸν εἶναι φιλίαν συμ-
μένειν ... (C 2) εἰκότως ἂν τοὺς ἐρῶντας μᾶλλον ἂν φοβοῖο· ... (233 C 6)
εἰ δ' ἄρα σοι τοῦτο παρέστηκεν, ὡς οὐχ οἷόν τε ἰσχυρὰν φιλίαν γενέσθαι
ἐὰν μή τις ἐρῶν τυγχάνῃ, (D 1) ἐνθυμεῖσθαι χρὴ ὅτι οὔτ' ἂν τοὺς ὑεῖς
περὶ πολλοῦ ἐποιούμεθα οὔτ' ἂν τοὺς πατέρας καὶ τὰς μητέρας, οὔτ' ἂν
πιστοὺς φίλους ἐκεκτήμεθα, οἳ οὐκ ἐξ ἐπιθυμίας τοιαύτης γεγόνασιν
ἀλλ' ἐξ ἑτέρων ἐπιτηδευμάτων ...

where the particle first of all recalls the earlier reference to the same condition, but at the same time intimates that this condition of fear comes within the scope of the instruction the hearer has meanwhile received, thus leading up to considerations which may help to overcome it.

In three leading questions the hearer is expressly asked to agree to a proposition in the light of previous information: at 10.22

ἐγὼ δὲ ἑωρακὼς μὲν ἐκεῖνο τοῦτον ποιήσαντα ὃ καὶ ὑμεῖς ἴστε, αὐτὸς δὲ
σώσας τὴν ἀσπίδα, ἀκηκοὼς δὲ οὕτως ἀνόσιον καὶ δεινὸν πρᾶγμα, με-
γίστης δὲ οὔσης μοι τῆς συμφορᾶς εἰ ἀποφεύξεται, τούτῳ δ' οὐδενὸς
ἀξίας εἰ κακηγορίας ἁλώσεται, οὐκ ἄρα δίκην παρ' αὐτοῦ λήψομαι;

'*in the light of* (all the information recalled by the participles) can it be that I will not ...?', i.e. '... is it not *clear* that I should ...?';

in 12.36 in an anacolouthon presumably intended to convey pathos

> οὐκ οὖν δεινὸν εἰ τοὺς μὲν στρατηγούς, οἳ ἐνίκων ναυμαχοῦντες, ὅτε
> διὰ χειμῶνα οὐχ οἷοί τ' ἔφασαν εἶναι τοὺς ἐκ τῆς θαλάττης ἀνελέσθαι,
> θανάτῳ ἐζημιώσατε, ἡγούμενοι χρῆναι τῇ τῶν τεθνεώτων ἀρετῇ παρ'
> ἐκείνων δίκην λαβεῖν, τούτους δέ, οἳ ἰδιῶται μὲν ὄντες καθ' ὅσον ἐδύ-
> ναντο ἐποίησαν ἡττηθῆναι ναυμαχοῦντας, ἐπειδὴ δὲ εἰς τὴν ἀρχὴν κατ-
> έστησαν, ὁμολογοῦσιν ἑκόντες πολλοὺς τῶν πολιτῶν ἀκρίτους ἀποκτιν-
> νύναι, οὐκ ἄρα χρὴ αὐτοὺς καὶ τοὺς παῖδας ὑφ' ὑμῶν ταῖς ἐσχάταις
> ζημίαις κολάζεσθαι;

And finally, in a supposition marked by ἄν with indicative as unreal, and
with another anacolouthon, at 31.28 in

> 27 Ἀκούω δ' αὐτὸν λέγειν ὡς, εἴ τι ἦν ἀδίκημα τὸ μὴ παραγενέσθαι ἐν
> ἐκείνῳ τῷ καιρῷ, νόμος ἂν ἔκειτο περὶ αὐτοῦ διαρρήδην, ὥσπερ καὶ περὶ
> τῶν ἄλλων ἀδικημάτων. οὐ γὰρ οἴεται ὑμᾶς γνώσεσθαι ὅτι διὰ τὸ μέγε-
> θος τοῦ ἀδικήματος οὐδεὶς περὶ αὐτοῦ ἐγράφη νόμος. τίς γὰρ ἄν ποτε
> ῥήτωρ ἐνεθυμήθη ἢ νομοθέτης ἤλπισεν ἁμαρτήσεσθαί τινα τῶν πολιτῶν
> τοσαύτην ἁμαρτίαν; (28) οὐ γὰρ ἂν δήπου, εἰ μέν τις λίποι τὴν τάξιν μὴ
> αὐτῆς τῆς πόλεως ἐν κινδύνῳ οὔσης ἀλλ' ἑτέρους εἰς τοῦτο καθιστάσης,
> ἐτέθη νόμος ὡς μεγάλα ἀδικοῦντος, εἰ δέ τις αὐτῆς τῆς πόλεως ἐν κιν-
> δύνῳ οὔσης λίποι τὴν πόλιν αὐτήν—οὐκ ἂν ἄρα ἐτέθη; <ἢ Dobree> σφό-
> δρα γ' ἄν, εἴ τις ᾤήθη τινὰ τῶν πολιτῶν ἁμαρτήσεσθαί τι τοιοῦτόν ποτε.

> '... the offence is so rank that there is no law against it, for what legislator
> could ever have expected a citizen to commit it? *If* he had (ἄν), *then* we surely
> would not have the situation that there is a law against desertion when we are
> in the attack, but not against desertion when we are in the defence.'[1]

Perhaps ἄρα may be said to stress the connexion; a proposition is recom-
mended by an appeal to the coherence of the available information; its
denial would involve paradox.[2]

4.2. *Herodotus*

In Herodotus ἄρα is, with sixty-eight instances, considerably more frequent than in Lysias, though rather less frequent than in Plato. We shall

---

[1] Thalheim prints a question mark, noting that *editores plerique pone* ἐτέθη *non in-
terrogant*; he is followed in this by Gernet-Bizos, though their own translation takes no
account of it. The effect would be '*If* he had, would a law have been passed against ...,yet
would no law *then* have been passed against ...? It would have by all means—if the need
for it had been foreseen.' These editors also reject Dobree's addition of ἢ. Neither of these
differences with Hude affects the interpretation of ἄρα very much.

[2] This context invites comparison with another dichotomy of which the second half at
least is interrogative, again with anacolouthon but now in a directive as opposed to a declarative utterance, in Herodotus 5.49.8 quoted below at p. 138.

now try to apply to these Herodotean instances our hypothesis that the uses of ἄρα can be reduced to a basic value of maintaining consistency of viewpoint or coherence of propositional content, which may work out as an informal species of implication, whether what might loosely be called 'mutual' implication or, in contexts of argument, with a clear distinction between premise or premises and conclusion, 'one-way' implication.

In what follows these instances are ordered according to the type of context in which they appear. Within each section the order is roughly from what seem to be comparatively simple and unambiguous instances to more complex or ambivalent ones. The indeterminacy involved may in part be 'subjective', i.e. testify to the poverty of our understanding, but I would submit that an at least equally large part of it is 'objective', in other words that the use of the particle in a given instance may be motivated by several distinct but compatible factors.

4.2.1. *In direct speech*

4.2.1.1. *In a reply*

The use, familiar from Homer,[1] of ἄρα marking the 'realization' following upon a new item of information, is found in H. all bound up within direct speech, more precisely within an exchange of speeches, when one speaker draws an implication from the other's speech—a situation comparable to that in Platonic dialogue insofar as the addressee is supposed to be bound by his own previous utterance to agree with the speaker:

8.111.2
> πρῶτοι γὰρ ''Ανδριοι νησιωτέων αἰτηθέντες πρὸς Θεμιστοκλέος χρήματα οὐκ ἔδοσαν ἀλλὰ προϊσχομένου Θεμιστοκλέος λόγον τόνδε ὡς ἥκοιεν 'Αθηναῖοι περὶ ἑωυτοὺς ἔχοντες δύο θεοὺς μεγάλους Πειθώ τε καὶ 'Αναγκαίην οὕτω τέ σφι κάρτα δοτέα εἶναι χρήματα ὑπεκρίναντο πρὸς ταῦτα λέγοντες ὡς κατὰ λόγον ἦσαν ἄρα αἰ 'Αθῆναι μεγάλαι τε καὶ εὐδαίμονες ⟨αἳ Stein⟩ καὶ θεῶν χρηστῶν ἥκοιεν εὖ, ἐπεὶ 'Ανδρίους γε ...

> 'clearly, obviously': it was apparently according to reason, and to Themistocles' account—λόγον perhaps comprehends both—that the Athenians were prosperous ...

With reference to a future occurrence:

8.57.2
> ἐνταῦθα δὴ Θεμιστοκλέα ... εἴρετο Μνησίφιλος ... ὅ τι σφι εἴη βεβουλεύμενον, πυθόμενος δὲ πρὸς αὐτοῦ ὡς εἴη δεδογμένον ἀνάγειν τὰς νέας

---

[1] Cf. *GP* 35 f.

πρὸς τὸν Ἰσθμὸν καὶ πρὸ τῆς Πελοποννήσου ναυμαχέειν εἶπε· οὔ τοι
ἄρα ἦν ἀπάρωσι τὰς νέας ἀπὸ Σαλαμῖνος οὐδὲ περὶ μιῆς ἔτι πατρίδος
ναυμαχήσεις ...

'do not think, in that case, that you will ...', 'know that, if so, it follows you
will not ...'

The next two contexts each contain, in addition to an instance of ἄρα
similar to those above, at least one other instance:

7.130.2

(1) εἰρομένου Ξέρξεω εἰ ..., εἶπον· βασιλεῦ ... Ξέρξην δὲ λέγεται εἰπεῖν
πρὸς ταῦτα· σοφοὶ ἄνδρες εἰσὶ Θεσσαλοί· (2) ταῦτ' ἄρα πρὸ πολλοῦ
ἐφυλάσσοντο γνωσιμαχέοντες καὶ τἆλλα καὶ ὅτι χώρην ἄρα εἶχον εὐ-
αἱρετόν τε καὶ ταχυάλωτον· τὸν γὰρ ποταμὸν πρῆγμα ἂν ἦν μοῦνον ἐπ-
εῖναί σφεων ἐπὶ τὴν χώρην, ..., ὥστε ...

With the *first* ἄρα Xerxes presents what occurs to him as a necessary
inference with reference to the Thessalians, from the information provided about their country. The *second* ἄρα could either mark (1) a consideration, whether expressed or not, of the Thessalians *χώρην ἄρα ἔχομεν
κτλ.*, i.e. a shift to their point of view; or (2) another component of Xerxes'
insight ἐφυλάσσοντο ... ὅτι χώρην ... εἶχον: Xerxes realizes 'that they
took shelter, *apparently* because ...';[1] or both.

3.34.3 *bis* & 4

(1) Πρηξάσπεα ... (2) ... τὸν δὲ εἰπεῖν ὦ δέσποτα τὰ μὲν ἄλλα πάντα
μεγάλως ἐπαίνεαι τῇ δὲ φιλοινίῃ σέ φασι πλεόνως προσκεῖσθαι. (3) τὸν
μὲν δὴ λέγειν ταῦτα περὶ Περσέων τὸν δὲ θυμωθέντα τοιοῖσδε ἀμείβε-
σθαι· νῦν ἄρα μέ φασι Πέρσαι οἴνῳ προσκείμενον παραφρονέειν καὶ
οὐκ εἶναι νοήμονα· οὐδ' ἄρα σφέων οἱ πρότεροι λόγοι ἦσαν ἀληθέες·
(4) πρότερον γὰρ δὴ ἄρα Περσέων οἱ συνέδρων ἐόντων καὶ Κροίσου εἴρετο ὁ Καμβύσης ...

' "Now it comes out that Persians say ... and it appears that ... were un-
truthful." For before this, as it appeared ... '.

The first two instances are unproblematic; as for the third, one difficulty is
that of distinguishing between the contributions of γάρ and of ἄρα. For
the combination γὰρ ἄρα cf. Cambyses' explanation of his own behaviour at 3.65.3 quoted below;[2] but a difference is that h.l. one use of ἄρα

---

[1] Or even 'because, *apparently*, ...'; though the position of ἄρα shows an adverb-like
freedom (not second in clause in thirteen instances, not counting 8.106.2 (δὲ ἄρα): 1.112.2,
3.64.4 & 65.3 & 70.1, 4.45.4 & 64.3, 6.62.1 & 100.1, 7.35.3 & 130.2, 8.8.1 & 2 & 136.2),
the tendencies determining the order of σύνδεσμοι in the widest sense at the beginning of
clauses may yet be too strong to allow for such fine distinctions.

[2] P. 124.

might be (1) to maintain the perspective of Cambyses even after we have shifted back from Cambyses as speaker to Herodotus as narrator: 'what he was alluding to is that ...'. Another use, which our paraphrase is intended to convey, might be to intimate that (2) the new item is not just supplementary, background information such as it is often marked by γάρ alone, but is of a piece with what precedes, and more or less a drawing out of the implications of this, so as to complete the picture: 'we note that ...'.

4.2.1.2. *Within a single speech*

In other contexts the occasion for the statement marked by ἄρα is not provided by another utterance but specified within the same utterance. One context is intermediate in that it can be read as a reply to a claim which is quoted in the reply; here the addressees are confronted with the new information disproving their claim.

9.58.2

ὦ παῖδες Ἀλεύεω ... ὑμεῖς γὰρ ... ἐλέγετε Λακεδαιμονίους οὐ φεύγειν ἐκ μάχης ἀλλὰ ἄνδρας εἶναι τὰ πολέμια πρώτους· τοὺς πρότερόν τε μετ-ισταμένους ἐκ τῆς τάξιος εἴδετε νῦν τε ... ὁρῶμεν διαδράντας, διέδεξάν τε ... ὅτι οὐδένες ἄρα ἐόντες ἐν οὐδαμοῖσι ἐοῦσι Ἕλλησι ἐναπεδεικ-νύατο

'apparently, clearly': the summing up which makes sense of the data is ...

Another context, but in the same connection, suggests that the use of ἄρα is not primarily bound up with the relation between speaker and hearer but with that between the contents of propositions: here it bears on the same statements, now addressed to the people they have reference to rather than to a third party.

9.48.2

ὦ Λακεδαιμόνιοι, ὑμεῖς δὴ λέγεσθε εἶναι ἄνδρες ἄριστοι ὑπὸ τῶν τῇδε ἀνθρώπων ἐκπαγλεομένων ὡς οὔτε φεύγετε ἐκ πολέμου οὔτε τάξιν ἐκ-λείπετε μένοντές τε ἢ ἀπόλλυτε τοὺς ἐναντίους ἢ αὐτοὶ ἀπόλλυσθε. τῶν δ' ἄρ'[1] ἦν οὐδὲν ἀληθές· πρὶν μὲν γὰρ ἢ συμμεῖξαι ἡμέας ἐς χειρῶν τε νόμον ἀπίκεσθαι καὶ δὴ φεύγοντας καὶ στάσιν ἐκλείποντας ὑμέας εἴ-δομεν ...

'none of this, (as) it now appears, was true': what accounts for experience, and puts earlier conceptions in their place, is that ...

---

[1] The only instance with elision among 29 instances in Herodotus of ἄρα before a vowel (Powell).

In a piece of 'discourse' which in the nature of things is confined to monologue:

7.35.2

ὦ πικρὸν ὕδωρ δεσπότης τοι δίκην ἐπιτιθεῖ τήνδε ὅτι μιν ἠδίκησας οὐδὲν
πρὸς ἐκείνου ἄδικον παθόν· καὶ βασιλεὺς μὲν Ξέρξης διαβήσεταί σε ἤν
τε σύ γε βούλῃ ἤν τε μή· σοὶ δὲ κατὰ δίκην ἄρα οὐδεὶς ἀνθρώπων θύει
ὡς ἐόντι καὶ θολερῷ καὶ ἁλμυρῷ ποταμῷ

'clearly', 'it appears': not so much from the previous words as from the
circumstances related in these.

In one context of direct speech we have another instance of the collocation γὰρ ἄρα.[1] The general purport is one of interpretation,[2] which may
be regarded as a form of implication (γάρ): the speaker, i.e. Cambyses,
reports his own actions together with his later understanding of them:

3.65.3

δείσας δὲ μὴ ... ἐποίησα ταχύτερα ἢ σοφώτερα· ἐν τῇ γὰρ ἀνθρωπηίῃ
φύσι οὐκ ἐνῆν ἄρα τὸ μέλλον γίνεσθαι ἀποτρέπειν, ἐγὼ δὲ ὁ ματαῖος ...

'for, as it could be observed here again, it was[3] not in human nature ...'

Here the clause containing ἄρα holds the information in the light of which
the hearer is invited to interpret the course of events, but again the question arises what is expressed by ἄρα and what by γάρ. In the present
context, in contrast with 3.34.4, no distinction or specification of point of
view is involved, but the other tentative interpretation of ἄρα given there
seems worth considering here as well: it is at least conceivable that the
new item is characterized by γάρ as subordinate and explanatory, and at
the same time by ἄρα as the, or a, way to make sense of what is given,
whether generally as the most economical hypothesis accounting for the
data, or, in several contexts, more particularly as a drawing out of the
implications of the information that was available.

We could go one step further and, taking account of the received derivation of γάρ from γε and ἄρα,[4] venture the hypothesis that γάρ *delimits*
whereas ἄρα *extends*: i.e. 'so much is clear (γάρ), and it is actually confirmed by the events (ἄρα), that ...'. This would yield a neat parallel with
γοῦν, and would oblige us to define the difference between γοῦν and γάρ.
Drawing on the account of οὖν given above[5] we might submit as the

---

[1] Cf. 3.34.4, quoted 122 above.
[2] Cf., in narrative, with ὡς, 4.205 at 133-4 below.
[3] Note the past tense, suggesting what was there all along but only came out now.
[4] Cf. *GP* 56.
[5] P. 87.

distinctive feature of γοῦν that it basically delimits a *topic* or the *range* of a *claim*, of γάρ that it basically delimits the range of what may be treated as *evident* or at least *plausible*; what the speaker estimates as acceptable and offers as minimally controversial.

These instances of ἄρα within single speeches, just like those in conversation quoted earlier, invite comparison with the Platonic use in arguments. We now come to uses more akin to those which we have provisionally called 'dissociative' and 'anticipatory'.

4.2.2. At transition to direct or reported speech

4.2.2.1. In announcing direct speech

4.134.1

> ... εἴρετο ὁ Δαρεῖος τῶν ἀντιπολέμων τὸν θόρυβον, πυθόμενος δέ σφεας τὸν λαγὸν διώκοντας εἶπε ἄρα πρὸς τούς περ ἐώθεε καὶ τὰ ἄλλα λέγειν· οὗτοι ὦνδρες ἡμέων πολλὸν καταφρονέουσι καί μοι νῦν φαίνεται Γωβρύης εἶπαι περὶ τῶν Σκυθικῶν δώρων ὀρθῶς.

It is possible to take ἄρα here as conveying that Darius replies 'as we expect him to', i.e. at least in the sense that the *fact* of his speaking is as expected, and wherever applicable, as it is h.l., also in that the *content* of his utterance is as one can understand or may have anticipated. But I submit that underlying this there is a more fundamental use of the particle to mark what follows as part and parcel of a different perspective. In this case the perspective is that of Darius, from whom a λόγος in the limited sense of a direct speech within Herodotus' λόγος in a wider sense is here announced. In two similar contexts the same basic use is compatible with slightly different final interpretations:

1.141.2

> (1) Ἴωνες δὲ καὶ Αἰολέες ... ἐς γῆν, (2) ὡς δὲ ψευσθῆναι τῆς ἐλπίδος λαβεῖν ἀμφίβληστρον καὶ περιβαλεῖν τε πλῆθος πολλὸν τῶν ἰχθύων καὶ ἐξειρύσαι ἰδόντα δὲ παλλομένους εἰπεῖν ἄρα αὐτὸν πρὸς τοὺς ἰχθῦς ... ὀρχεόμενοι .(3) Κῦρος μὲν ... πείθεσθαι Κύρῳ.

> 'he said, as you can understand / may have anticipated', 'he of course said'.

It may not be too fanciful to recognize as a use served by the particle in this context, in addition to that of (1) announcing an extraneous ingredient in the form of a direct speech, that of (2) marking the link between parable and actual situation, and so the point which the listener should now come to *realize*. And in

9.9.2

(8.1 ...οἱ ἔφοροι ... ἀνεβάλλοντο ... ὑποκρίνασθαι) τέλος δὲ τῆς τε ὑπο-
κρίσιος καὶ ἐξόδου τῶν Σπαρτιητέων ἐγένετο τρόπος τοιόσδε· ... Χίλεος
ἀνὴρ Τεγεήτης ... τῶν ἐφόρων ἐπύθετο πάντα λόγον τὸν δὴ οἱ Ἀθηναῖοι
ἔλεγον, ἀκούσας δὲ [ταῦτα] ὁ Χίλεος ἔλεγε ἄρα σφι τάδε· ...

the context makes it easy for the hearer to attribute to ἄρα overtones of
(1) 'he said, as one can imagine', 'his reply, understandably, was ...',
implying some amount of endorsement on the part of the narrator, i.e.
Herodotus; or of (2) 'then, it appears, he said', 'then he must have said',
the reply providing the link between the Spartans' earlier evasive procras-
tination and later decisive action.

4.2.2.2. *In introducing oblique speech and other embedded propositions*

While the use of ἄρα in announcing direct speech is in the nature of
things likely to be prior to that in discourse formally marked as being a
transformation of direct speech, its reality may be confirmed by the latter
type, which unlike the former is common between Herodotus and Plato.
A straightforward example of what we may call 'intensional' ἄρα is

1.111.5

πυνθάνομαι τὸν πάντα λόγον θεράποντος ὃς ἐμὲ προπέμπων ἔξω πόλιος
ἐνεχείρισε τὸ βρέφος, ὡς ἄρα Μανδάνης τε εἴη παῖς ... καὶ ..., καί ...·
νῦν τε ὅδε ἐστί. ἅμα τε ταῦτα ἔλεγε κτλ.

Here ἄρα is 'intensional' in the sense of signifying that the following
clause belongs to the λόγος, down to ἅμα ... ἔλεγε. It is all the more
appropriate as the adjunct clause ὃς ... τὸ βρέφος has intervened, which
might be followed by a clause introduced by ὡς calling for a different,
e.g. a causal or temporal interpretation; without the particle the status of
the clause would not have become unambiguous before the oblique optative εἴη. In

8.135.1

τότε δὲ θῶμά μοι μέγιστον γενέσθαι λέγεται ὑπὸ Θηβαίων ἐλθεῖν ἄρα
τὸν Εὐρωπέα Μῦν ... καὶ ἐς τοῦ Πτῴου Ἀπόλλωνος τὸ τέμενος,

(word for word:) 'And then there is said by the Thebans to have occurred
what is to me a cause for wonder: that, as they have it, ...', '... that, if it is
true, ...',

the particle helps to mark off the story of the Thebans from the comment
of Herodotus; or, in more grammatical terms, to define the relation be-

tween the reference of the two infinitives ἐλθεῖν and γενέσθαι, which has not been specified by syntactical means.

Yet another special motivation for the use of ἄρα at issue is found at

8.136.2
> (1 ὁ Μαρδόνιος ...) τοὺς γὰρ Ἀθηναίους οὕτω ἐδόκεε μάλιστα προσκτήσεσθαι, λεών τε πολλὸν ἄρα ἀκούων εἶναι καὶ ἄλκιμον τά τε κατὰ τὴν θάλασσαν συντυχόντα σφι παθήματα κατεργασαμένους μάλιστα Ἀθηναίους ἐπίστατο. (3) τούτων δὲ προσγενομένων κατήλπιζε ...

in a context in which (1) the indirect statement is governed by the in a sense 'passive' ἀκούειν, 'hearing (it said) that ...', rather than by 'active' λέγειν or εἰπεῖν, and (2) a part of this indirect statement *precedes* this governing verb, therefore has not been marked as being such.—It is perhaps worth considering whether this context is in addition susceptible to a final interpretation 'being informed, *apparently*, that ...'. At

7.152.3
> ἐγὼ δὲ ὀφείλω λέγειν τὰ λεγόμενα, πείθεσθαί γε μὲν οὐ παντάπασιν ὀφείλω, καί μοι τοῦτο τὸ ἔπος ἐχέτω ἐς πάντα λόγον· ἐπεὶ καὶ ταῦτα λέγεται ὡς ἄρα Ἀργεῖοι ἦσαν οἱ ... ἐπειδή ... πᾶν δὴ βουλόμενοι ...:

'intensional' ἄρα seems all the more apt as H. is concluding a chapter of 'meta'-statements *about* his own λόγοι here to proceed with the λόγοι themselves.

The embedded propositions need not have been given verbal expression; at

1.77.4
> (1) Κροῖσος ... (3) ἐνένωτο τὸν χειμῶνα παρεὶς ἅμα τῷ ἦρι στρατεύειν ἐπὶ τοὺς Πέρσας. (4) καὶ ὁ μὲν ταῦτα φρονέων ὡς ἀπίκετο ἐς τὰς Σάρδις ἔπεμπε κήρυκας ... προερέοντας ἐς πέμπτον μῆνα συλλέγεσθαι ἐς Σάρδις, τὸν δὲ παρεόντα καὶ μαχεσάμενον στρατὸν Πέρσῃσι ... πάντα ἀπεὶς διεσκέδασε οὐδαμὰ ἐλπίσας μή κοτε ἄρα ἀγωνισάμενος οὕτω παραπλησίως Κῦρος ἐλάσῃ ἐπὶ Σάρδις

the particle seems to invite the hearer to adopt Croesus' point of view, in particular by realizing the bearing of ἀγωνισάμενος on ἐλάσῃ: that he would ἐλαύνειν, and especially that he would do so when ἀγωνισάμενος, was not a matter for (Croesus') ἐλπίς. At the same time an interpretation relating ἄρα to ἐλάσῃ alone, i.e. 'that Cyrus would appear to ...', 'that he would, as he in fact turned out to ...', implicitly characterizing the event as unaffected by any deliberations of Croesus, need not be ruled out.

4.2.3. *Conditional clauses*

4.2.3.1. εἰ ἄρα

An affinity of ἄρα with statements which the speaker does not accept personal responsibility for but e.g. (1) presents as resting on evidence just as accessible to the addressee as to himself, or (2) assumes for the sake of the argument, accounts for its fairly regular occurrence with propositions he is prepared to entertain, regardless of whether he considers them (1) probable, as at 7.10 θ 3 & 159, or (2) improbable,[1] as at 5.106.4 & 7.9 γ 1, all to be quoted presently. All the same it is to be expected that what we have referred to as the overtones of uses of the particle in particular contexts come out somewhat differently in these two cases. In (2) the operative notion seems to be the perspective on a different universe of discourse, or possible world: thus, with the optative mood expressly calling attention to the hypothetical character of the proposition, at

7.9 γ 1

> εἰ δὲ ἄρα ἔγωγε ψευσθείην γνώμῃ
>
> '… but if I *should* be mistaken …',

and with an indicative mood but with the speaker dissociating himself from the supposition by lexical means, at

7.16 γ 1

> εἰ δὲ ἄρα μή ἐστι τοῦτο τοιοῦτον οἷον ἐγὼ διαιρέω,

where in addition an 'as you mentioned earlier' may be hinted at, i.e. a reference to 15.3 εἰ ὦν θεός ἐστι ὁ ἐπιπέμπων;[2] also

5.106.4

> ἀρχὴν δὲ ἔγωγε οὐδὲ ἐνδέκομαι τὸν λόγον ὅκως … εἰ δ' ἄρα τι τοιοῦτο ποιεῦσι καὶ σὺ τὸ ἐὸν ἀκήκοας
>
> '… but assuming it to be true …',[3]

and at 4.32

> … οὔτε τινὲς ἄλλοι … εἰ μὴ ἄρα Ἰσσηδόνες· ὡς δ' ἐγὼ δοκέω οὐδ' οὗτοι …
>
> '… unless it would turn out that …'.

---

[1] Cf. KG 2.324-5.

[2] Cf. 7.159 quoted below p. 129.

[3] Cf. 2.28.5 (1 τοῦ δὲ Νείλου τὰς πηγὰς … οὐδεὶς ὑπέσχετο εἰδέναι εἰ μὴ … ὁ γραμματιστὴς τῶν ἱρῶν χρημάτων τῆς Ἀθηναίης· (2) οὗτος δ' ἔμοιγε παίζειν ἐδόκεε φάμενος εἰδέναι ἀτρεκέως· ἔλεγε δὲ ὧδε …) οὗτος μὲν δὴ ὁ γραμματιστὴς εἰ ἄρα ταῦτα γινόμενα ἔλεγε κτλ.

The characteristic effect, clearly relevant to the Platonic use in inferences submitted for ὁμολογία, is that of *deferring to any evidence to the contrary.*

In the case (1) of propositions presented as probable, such as

7.10 θ 3

  εἰ μὴ ἄρα καὶ πρότερον κατ' ὁδόν ...

the hearer is invited to adopt the speaker's point of view and accept the proposition as natural and plausible in its context; this use is akin both to Homeric contexts containing clauses interpreted as causal such as

A 94-6

  ἀλλ' ἕνεκ' ἀρητῆρος ὃν ἠτίμησ' Ἀγαμέμνων

  ...

  τοὔνεκ' ἄρ' ἄλγε' ἔδωκεν ἑκηβόλος,

where the particle is equally at home in what has come to be analysed as the 'subordinate' as in the independent clause,[1] and to the Platonic application to information supposed to suggest itself, regardless of the expectations and preferences of the speaker and hearer.

Elsewhere grounds for accepting the hypothesis have been given in the preceding context, and ἄρα may be taken, over and above its neutral use as *ex hypothesi*, to hint at this: thus at

7.159

  ἀλλ' εἰ μὲν βούλεαι βοηθέειν τῇ Ἑλλάδι ἴσθι ἀρξόμενος ὑπὸ Λακεδαι-
  μονίων· εἰ δ' ἄρα μὴ δικαιοῖς ἄρχεσθαι σὺ δὲ μηδὲ βοηθέειν,

Gelon had quite unambiguously stipulated in 158.5 ἐπὶ δὲ λόγῳ τοιῷδε τάδε ὑπίσχομαι ... πέμψαιμι. An equally relevant possibility, however, is that the range of ἄρα here includes the subsequent main clause. An overexposed outsize projection might be 'but (1) let's suppose that, (2) as you say, you do not choose to ...; (3) in that case, (4) clearly, you will not ... either'.

In one context it becomes quite clear that the motivation of ἄρα in conditional clauses cannot be accounted for entirely in terms of the supposed probability or improbability of the proposition involved: at

8.100.3

  (1 Μαρδόνιος δὲ ὁρῶν μὲν Ξέρξην ... ὑποπτεύων δὲ αὐτὸν δρησμὸν βου-
  λεύειν ... προσέφερε τὸν λόγον τόνδε· (2) δέσποτα ... (3) εἰ μέν νυν δοκέει ... εἰ δὲ καὶ δοκέει ... μὴ δὲ δυσθύμει ... μάλιστα μέν νυν ταῦτα

---

[1] Cf. A 56 κήδετο γὰρ Δαναῶν ὅτι ῥα θνήσκοντας ὁρᾶτο. The listener is initiated to the viewpoint of Apollo.

ποίεε· εἰ δ᾽ ἄρα τοι βεβούλευται αὐτὸν ἀπελαύνοντα ἀπάγειν τὴν στρατιήν ...

'and should it be your resolve ...', 'in case you have decided ...', 'if by any chance your decision is ...'

this proposition is marked by the particle as 'offering itself' not because Mardonius feels any urge to pronounce on its likelihood, but as a seemingly casual, and so the most cautious, way to mention an alternative which his lord and sovereign has not brought up and which Mardonius is privately opposed to. And in

9.60.3

(2 δίκαιοί ἐστε ὑμεῖς πρὸς τὴν πιεζομένην μάλιστα τῶν μοιρέων ἀμυνέοντες ἰέναι,) εἰ δ᾽ ἄρα αὐτοὺς ὑμέας καταλελάβηκε ἀδύνατόν τι βοηθέειν ...

'but if it happens that ...'

the particle seems to convey that the contingency mentioned in the conditional clause is not subject to the judgement of the speaker, and provides an exception to the consequence which would obtain but for such force majeure: that the Athenians would prove themselves to be ἄδικοι by not coming to reinforce the Spartans.

4.2.3.2. ἦν ἄρα

In 9.104

Μιλησίοισι δὲ προσετέτακτο μὲν ⟨ἐκ⟩ τῶν Περσέων τὰς διόδους τηρέειν σωτηρίης εἵνεκά σφι ὡς ἦν ἄρα σφέας καταλαμβάνῃ οἷά περ κατέλαβε ἔχοντες ἡγεμόνας σῴζωνται ἐς τὰς κορυφὰς τῆς Μυκάλης. ἐτάχθησαν μέν νυν ἐπὶ τοῦτο τὸ πρᾶγμα οἱ Μιλήσιοι τούτου τε εἵνεκεν καὶ ἵνα μὴ παρεόντες ἐν τῷ στρατοπέδῳ τι νεοχμὸν ποιέοιεν· οἱ δὲ πᾶν τοὐναντίον τοῦ προστεταγμένου ἐποίεον

'in order that, should such a fate overtake them as did in fact overtake them', '... if things turned out as in fact they did',

the particle hints at the coherence of the general picture, more particularly between their provisions for safety (σωτηρίης) and the prospect which inspired these; perhaps also between this prospect and the event.[1]

---

[1] It should be noted that the conditional clause in which it appears contains what is virtually the only new information in these two sentences: cf. 99.3 (1 τοῦτο μὲν ...) τοῦτο δὲ τὰς διόδους τὰς ἐς τὰς κορυφὰς τῆς Μυκάλης φερούσας προστάσσουσι τοῖσι Μιλησίοισι φυλάσσειν ὡς ἐπισταμένοισι δῆθεν μάλιστα τὴν χώρην· ἐποίευν δὲ τούτου εἵνεκεν ἵνα ἐκτὸς τοῦ στρατοπέδου ἔωσι. τούτους μὲν Ἰώνων τοῖσι καὶ κατεδόκεον νεοχμὸν ἄν τι ποιέειν δυνάμιος ἐπιλαβομένοισι τρόποισι τοιούτοισι προεφυλάσσοντο οἱ Πέρσαι—the sentence followed by the instance of ἄρα in a temporal clause with ὡς quoted p. 132 below.

At 5.124.2 in

λέγων ὡς ἄμεινον σφίσι εἴη ... ἢν ἄρα ἐξωθέονται

the use of ἄρα primarily indicates that the condition still comes under ὡς: '... supposing them to be ...'; perhaps it is at the same time related to that called 'anticipatory' above:[1] 'if it should turn out that ...'.

The question of the range of the particle, raised by 7.159 quoted in the previous section, is doubly relevant to

9.45.2

λέγω δὲ ὧν ὅτι Μαρδονίῳ ... τὰ σφάγια οὐ δύναται καταθύμια γενέσθαι· πάλαι γὰρ ἂν ἐμάχεσθε. νῦν δέ οἱ δέδοκται τὰ μὲν σφάγια ἐᾶν χαίρειν ἅμα ἡμέρῃ δὲ διαφαυσκούσῃ συμβολὴν ποιέεσθαι· καταρρώδηκε γὰρ μὴ πλεῦνες συλλεχθῆτε ὡς ἐγὼ εἰκάζω· πρὸς ταῦτα ἑτοιμάζεσθε· ἢν δὲ ἄρα ὑπερβάληται ... (3) ἢν δὲ ὑμῖν ὁ πόλεμος ὅδε κατὰ νόον τελευτήσῃ μνησθῆναί τινα χρὴ καὶ ἐμεῦ ... ὃς ... ἵνα μὴ ἐπιπέσωσι ὑμῖν [ἐξαίφνης] οἱ βάρβαροι μὴ προσδεκομένοισί κω.

Here the smallest range within which it is possible to make sense of the particle extends to the first alternative only: 'if (regardless of our predictions to, and preparations for, the contrary) it turns out that', but a richer interpretation is attained if we take it to bear on the *set* of alternatives: 'the preparation (ἑτοιμάζεσθαι) which is in keeping with alternative (1) is ..., with (2) is ...'.[2]

4.2.4. *Within the narrative*

4.2.4.1. *In temporal clauses*

The particle is not rarely found in temporal clauses introduced by ὡς.[3] It will here be suggested that these contexts involve an element of informal implication: that the content of the ἄρα-clause was to be expected in the light of previous information. By contrast the particle is not regularly found where there is verbatim repetition of old information: this is the province of οὖν, which assigns to such given items a new role in the

---

[1] P. 110.

[2] Or, if this is not a distinction without a difference, 'the preparation (ἑτοιμάζεσθαι) which is in keeping with these data is if (1), then ..., and if (2), then ...'. — With the instances quoted in this section cf. 3.45.4, 7.149.1, 8.109.5, 9.90.2.

[3] The preponderance of ὡς ἄρα over ἐπεὶ ἄρα could be construed as confirmation of the hypothesis that ἄρα regards the propositions involved rather than the subjects supposed to entertain these propositions. Cf. E.J. Bakker, unpublished MS.

ordering of topic and comment imposed by the speaker. A selection follows.[1]

7.116

> (115.1 ὁ στρατός ... ἀπίκετο ἐς τὴν Ἄκανθον ... (3) τὴν δὲ ὁδὸν ταύτην τῇ βασιλεὺς Ξέρξης τὸν στρατὸν ἤλασε ...) ὡς δὲ ἄρα ἐς τὴν Ἄκανθον ἀπίκετο ... ὁ Ξέρξης ... (117) ἐν Ἀκάνθῳ δὲ ἐόντος Ξέρξεω ...

Xerxes' arrival in Acanthus (ἀπίκετο) was implied by (1) the arrival of the army in Acanthus (ἀπίκετο) and (2) his having led it there (ἤλασε).

9.100.1

> (99.1 οἱ δὲ Πέρσαι ὡς εἶδον τοὺς Ἕλληνας παρασκευαζομένους ἐς μάχην ...) ὡς ἄρα παρεσκευάδατο τοῖσι Ἕλλησι (προσήισαν πρὸς τοὺς βαρβάρους)

i.e. as we expected the Greeks to be ready to attack, after being told that the Persians observed them preparing themselves for battle.

1.86.3

> (τῷ δὲ Κροίσῳ ... ἐσελθεῖν ... τὸ τοῦ Σόλωνος ὥς ..., τὸ ...) ὡς δὲ ἄρα μιν προσστῆναι τοῦτο

i.e. as it had been expressed in the previous sentence in the synonym ἐσελθεῖν.

1.27.1

> (26.3 πρώτοισι μὲν δὴ τούτοισι ἐπεχείρησε ὁ Κροῖσος μετὰ δὲ ἐν μέρεϊ ἑκάστοισι Ἰώνων τε καὶ Αἰολέων) ὡς δὲ ἄρα οἱ ἐν τῇ Ἀσίῃ Ἕλληνες κατεστράφατο ...

i.e. as the hearer has been prepared for.

8.106.3

> [2 &] 3 (1 ... ὁ Ἑρμότιμος ... εὑρίσκει τὸν Πανιώνιον ...) ἐπιγνοὺς δὲ ἔλεγε (ἄρα in δ) πρὸς αὐτὸν πολλοὺς καὶ φιλίους λόγους ... ὥστε ὑποδεξάμενον ἄσμενον τοὺς λόγους τὸν Παιώνιον κομίσαι τὰ τέκνα καὶ τὴν γυναῖκα. ὡς δὲ ἄρα πανοικίῃ μιν περιέλαβε ἔλεγε ὁ Ἑρμότιμος τάδε· ὦ πάντων ἀνδρῶν ἤδη μάλιστα ἀπ' ἔργων ἀνοσιωτάτων τὸν βίον κτησάμενε ...

'thus, as implied'.

8.59

> (58.2 ... ἀνέγνωσε χρηίζων ἔκ τε τῆς νεὸς ἐκβῆναι συλλέξαι τε τοὺς στρατηγοὺς ἐς τὸ συνέδριον) ὡς δὲ ἄρα (om. d) συνελέχθησαν ...

---

[1] Analogous accounts apply to 3.134.1, 9.8.1 (cf. 7.1) & 19.3 (cf. 15.3?) & 33.1 & 86.1.

'accordingly': the particle presents the statement συνελέχθησαν as related to, in this case the outcome of, the injunction to συλλέξαι reported in the previous sentence. This context could be assigned to a sub-species of uses of ἄρα in which the coherence cemented by the particle is that of narrative with direct speech: thus

1.112.2

ὡς δὲ οὐκ ἔπειθε ἄρα τὸν ἄνδρα δεύτερα λέγει ἡ γυνὴ τάδε· Ἐπεὶ τοίνυν οὐ δύναμαι σε πείθειν

'As it appeared (from his explanation) she couldn't persuade her husband ...'.

It is worth noting how ἄρα in the third person narrative statement corresponds to τοίνυν in the reported conversation.[1]

4.2.4.2. *Other narrative contexts*

While ἄρα shows a marked affinity to temporal ὡς-clauses, the use which we are surveying is not confined to these. With parataxis we have, in the context of two historical infinitives

2.141.3

τὸν δὲ ἱρέα ... ἐσελθόντα ἐς τὸ μέγαρον πρὸς τὤγαλμα ἀποδύρεσθαι οἷα κινδυνεύει παθεῖν, ὀλοφυρόμενον δ' ἄρα μιν ἐπελθεῖν ὕπνον ...

i.e. as stated, or at least implied in a near-synonym; and with a finite verb

5.87.2

(1 λέγεται μὲν ... ὁμολογέεται δὲ ... ἕνα ... ἐς τὴν Ἀττικὴν γενέσθαι (2) πλὴν ...) κομισθεὶς ἄρα ἐς τὰς Ἀθήνας ...

i.e. having arrived in Athens, as we already knew he had and as both parties agree he had. By the latter circumstance, incidentally, this instance is related to the use we have called 'intensional': 'it is said ... it is agreed that only one man ... arrived in Athens, except that one party has it that ... and the other has it that ...; now having arrived as stated, this man ...'.

A collocation with non-temporal ὡς invites comparison with the two instances discussed above of γὰρ ἄρα, to which it seems to supply a hypotactical near-equivalent:

4.205

ζῶσα γὰρ εὐλέων ἐξέζεσε ὡς ἄρα ἀνθρώποισι αἱ λίην ἰσχυραὶ τιμωρίαι πρὸς θεῶν ἐπίφθονοι γίνονται

---

[1] Cf. 86-7 above (general introd.) and 152 below (τοίνυν). — With the instances quoted in this section cf. 1.24.7, 2.140.1, 8.94.2, all with infinitive verbs.

'… as, *apparently*, …' 'in accordance with *what could here* again *be observed*, …',

a context which resembles 3.65.3 in offering an interpretation of what precedes, but like 3.34.4 is contributed by Herodotus as narrator.

There remain a sizable proportion of instances of ἄρα used in declarative main clauses in the course of Herodotus' narrative. These are neither easy to explain nor very similar to anything we have found in the *Phaedo*; all the same a brief discussion of them is in order here, since a failure to account for all these uses of the particle in older prose might with some justice be taken to falsify the entire approach to ἄρα outlined here.

We begin with an instance of explanation within the narrative which does not seem radically different from uses in arguments in Plato:

3.64.4

εἴρετο ὁ Καμβύσης ὅ τι τῇ πόλι οὔνομα εἴη, οἱ δὲ εἶπαν ὅτι Ἀγβάτανα· τῷ δὲ ἔτι πρότερον ἐκέχρηστο … ἐν Ἀγβατάνοισι τελευτήσειν τὸν βίον· ὁ μὲν δὴ ἐν τοῖσι Μηδικοῖσι Ἀγβατάνοισι ἐδόκεε τελευτήσειν γηραιός … τὸ δὲ χρηστήριον ⟨ἐν⟩ τοῖσι ἐν Συρίῃ Ἀγβατάνοισι ἔλεγε ἄρα.

'…, it appeared' or 'it appears'.

What accounts for the familiar look of this is (1) the fact that the means towards understanding and the grounds for accepting the statement containing ἄρα are all given before we get to this statement, so that the particle faces backwards, and (2) the absence here of any impediment to interpreting this statement as asserted by the narrator. One example suffices to show that (2) is not given with ἄρα as such:

4.45.4

ἡ δὲ δὴ Εὐρώπη οὔτε εἰ περίρρυτός ἐστι γινώσκεται … οὔτε ὁκόθεν τὸ οὔνομα ἔλαβε τοῦτο οὔτε ὅστις οἱ ἦν ὁ θέμενος φαίνεται εἰ μὴ ἀπὸ τῆς Τυρίης φήσομεν Εὐρώπης λαβεῖν τὸ οὔνομα τὴν χώρην· πρότερον δὲ ἦν ἄρα ἀνώνυμος ὥσπερ αἱ ἕτεραι.

An attempt to assimilate this to the received interpretation as 'therefore' is implied in the note 'führt öfter etwas noch nicht Gesagtes aber aus dem Vorhergehenden sich mit Notwendigkeit Ergebendes ein' of Abicht;[1] Powell's heading 'after all, as it turned out' similarly implies that the proposition is asserted. The comment of Stein 'falls man annimmt, dass der Name von der tyrischen Europe herrühre' may point to the same reading, but is compatible with both 'on this hypothesis' and 'by their account'. At the other extreme Van Groningen takes the particle to confirm a scepti-

---

[1] Whose somewhat surprising selection of parallels consists of 4.189.1, to be quoted presently, and 4.205 quoted p. 133 above.

cism on the part of Herodotus which is supposed to be apparent from the verb φήσομεν 'maintain' as well as from the last sentence of 45.5 τοῖσι γὰρ νομιζομένοισι αὐτῶν χρησόμεθα. While this seems more perceptive and less naive, it is questionable as a final interpretation of the context, and it would certainly be going too far as a reading of the particle as such; there is no need to assume that this characterizes the proposition any more specifically than as belonging not to Herodotus' ἀπόδεξις but to the νομιζόμενα αὐτῶν.

As for (1) above, the orientation of ἄρα back towards the preceding context does not apply to all or most instances of the particle in sections of narrative in the strictest sense, as distinct from exposition. A more complex connection is found in

6.62.1
(61.1 Ἀρίστωνι βασιλεύοντι ἐν Σπάρτῃ καὶ γήμαντι γυναῖκας δύο παῖδες οὐκ ἐγίνοντο, (2) καὶ οὐ γὰρ συνεγινώσκετο αὐτὸς τούτων εἶναι αἴτιος γαμέει τρίτην γυναῖκα, ὧδε δὲ γαμέει. ἦν οἱ φίλος ... ἀνήρ ... τούτῳ τῷ ἀνδρὶ ἐτύγχανε ἐοῦσα γυνὴ καλλίστη ... ἐξ αἰσχίστης γενομένη· (3) ἐοῦσαν γάρ μιν τὸ εἶδος φλαύρην ... (5) ... ἀπὸ μὲν δὴ ταύτης τῆς ἡμέρης μεταπεσεῖν τὸ εἶδος· γαμέει δέ [δή] μιν ἐς γάμου ὥρην ἀπικομένην Ἄγητος ὁ Ἀλκείδεω, οὗτος δὴ ὁ τοῦ Ἀρίστωνος φίλος. 62.1) τὸν δὲ Ἀρίστωνα ἔκνιζε ἄρα τῆς γυναικὸς ταύτης ἔρως· μηχανᾶται δὴ τοιάδε· ...

We have not been told in so many words that this lady was destined to become Ariston's third wife, but there have been one or two pointers: as a king he was presumably not in the habit of denying himself what he fancied, and previous marriages have not brought him all that he was hoping for. In the circumstances 'it was only natural', 'one can imagine' that Ariston conceived a passionate desire for this woman. At the same time the scope of the particle extends forward: 'you have to be aware ... in order to appreciate ...'. This facing forward is very much in evidence in

5.92 γ 2
ἀπικόμενοι δὲ οὗτοι ... αἴτεον τὸ παιδίον· ἡ δὲ Λάβδα ἐνεχείρισε αὐτῶν ἑνί· τοῖσι δὲ ἄρα ἐβεβούλευτο κατ' ὁδὸν τὸν πρῶτον αὐτῶν λαβόντα τὸ παιδίον προσουδίσαι· (3) ἐπείτε ὦν ἔδωκε φέρουσα ἡ Λάβδα τὸν λαβόντα τῶν ἀνδρῶν θείῃ τύχῃ προσεγέλασε τὸ παιδίον καὶ τὸν φρασθέντα τοῦτο οἰκτός τις ἴσχει ἀποκτεῖναι κατοικτίρας δὲ παραδιδοῖ τῷ δευτέρῳ ὁ δὲ τῷ τρίτῳ ... (4) ἀποδόντες ὦν ὀπίσω τῇ τεκούσῃ τὸ παιδίον καὶ ἐξελθόντες ἔξω ... ἀλλήλων ἅπτοντο καταιτιώμενοι καὶ μάλιστα τοῦ πρώτου λαβόντος ὅτι οὐκ ἐποίησε κατὰ τὰ δεδογμένα ...

'now what follows makes sense against the background information that ...':

anticipatory, i.e. looking forward to the stage reached by the end of our quotation, and preserving the relation with γάρ bearing on what follows

rather than what precedes, but with the difference that the new information is not presented as subordinate either to that which precedes or to that which follows. An interpretation which seems possible, but which alone would ascribe too limited a scope to ἄρα to do justice to the narrative connection, is 'the story has it', 'now it is supposed ...', indicating that the speaker does not accept responsibility for the statement.

The same situation within a brief compass is found in

1.111.1

τῷ δ' ἄρα καὶ αὐτῷ ἡ γυνὴ ἐπίτεξ ἐοῦσα πᾶσαν ἡμέρην τότε κως κατὰ δαίμονα τίκτει ...

'here it should be understood that',

where again the connection with γάρ is visible and relevant, and an 'anticipatory' interpretation comes naturally, and in

3.14.8

ὁ δὲ Ψαμμήνιτος ὡς εἶδε ... ἐπλήξατο τὴν κεφαλήν. ἦσαν δ' ἄρα αὐτοῦ φύλακοι οἳ τὸ ποιεύμενον πᾶν ... Καμβύσῃ ἐσήμαινον. θωμάσας δὲ ὁ Καμβύσης τὰ ποιεύμενα

'now it appears / you have to know / must take it that',

supplying a proposition r which is presupposed or implied by the context, here esp. by q, and which is required if you are to get the relation between p and q right.

In another wider connection at

6.100.1

Ἐρετριέες δὲ ... Ἀθηναίων ἐδεήθησαν σφίσι βοηθοὺς γενέσθαι· Ἀθηναῖοι δὲ ... τοὺς τετρακισχιλίους ... σφι διδοῦσι τιμωρούς. τῶν δὲ Ἐρετριέων ἦν ἄρα οὐδὲν ὑγιὲς βούλευμα οἳ μετεπέμποντο μὲν Ἀθηναίους ἐφρόνεον δὲ διφασίας ἰδέας· (2) οἱ μὲν γὰρ αὐτῶν ... ἄλλοι δὲ ... (3) μαθὼν δὲ τούτων ἑκάτερα ὡς εἶχε Αἰσχίνης ὁ Νόθωνος ... φράζει τοῖσι ἥκουσι Ἀθηναίων πάντα τὰ παρεόντα σφι πρήγματα προσεδέετό τε ἀπαλλάσσεσθαί σφεας ἐς τὴν σφετέρην ἵνα μὴ προσαπόλωνται, οἱ δὲ Ἀθηναῖοι ταῦτα Αἰσχίνῃ συμβουλεύσαντι πείθονται, καὶ οὗτοι μὲν διαβάντες ἐς Ὠρωπὸν ἔσῳζον σφέας αὐτούς· οἱ δὲ Πέρσαι κτλ.

'Now it must be understood ...'.

In two passages the information conveyed by the clause containing ἄρα is more loosely relevant to what follows, as an extension:

3.70.1

ὁ δὲ Ὀτάνης παραλαβὼν Ἀσπαθίνην καὶ Γωβρύην ... ἑωυτῷ ἐπιτηδεοτάτους ἐς πίστιν ἀπηγήσατο πᾶν τὸ πρᾶγμα· οἱ δὲ καὶ αὐτοὶ ἄρα ὑπώπτευον οὕτω τοῦτο ἔχειν ἀνενείκαντος δὲ τοῦ Ὀτάνεω τοὺς λόγους ἐδέξαντο

'it appeared' rather than 'it is, was said', and perhaps even more 'it appears', 'the course of events suggests, the story indicates that'; cf.

8.8.1

ἐν δὲ τούτῳ τῷ χρόνῳ ἐν ᾧ ..., ἦν γὰρ ἐν τῷ στρατοπέδῳ τούτῳ Σκυλλίης ... δύτης τῶν τότε ἀνθρώπων ἄριστος ..., οὗτος ὁ Σκυλλίης ἐν νόῳ μὲν εἶχε ἄρα καὶ πρότερον αὐτομολήσειν ἀλλ' οὐ γάρ οἱ παρέσχε ἐς τότε· ὅτεῳ μὲν δὴ τρόπῳ τὸ ἐνθεῦτεν ἔτι ἀπίκετο ἐς τοὺς Ἕλληνας οὐκ ἔχω εἰπεῖν ἀτρεκέως, θωμάζω δὲ εἰ τὰ λεγόμενά ἐστι ἀληθέα· λέγεται γὰρ ὡς ... δὺς ἐς τὴν θάλασσαν οὐ πρότερον ἀνέσχε πρὶν ἢ ἀπίκετο ἐπὶ τὸ Ἀρτεμίσιον ... λέγεται μέν νυν καὶ ἄλλα ψεύδεσι ἴκελα περὶ τοῦ ἀνδρὸς τούτου, τὰ δὲ μετεξέτερα ἀληθέα· περὶ μέντοι τούτου γνώμη μοι ἀποδεδέχθω πλοίῳ μιν ἀπικέσθαι ἐπὶ τὸ Ἀρτεμίσιον.

'apparently' rather than 'allegedly', whether 'as it then appeared' or 'as it now appears'; but perhaps also 'you have to be aware, in order to appreciate the following'.

Much less transparent is

4.64.3

(1 ὅσους δ' ἂν φονεύσῃ ... τούτων τὰς κεφαλὰς ἀποφέρει τῷ βασιλέϊ· ἀπενείκας μὲν γὰρ κεφαλὴν τῆς ληίης μεταλαμβάνει τὴν ἂν λάβωσι μὴ ἐνείκας δὲ οὔ· (2) ἀποδείρει δὲ αὐτὴν τρόπῳ τοιῷδε ... 3) πολλοὶ δὲ αὐτῶν ἐκ τῶν ἀποδαρμάτων καὶ χλαίνας ἐπιέννυσθαι ποιεῦσι συρράπτοντες κατά περ βαίτας· πολλοὶ δὲ ἀνδρῶν ἐχθρῶν τὰς δεξιὰς χεῖρας νεκρῶν ἐόντων ἀποδείραντες αὐτοῖσι ὄνυξι καλύπτρας τῶν φαρετρέων ποιεῦνται· δέρμα δὲ ἀνθρώπου καὶ παχὺ καὶ λαμπρὸν ἦν ἄρα, σχεδὸν δερμάτων πάντων λαμπρότατον λευκότητι· πολλοὶ δὲ καὶ ὅλους ἄνδρας ἐκδείραντες ... ἐφ' ἵππων περιφέρουσι.

There is plainly no inference involved here, and it is not immediately evident why the characterization of human skin should be inserted precisely where it is, or whether it should be made to bear on the preceding or on the following item of description. Perhaps a paraphrase 'to appreciate this, one has to realize' is tenable yet not too unspecific to be helpful. Herodotus in the course of his narrative sees the need to call attention to the qualifications of human skin for the uses it is put to by the Scythians; in addition to the thickness required for holding arrows it has a bright hue suitable for ornaments, which brings Herodotus to the last, purely decorative use that he mentions.

Two somewhat similar contexts are

4.189.1

(187.2 οἱ γὰρ δὴ τῶν Λιβύων νομάδες ... (188) θυσίαι δὲ τοῖσι νομάσι εἰσὶ αἵδε ... τούτοισι μέν νυν πάντες Λίβυες θύουσι, ἀτὰρ οἱ περὶ τὴν Τριτωνίδα λίμνην νέμοντες τῇ Ἀθηναίῃ μάλιστα ...) τὴν δὲ ἄρα ἐσθῆτα

καὶ τὰς αἰγίδας τῶν ἀγαλμάτων τῆς Ἀθηναίης ἐκ τῶν Λιβυσσέων ἐποιή-
σαντο οἱ Ἕλληνες· πλὴν γὰρ ἢ ὅτι σκυτίνη ἡ ἐσθὴς τῶν Λιβυσσέων καὶ
... τὰ δὲ ἄλλα πάντα κατὰ τὠυτὸ ἔσταλται· καὶ δὴ καὶ τὸ οὔνομα κατ-
ηγορέει ὅτι ἐκ Λιβύης ἥκει ἡ στολὴ τῶν Παλλαδίων ...

'and so': it is *in keeping* with this, whether we choose to regard it as a *sign*
or as a *consequence* of it, that ...&c.;

and 2.58

ἔστι δὲ καὶ τῶν ἱρῶν ἡ μαντικὴ ἀπ' Αἰγύπτου ἀπιγμένη. πανηγύριας δὲ
ἄρα[1] καὶ πομπὰς καὶ προσαγωγὰς πρῶτοι ἀνθρώπων Αἰγύπτιοί εἰσι οἱ
ποιησάμενοι καὶ παρὰ τούτων Ἕλληνες μεμαθήκασι. τεκμήριον δέ μοι
τούτου τόδε· ...

In both contexts it is clear that the statement containing ἄρα has a news
value of its own, as opposed to supporting that which precedes it; compare, and contrast, (πλὴν) γὰρ (ἢ ὅτι) and καὶ δὴ καί in the first, and
τεκμήριον δέ μοι τούτου in the second passage. On the other hand it
would be at least equally one-sided to regard the preceding statements as
merely supporting that containing ἄρα, as in contexts of inference: the
content of the statements themselves militates against this, and the sequel
just quoted is not more compatible with this than it is with the reverse.
There is a significant compatibility, a coherence, and thus a mutual confirmation among statements making sense as forming a whole.

We end with a syntactically and semantically complex connection in a
question at

5.49.8

ἀλλὰ περὶ μὲν χώρης ἄρα οὐ πολλῆς οὐδὲ οὕτω χρηστῆς ... χρεόν ἐστι
ὑμέας μάχας ἀναβάλλεσθαι πρός τε Μεσσηνίους ἐόντας ἰσοπαλέας καὶ
... παρέχον δὲ τῆς Ἀσίης πάσης ἄρχειν εὐπετέως ἄλλο τι αἱρήσεσθε;

This last sentence of a long speech urging war consists in a double question, the first part of which is only formally a question but in effect supplies the premiss to an εἰκός-argument:[2] 'Is it necessary to put up a hard
fight for a small prize, and when there is much to be gained with little
effort will you choose differently?' What is expressed in this first part is
common knowledge, yet within the speech the information is new. While

---

[1] The observation that a πομπή introduced to the Greeks from Egypt was discussed in
2.49.1 might suggest a rudimentary form of induction, previous information adding up to a
general assessment; but this would still be a final interpretation of one context rather than
an approximation to the value of ἄρα. (In spite of all this: is ἄμα at all possible?)

[2] Alternatively the sentence just might be analysed as consisting of a statement of fact
balanced by a question, but the predicate χρεόν ἐστι is in this context more easily read as a
question.

it is conceivable that ἄρα might serve to remind the addressee of this, a richer interpretation is achieved by taking the scope of the particle to be the sentence as a whole,[1] so that the leading question comes to suggest that doing the one thing but not the other thing does not square; that it would not be a sequence of actions between which an ἄρα-relation could obtain, so to speak.[2]

5. ἄρα *in general*

The use of ἄρα shows a wide variety, but it seems possible to reduce this to a value of signifying that the proposition which contains the particle belongs to a distinct perspective and in a connection which is not just that imparted by the speaker, and that it is to be accepted or assumed, not e.g. as being self-evident, in which case δή would apply, but on any kind of external grounds. Its particular aptitude to mark the progress 'du connu à l'inconnu' which Des Places gives as one subspecies of its use[3] is only a special application of its appropriateness to contexts in which the ground for entertaining the proposition is not a supposedly known fact, but either itself assumed as a hypothesis, or simply residing in the words of some other speaker. When ἄρα is used in a statement, i.e. in asserting a proposition, what may be called its assertiveness may range from a mere 'allegedly' to something approaching 'manifestly'; but even in these declarative uses its force is more adequately defined in terms of the 'acceptance' than of the 'truth' of the statements involved. Both the interpretation of any such statement as positive and true, and the popular characterization of such a statement as 'surprising',[4] wherever they apply are based on the entire context and cannot be justified by reference to the value of ἄρα as such. The entire context in the case of ἄρα more often than with some other particles includes the sequel as well as the preceding context. This has to do with the fact that the general force of maintaining a consistent perspective and a coherent view is prior to the particular form of logical implication with a clear distinction between premises and conclusions which from our modern vantage-point seems to occupy the foreground.

---

[1] Alternatively one might take the particle to bear on the relation between this final sentence and what precedes. There is little to choose, since the absolute accusative παρέχον ... εὐπετέως introducing the final question is the shortest possible summary of all that precedes.

[2] Cf. Lys. 31.28 quoted above at p. 120.

[3] Des Places 237.

[4] Denniston *GP* 35, after Hartung (1832) 430.

CHAPTER FOUR

ΔΗ

1. *A distinctive use*: *visualizing*

Of the four particles here discussed which are often credited with an inferential force, δή is the commonest, but also the one for which this inferential force is appealed to in the smallest proportion of its occurrences. This may be one reason why the particle is not discussed by Des Places.

One type of context which may provide a clue to the function of δή is that of visual perception and visibility, denoted by verbs of seeing or appearing, whether these are used in their strict sense or more loosely:

81 D 1
    ... περὶ ἃ δὴ καὶ ὤφθη ἄττα ψυχῶν σκιοειδῆ φαντάσματα[1]
76 A 1
    Δυνατὸν γὰρ δὴ τοῦτό γε ἐφάνη...

or by the adjective δῆλος:

80 A 8
    – Ποτέρῳ οὖν ἡ ψυχὴ ἔοικεν;
    – Δῆλα δή, ὦ Σ., ὅτι ἡ μὲν ψυχὴ τῷ θείῳ, ...
82 A 7, 9
    – Οὐκοῦν ... δῆλα δὴ καὶ τἆλλα ᾗ ἂν ... ἴοι...;
    – Δῆλον δή, ... · πῶς δ' οὔ;

In other contexts δή accompanies not a word connoting vision, but a reference to a visible object present in the situation of the utterance: at 60 A 5

    ὕστατον δή σε προσεροῦσι νῦν οἱ ἐπιτήδειοι

---

[1] Robin translates 'c'est un fait', Gallop 'actually', following Hackforth, who explains (p. 89 n. 2) that 'by ὥσπερ λέγεται and δή (semi-ironical) Socrates maintains a non-committal attitude on these ghostly apparitions'. I think this ironic reserve is more relevant to ὥσπερ λέγεται, which should be construed to refer backwards, qualifying the soul's alleged 'fear of the invisible and of Hades' (φόβῳ τοῦ ἀιδοῦς τε καὶ ῞Αιδου ὥσπερ λέγεται C 11) and perhaps calling attention especially to the popular etymology implied in this punning expression. By contrast the observation introduced by δή should not be called in doubt: it supplies 'an interesting illustration of the manner in which Plato will take some popular belief, as he often takes some popular expression, and fill it with a deeper meaning of his own', in the words of Archer-Hind, followed by Wohlrab. In this role of appealing to the evidence δή is strengthened by καί, which points to the conformity between what is alleged and what is observed.

it marks the entrance of Socrates' friends; at 89 B 4

Αὔριον δή ... τὰς καλὰς ταύτας κόμας ἀποκερῇ

Socrates is fingering the hairs which call forth his reflection. At 69 D 2 such an object may just possibly be present in the person of the speaker himself:

οὗτοι δ' εἰσὶν ... οἱ πεφιλοσοφηκότες ὀρθῶς. ὧν δὴ καὶ ἐγὼ ... προυθυμήθην γενέσθαι·

at 63 E 8 it is found in the audience:

Ἔα αὐτόν, ἔφη. ἀλλ' ὑμῖν δὴ τοῖς δικασταῖς βούλομαι ἤδη τὸν λόγον ἀποδοῦναι ...

I take it that δή in such contexts as these serves to direct the hearer to what meets the eye, and I submit that the basic value of the particle relates to what is visible to the mind's eye as well as to the organ of sight, and accordingly both to propositions contained in sentences and clauses and to physical objects referred to by means of nouns and pronouns and nominal phrases. This would imply that the interpretations of Kühner-Gerth: 'offenbar, bekanntlich, ja',[1] and of Brugmann-Thumb: 'δή wies auf das dem Sprechenden[2] gegenwärtig Vorliegende und ihm klar vor Augen Liegende hin'[3] are more to the point than Denniston's 'the essential meaning seems clearly to be 'verily', 'actually', 'indeed'. δή denotes that a thing really and truly is so: or that it is very much so'.[4] On the other hand I would concur with Denniston in rejecting the derivation, countenanced by these German grammarians, of this and other uses from a *temporal* basic meaning.

2. *Evidential*

Before turning to 'logical' and/or 'connective' δή I shall illustrate the application of δή to what is evident in some non-sensory way by examples from the *Phaedo*.

---

[1] § 500.3, p. 126; cf. § 500.1, p. 122: 'Bekanntes, Offenbares, *Augenscheinliches*' (italics JMvO).
[2] It would be more accurate to say: 'auf dasjenige was von dem Sprechenden als dem Hörenden gegenwärtig Vorliegend(es) (...) vorgestellt wird hin', just as, in a more explicit and emphatic way, ἰδού 'look' does. 'Here you have ... ', cf. French 'voici' and 'voilà'.
[3] § 631, p. 630.
[4] *GP* 203-4.

2.1. *Quoting*

δή is obviously appropriate when quoting one's interlocutor's very own words:

115 C 3
θάπτωμεν δέ σε τίνα τρόπον; – ... ἐρωτᾷ δὴ πῶς με θάπτῃ.

85 E 2
ἐμοὶ ... οὐ πάνυ φαίνεται ἱκανῶς εἰρῆσθαι.– ... ἀλλὰ λέγε ὅπῃ δὴ οὐχ ἱκανῶς.[1]

At 86 E 6 the particle may be facing both ways,

... ἀλλ' ἄγε, ἦ δ' ὅς, ὦ Κέβης, λέγε, τί ἦν τὸ ...
– Λέγω δή, ἦ δ' ὃς ὁ Κέβης. ἐμοὶ γὰρ φαίνεται ...

i.e. it may pick up Socrates' λέγε and at the same time point forward to Cebes' actual reply ἐμοὶ γὰρ φαίνεται κτλ.

2.2. *Naming*

δή is also used when the proper word for, or name of, a thing is appended to a description of it:

80 C 3
... ἐπειδὰν ἀποθάνῃ ὁ ἄνθρωπος, τὸ μὲν ὁρατὸν αὐτοῦ, τὸ σῶμα, ..., ὃ δὴ νεκρὸν καλοῦμεν, ...

96 A 8
... ταύτης τῆς σοφίας ἣν δὴ καλοῦσι περὶ φύσεως ἱστορίαν·

109 B 8
... αὐτὴν δὲ τὴν γῆν καθαρὰν ἐν καθαρῷ κεῖσθαι τῷ οὐρανῷ ἐν ᾧπέρ ἐστι τὰ ἄστρα, ὃν δὴ αἰθέρα ὀνομάζειν τοὺς πολλοὺς τῶν περὶ τὰ τοιαῦτα εἰωθότων λέγειν ...

113 C 1
... ὁ τέταρτος ἐκπίπτει ..., ὃν δὴ ἐπονομάζουσι Στύγιον, καὶ τὴν λίμνην ... Στύγα·

'... which, as we all know, is called ...'.

---

[1] At 96 A 3 in (95 E 4) Καὶ ὁ Κέβης ... ἔφη ...· ἔστι δὲ ταῦτα ἃ λέγω. ὁ οὖν Σωκράτης ... ἔφη ...· ... ἐγὼ οὖν ...· ἔπειτα ἄν τί σοι χρήσιμον φαίνεται ὧν ἂν λέγω, πρὸς τὴν πειθὼ περὶ ὧν δὴ λέγεις χρήσῃ we have the same usage of δή if, with Burnet, we adopt Baumann's conjecture δὴ λέγεις, which would explain both λέγεις (T, Stob.) and ἂν λέγῃς (BW) as attempts to remedy an initial corruption to ἂν λέγεις. For variation between ἄν and δή cf. W.J. Verdenius in *Mnemosyne* (IV) 11 (1958) 228-9 who, referring to Schanz, *Novae commentationes Platonicae*, Würzburg 1871, pp. 50-2, compares *Ly.* 204 A 3 ... λόγοις ὧν ἡδέως ἄν (T) / δή (B) σοι μεταδιδοῖμεν.

2.3. *Empirical*

The particle is used in referring to a well-known empirical fact:

60 A 4

τοιαῦτ' ἄττα εἶπεν, οἷα δὴ εἰώθασιν αἱ γυναῖκες ...

'... as women will do – you know what they're like ...'.

81 D 1

ψυχή ... περὶ τὰ μνήματα ... κυλινδουμένη, περὶ ἃ δὴ καὶφθη ἄττα ψυ-
χῶν σκιοειδῆ φαντάσματα...

110 B 8

... χρώμασιν ... ὧν καὶ τὰ ἐνθάδε εἶναι χρώματα ὥσπερ δείγματα, οἷς
δὴ οἱ γραφῆς καταχρῶνται ...

68 A 4

... παιδικῶν ... ἀποθανόντων πολλοὶ δὴ ἑκόντες ἠθέλησαν εἰς Ἅιδου
μετελθεῖν

—though the combination of δή with πολύς is stereotyped, and to that
extent less significant, just as is that of δή with μάλιστα and other super-
latives: e.g.

90 B 9

καὶ μάλιστα δὴ οἱ περὶ τοὺς ἀντιλογικοὺς λόγους διατρίψαντες οἶσθ'
ὅτι τελευτῶντες οἴονται ...

2.4. *Motivated by the speaker's previous words*

Most often, however, a justification for presenting a notion as evident
may be found in the speaker's own preceding words. We can see that the
exact scope of the particle is not always easy to define, and in particular,
that there is no hard and fast dividing-line between cases of δή marking
phrases referring to objects and of δή marking clauses expressing propositions, for instance at 59 B 6:

πάντες οἱ παρόντες ... οὕτω διεκείμεθα ... εἰς δὲ ἡμῶν καὶ διαφερόντως,
'Απολλόδωρος ... – ... Ἔτυχον δέ ... τινες παραγενόμενοι; – Οὗτός τε
δὴ ὁ 'Απολλόδωρος τῶν ἐπιχωρίων παρῆν καί ...

This is only one out of many instances of what may be called anaphoric
δή, i.e. δή accompanying a demonstrative pronoun or otherwise deictic
expression referring the hearer to, and more often than not summarizing,
an earlier expression:

'this Apollodorus that we mentioned';

yet even here the interpretation

> ('who were present?'–) 'this Apollodorus was obviously present (as I implied just now in πάντες ... Ἀπολλόδωρος)'

is not implausible.

What follows is a sample of evidential δή motivated within the same utterance.

62 B 4

λόγος, ὡς ἔν τινι φρουρᾷ ἐσμεν οἱ ἄνθρωποι καὶ οὐ δεῖ δὴ ἑαυτὸν ἐκ ταύτης λύειν ...

The point of a φρουρά is not that you desert from it.

72 A 7

ὁμολογεῖται ἄρα ἡμῖν καὶ ταύτῃ τοὺς ζῶντας ἐκ τῶν τεθνεώτων γεγονέναι οὐδὲν ἧττον ἢ τοὺς τεθνεῶτας ἐκ τῶν ζώντων, τούτου δὲ ὄντος ἱκανόν που ἐδόκει τεκμήριον εἶναι ὅτι ἀναγκαῖον τὰς τῶν τεθνεώτων ψυχὰς εἶναί που, ὅθεν δὴ πάλιν γίγνεσθαι

Their γίγνεσθαι was implied in the γεγονέναι I just ascribed to them.

82 D 6

ἡγούμενοι οὐ δεῖν ἐναντία τῇ φιλοσοφίᾳ πράττειν ... ταύτῃ δὴ τρέπονται ἐκείνῃ ἑπόμενοι, ᾗ ἐκείνη ὑφηγεῖται.

If you think you shouldn't oppose it, you naturally follow its lead.

89 E 1

ἡ ... μισανθρωπία ἐνδύεται ἐκ τοῦ σφόδρα τινὶ πιστεῦσαι ... ἔπειτα ὀλίγον ὕστερον εὑρεῖν τοῦτον ... ἄπιστον, καὶ αὖθις ἕτερον· καὶ ὅταν τοῦτο πολλάκις πάθῃ τις ..., τελευτῶν δὴ θαμὰ προσκρούων μισεῖ τε πάντας ...

The main clause involves the obvious in several ways: τελευτῶν merely makes explicit what ὅταν ... πολλάκις with aorist might have led us to expect anyway; θαμὰ προσκρούων summarizes and visualizes[1] the experience of repeated disappointment just described, and with μισεῖ τε πάντας the aetiology of μισανθρωπία comes full circle.

91 D 4

... πολυχρονιώτερόν γε εἶναι ψυχὴν σώματος, ἀλλὰ τόδε ἄδηλον παντί, μὴ πολλὰ δὴ σώματα καὶ πολλάκις κατατρίψασα ἡ ψυχὴ τὸ τελευταῖον σῶμα καταλιποῦσα νῦν αὐτὴ ἀπολλύηται ...

---

[1] προσκρούω 'be offended, rebuffed' rather than (LSJ) 'take offence, be angry'. "repeated (hard) knocks" Hackforth, Gallop.

If soul is longer-lived than body, it is clear (δή) that she may wear out quite a few bodies, and yet obscure (ἄδηλον) whether she will survive the last of them.

93 E 1: it being agreed (D 1-7) that ψυχή = ἁρμονία = ἡρμόσθαι, and that none of these admits of more or less,

> οὐκοῦν ψυχὴ ἐπειδὴ οὐδὲν μᾶλλον οὐδ' ἧττον ἄλλη ἄλλης αὐτὸ τοῦτο, ψυχή, ἐστίν, οὐδὲ δὴ μᾶλλον οὐδὲ ἧττον ἥρμοσται;

As often, we have a reshuffle rather than a move.

95 D 3

> ... αὐτὸ τὸ εἰς ἀνθρώπου σῶμα ἐλθεῖν ἀρχὴ ἦν αὐτῇ ὀλέθρου, ὥσπερ νόσος· καὶ ταλαιπωρουμένη τε δὴ τοῦτον τὸν βίον ζῴη καὶ ...

101 B 1

> ... τῇ κεφαλῇ σμικρᾷ οὔσῃ τὸν μείζω μείζω εἶναι, καὶ τοῦτο δὴ τέρας εἶναι, τὸ σμικρῷ τινι μέγαν τινὰ εἶναι ...

2.5. Self-evidential

Finally, δή is found in contexts devoid of any explicit consideration which might induce us to accept the truth of the statement in question as evident; it is simply being taken for granted that we shall acknowledge it as such: the statement is supposed to be *self*-evident.

Here, as it has been felicitously expressed,[1] δή may equal ἴσθ' ὅτι just as easily as οἶσθ' ὅτι:

70 E 4

> ... οἷον τὸ καλὸν τῷ αἰσχρῷ ἐναντίον που καὶ δίκαιον ἀδίκῳ, καὶ ἄλλα δὴ μυρία οὕτως ἔχει.

91 B 2

> εἰ μὲν τυγχάνει ἀληθῆ ὄντα ἃ λέγω, καλῶς δὴ ἔχει τὸ πεισθῆναι·

'If what I am saying happens to be the truth, it is obviously good to have been persuaded of it'—a fairly trivial statement, not likely to be disputed.

The chief interest of these occurrences is in the light they throw on the rhetorical uses δή may be put to. In contexts such as those quoted under 4.2.2 & 3 above, the particle at times seems almost to offer an apology for stating the obvious – for the kind of redundancy which is natural in ordinary speech: 'the visible part of dead man, the body, which, needless to

---

[1] By Professor C.J. Ruijgh in a personal communication.

say, we call a corpse';[1] 'the colours here below, used, I need not tell you, by painters'.[2] What we may call self-evidential δή, on the other hand, could just as soon unconsciously reveal a deep conviction shared by the participants in the conversation, or, less harmlessly, bluff the other party into granting a point which is not as uncontroversial as it may seem to be.

3. *In arguments*

According to Denniston[3] δή as a connective 'like οὖν, expresses *post hoc* and *propter hoc*, and anything between the two, tending on the whole to denote a less strictly logical sequence than οὖν. The *propter hoc* is subsequently referred to in *GP* as its logical connective sense, the *post hoc* as temporal; in addition to these we are acquainted with 'progressive' δή,[4] which 'expresses something intermediate between temporal and logical connexion, and marks the progression from one idea to a second of which the consideration naturally follows'.

For the connective use of δή with 'full logical force' three Platonic references are given.[5] That at *Phdr.* 245 C 7 is very plausible:

ψυχὴ πᾶσα ἀθάνατος. τὸ γὰρ αὐτοκίνητον[6] ἀθάνατον· τὸ δ' ἄλλο κινοῦν καὶ ὑπ' ἄλλου κινούμενον, παῦλαν ἔχον κινήσεως, παῦλαν ἔχει ζωῆς. Μόνον δὴ τὸ αὐτὸ κινοῦν, ἅτε οὐκ ἀπολεῖπον ἑαυτό, οὔποτε λήγει κινούμενον, ἀλλὰ καί ...

It is tempting to read this as the conclusion to a proof by elimination, and translate 'therefore'. But in fact we are only at the beginning of an argument, which continues: '(what moves itself never ends its movement, but also) provides all other moving things with a source and origin of motion. Now an origin is unoriginated, and since it is unoriginated it must be indestructible, i.e. immortal, and this is soul'. The beginning is a little less straightforward, but I think it can be understood as follows: (1) 'soul is immortal' – to be proved; (2) 'what moves itself is immortal' – would be sufficient ground for believing (1) if we could prove it; (3) 'what moves other things and is moved by something elso may end its movement and lose its life' – this is not what we are looking for; (4) '*obviously*, it is only what moves itself which can*not* desert itself and stop moving (but still

---

[1] 80 C 3, p. 142 above.
[2] 110 B 8, p. 143 above.
[3] *GP* p. 237-8.
[4] P. 239.
[5] P. 239.
[6] V.l. ἀεικίνητον.

can move other things)'– this is our candidate for the function soul is required to perform.

By contrast Denniston's quotation of *Euthyd.* 275 B 2

ἔστι δὲ νέος· φοβούμεθα δὴ περὶ αὐτῷ

would seem to be far more apt as an illustration of 'progressive' δή, in so far as this 'marks the progression to a second idea of which the consideration naturally follows'. At the same time it shows very clearly that this use cannot sensibly be classified as 'intermediate between temporal and logical connexion', for the notion of a continuum leading from *post hoc* to *propter hoc*, while it is entirely appropriate to the description of events in time, simply does not apply here: there *is* no *post hoc* in fact, but only in the trivial sense that one statement by one speaker necessarily either precedes or follows another. We have fallen victims to the widespread loose and vague use of the word logical, for neither the connexion between the two statements nor that between the two facts, that 'he is young' and that 'we are afraid for him', has anything to do with logic.

Moreover, even granting that we do have a 'progression to a second idea of which the consideration naturally follows', there is still no need to invent a separate category to cover this; δή is sufficiently motivated as conveying that the second statement is obviously acceptable, given the first.

The same applies to Denniston's third reference, *Phdr.* 239 A, which actually covers two instances, at A 1 and A 7:

(A 1) it is presupposed that sexual desire is a slavery to pleasure and a disease,

νοσοῦντι δὲ πᾶν ἡδὺ τὸ μὴ ἀντιτεῖνον, κρεῖττον δὲ καὶ ἴσον ἐχθρόν. οὔτε δὴ κρείττω οὔτε ἰσούμενον ἑκὼν ἐραστὴς παιδικὰ ἀνέξεται ...

—and (A 7) not only that, but it is in the lover's interest to keep his favourite in this inferior condition:

τοσούτων κακῶν καὶ ἔτι πλειόνων κατὰ τὴν διάνοιαν ἐραστὴν ἐρωμένῳ ἀνάγκη γιγνομένων τε καὶ φύσει ἐνόντων τῶν μὲν ἥδεσθαι, τὰ δὲ παρασκευάζειν, ἢ στέρεσθαι τοῦ παραυτίκα ἡδέος. φθονερὸν δὴ ἀνάγκη εἶναι ...

he will inevitably try to confirm the other's failings; he will obviously be jealous of all potential forces for good.

It looks as if we can dispense with the category of progressive δή as well as with that of logical δή—and, incidentally, with that of temporal δή.[1] To explain the occurrences of the particle brought under these headings all that we need is an evidential meaning and the recognition that, regardless of the presence or absence of any coordinator or connector, it is natural to expect that the supposed self-evidence of the statement finds some support in the preceding statement(s). It remains to apply this reduced conceptual apparatus to all syntactically comparable occurrences in the *Phaedo*.

4. *Quasi-connective instances from* Phaedo

At some places in the *Phaedo* verbal repetition or an anaphoric pronoun helps to make a notion more evident. At one of these the scope of the particle is clearly limited to the nominal phrase in which it occurs:

98 B 7[2]

... οὐκ ἂν ἀπεδόμην πολλοῦ τὰς ἐλπίδας ...
... Ἀπὸ δὴ θαυμαστῆς ἐλπίδος ... ᾠχόμην φερόμενος ...

'I would not have sold my hopes for a large sum; you can see it was a marvellous hope I was deceived of'.

At 106 E 1

... εἴ τι ... ἀθάνατόν ἐστιν, παρὰ πάντων ἂν ὁμολογηθείη μηδέποτε ἀπόλλυσθαι.
– Παρὰ πάντων μέντοι νὴ Δί', ἔφη, ...
– Ὁπότε δὴ τὸ ἀθάνατον καὶ ἀδιάφθορόν ἐστιν, ἄλλο τι ψυχὴ ἤ, εἰ ἀθάνατος ..., καὶ ἀνώλεθρος ἂν εἴη;

the scope is probably just the subordinate clause.

At 97 D 5

(97 B 8) ... ἀκούσας ... τινός ... λέγοντος ὡς ... νοῦς ἐστιν ὁ ... αἴτιος, ταύτῃ δὴ τῇ αἰτίᾳ ἥσθην τε καὶ ἔδοξέ μοι ...
ταῦτα δὴ λογιζόμενος ἅσμενος ηὑρηκέναι ᾤμην διδάσκαλον τῆς αἰτίας ...

it is most likely to extend over the first main clause, which approximates to a summary.

84 B 4 ss. rounds off an argument which began as long ago as 77 D 7-E 1, on whether we stand in danger of having our souls scattered by the winds (διαφυσᾶν 77 D 8-E 1) at our death. The conclusion has been anticipated at 80 D 5-E 1 in

---

[1] See p. 150 below.
[2] Cf. W.J. Verdenius, *Mnemosyne* IV 11 (1958) 230.

ἡ δὲ ψυχὴ ἄρα ... ἡ τοιαύτη καὶ οὕτω πεφυκυῖα ἀπαλλαττομένη τοῦ σώματος εὐθὺς διαπεφύσηται καὶ ἀπόλωλεν, ὥς φασιν οἱ πολλοὶ ἄνθρωποι; ... πολλοῦ γε δεῖ ...

It is confirmed from 84 A 8 onwards,

... τὸ ἀληθὲς ... θεωμένη καὶ ὑπ' ἐκείνου τρεφομένη ... ἐκ δὴ τῆς τοιαύτης τροφῆς οὐδὲν δεινὸν μὴ φοβηθῇ ... ὅπως μὴ ... διαφυσηθεῖσα ... οἴχηται ...

where δή may recall that we have seen it before, and in particular that the *terms* in which it is expressed are familiar: τροφῆς (B 4) after τρεφομένη (B 1), but even more significantly the various forms of the verb διαφυσᾶν, which in Plato is confined to these three passages.

59 A 1

οὔτε ... ἔλεος εἰσῄει· εὐδαίμων γάρ μοι ἐφαίνετο ... διὰ δὴ ταῦτα οὐδὲν πάνυ μοι ἐλεεινὸν εἰσῄει ...

is interesting in that διὰ ταῦτα takes care of the consecutive or causal connection. δή probably helps to set this apart from what is mere repetition:

'I did not feel sorry ... here you have *why* I did not feel sorry'.

δή is also combined with διὰ ταῦτα, now following the demonstrative pronoun, *in apodosi* at 98 E 3

ἐπειδὴ 'Αθηναίοις ἔδοξε βέλτιον εἶναι ... διὰ ταῦτα δὴ καὶ ἐμοὶ βέλτιον αὖ δέδοκται

where the connecting is done by ἐπειδή; with the same conjunction, but now without the adjunct διὰ ταῦτα, apodotic δή is found at 60 C 7

ἐπειδὴ (ὑπὸ τοῦ δεσμοῦ) ἦν ἐν τῷ σκέλει τὸ ἀλγεινόν, ἥκειν δὴ φαίνεται ἐπακολουθοῦν τὸ ἡδύ ...

and at 93 E 1 quoted above.[1]

Elsewhere repetition and anaphora are less conspicuous; in compensation, 112 B 3 has at least a visualizing aspect:

ἡ δὲ αἰτία ἐστὶν τοῦ ἐκρεῖν τε ... καὶ εἰσρεῖν ... ὅτι πυθμένα οὐκ ἔχει ... τὸ ὑγρὸν τοῦτο. αἰωρεῖται δὴ καὶ κυμαίνει ἄνω καὶ κάτω ...

flowing in and out is an analytical description, which merely implies, and at once explains, that the *content* of a body of liquid is altered; tossing and

---

[1] P. 145.

swelling is to some extent a more graphic description of the same process, but now we see its *volume* and *surface* in perpetual change and motion.

95 B 3

... πάνυ ἐθαύμαζον εἴ τι ἕξει τις χρήσασθαι τῷ λόγῳ αὐτοῦ· πάνυ οὖν μοι ἀτόπως ἔδοξεν εὐθὺς τὴν πρώτην ἔφοδον οὐ δέξασθαι τοῦ σοῦ λόγου. ταὐτὰ δὴ οὐκ ἂν θαυμάσαιμι καὶ τὸν τοῦ Κάδμου λόγον εἰ πάθοι.

'I was surprised at what you did to an earlier λόγος; I would not now be surprised if you did this again.'

With δή, which brings ταὐτά especially into relief, Cebes intimates that his present disposition is sufficiently motivated by his past experience.

99 E 4

Ἔδοξε τοίνυν[1] μοι ... δεῖν εὐλαβηθῆναι μὴ ... τὴν ψυχὴν τυφλωθείην βλέπων πρὸς τὰ πράγματα ... ἔδοξε δή μοι χρῆναι εἰς τοὺς λόγους καταφυγόντα ἐν ἐκείνοις σκοπεῖν τῶν ὄντων τὴν ἀλήθειαν.

δή makes the flight into the λόγοι appear to be the obvious, or indeed the only, alternative to looking the blinding πράγματα or ὄντα straight in the face.

91 E 1

... ἆρα ἄλλ᾽ ἢ ταῦτ᾽ ἐστίν, ὦ Σ. τε καὶ Κ., ἃ δεῖ ἡμᾶς ἐπισκοπεῖσθαι; – Συνωμολογείτην δὴ ταῦτ᾽ εἶναι ἄμφω. – Πότερον οὖν, ἔφη, πάντας τοὺς ... ἢ ...

This is set down by Denniston[2] as an example of δή being 'clearly temporal', where it 'marks a new stage in a narrative'. I submit that it is more likely to convey that they *duly* agreed, as they were expected to do, and were indeed invited to do by ἆρ᾽ ἄλλ᾽ ἤ.

One passage remains, which is particularly interesting in that it contains two instances of δή alternating with two instances of ἄρα:[3]

104 D 5-E 6

ἃ ἂν ἡ τῶν τριῶν ἰδέα κατάσχῃ, ἀνάγκη αὐτοῖς ... εἶναι ... περιττοῖς . – πάνυ γε.
– ἐπὶ τὸ τοιοῦτον δή, φαμέν, ἡ ἐναντία ἰδέα ἐκείνη τῇ μορφῇ ἣ ἂν τοῦτο ἀπεργάζηται οὐδέποτ᾽ ἂν ἔλθοι. – οὐ γάρ. –εἰργάζετο δέ γε ἡ περιττή; – ναί. – ἐναντία δὲ ταύτῃ ἡ τοῦ ἀρτίου; – ναί. – ἐπὶ τὰ τρία ἄρα ἡ τοῦ ἀρτίου ἰδέα οὐδέποτε ἥξει. – οὐ δῆτα. – ἄμοιρα δὴ τοῦ ἀρτίου τὰ τρία. – ἄμοιρα. – ἀνάρτιος ἄρα ἡ τριάς. – ναί.

---

[1] Cf. p. 154 below.
[2] *GP* 238.
[3] For which see p. 104 above.

The first δή (D 9) marks as a truth plain to see what later turns out to serve as a premiss. Following two substitutions a conclusion is reached with the first ἄρα at E1. This is restated in a succinct and technical formula with the second ἄρα at E 5: 'the triad' (ἡ τριάς E 5) instead of 'three' (τὰ τρία E 1), an abstract negative 'uneven' (ἀνάρτιος E 5) instead of the ordinary language *verbum proprium* 'odd' (περιττοῖς D 7). Between the two ἄρα-sentences of E 1 and E 5 we get the same statement in yet a different wording (at E 3), the point of which must be to ease the transition between the other two, retaining two nominal phrases from the one that precedes but anticipating the word order of the one that follows.

δή suggests—aptly, in such a context of paraphrase—that there is nothing left to prevent our understanding the sentence it forms part of, and acknowledging its truth.

CHAPTER FIVE

TOINYN

1. *Distinctive uses in* Phaedo

Of τοίνυν it is stated by Denniston[1] that 'its logical force is for the most part not very strong, rather weaker, on the whole, than that of οὖν, which comes nearest to it in meaning'. Its uses are then divided into (I) logical[2] and (II) transitional,[3] though it is conceded that (II) 'merges imperceptibly into' (I), and that 'no sharp line can be drawn between' the two.[4] We shall deal with some of the examples in *GP* taken from other dialogues than the *Phaedo* later on, but it may be instructive to test some general observations against the *Phaedo* first.

1.1. *Introductory*

'τοίνυν (...) in Plato, speaking generally, is much commoner in dialogue than in continuous speech'.[5] Species of its use in dialogue are given under a number of headings, among them 'introducing an answer' represented 'as springing from the actual words, or general attitude, of the previous speaker',[6] 'responding to an invitation to speak',[7] 'rejoinder introduced by τοίνυν' conveying 'a comment on, or criticism of, the previous speaker's words',[8] 'introducing a fresh item in a series'.[9]

An affinity with the beginning of an utterance is marked in the *Phaedo*: the only exception among twenty-one instances is

109 A 6

(D 2) περὶ γῆς ... – (D 8) ὁ βίος μοι δοκεῖ ὁ ἐμός ... τῷ μήκει τοῦ λόγου οὐκ ἐξαρκεῖν. τὴν μέντοι ἰδέαν τῆς γῆς οἵαν πέπεισμαι εἶναι ... οὐδέν με κωλύει λέγειν. – ᾽Αλλ᾽ ... καὶ ταῦτα ἀρκεῖ. – Πέπεισμαι τοίνυν ... ἐγὼ ὡς πρῶτον μέν, ... πρῶτον μὲν τοίνυν ... τοῦτο πέπεισμαι

---

[1] *GP* 568.
[2] P. 569.
[3] P. 574.
[4] Ib.
[5] *GP* 569.
[6] Ib.
[7] P. 571.
[8] P. 572.
[9] P. 575.

which merely resumes the unexceptional 108 E 4. This tendency has it parallels outside Plato: 'All the 80 Aristophanic examples occur near the opening of an answer' (*GP* 569), 'Xenophon's occasional use of τοίνυν at the opening of a set speech' (*GP* 573). An interesting corollary is that when Denniston refers to 'the connective force' of the particle,[1] this should probably be taken to apply neither to coordination nor to the role, sometimes assigned to connectors, of marking a connection between propositions normally expressed by the same speaker and often within the same utterance, but to a third function, that of defining one's position in relation to that stated by the preceding speaker.

1.2. *Volitional*

An important observation made by Des Places and quoted by Denniston about the distribution of τοίνυν is that 'in about half the Platonic instances it goes with imperative or hortative subjunctive (Des Places)'.[2] The proportion in the *Phaedo* is rather smaller: with imperative five out of 21 instances (60 D 8, 70 D 7, 72 A 11, 96 A 6, 104 B 6), with the subjunctive only one (90 D 9). Several other pasages, however, invite comparison with these six. Thus we find two instances of a first person indicative with τοίνυν, at 89 C 9 and 115 C 2:

89 C 9
 'Αλλ'.... πρὸς δύο λέγεται οὐδ' ὁ 'Ηρακλῆς οἷός τε εἶναι. –'Αλλὰ καὶ ἐμέ ... τὸν 'Ιόλεων παρακάλει ... – Παρακαλῶ τοίνυν, ... οὐχ ὡς 'Ηρα- κλῆς, ἀλλ' ὡς 'Ιόλεως τὸν 'Ηρακλῆ.

and 115 C 2
 (B 2) ... τί δὲ τούτοις ἢ ἐμοὶ ἐπιστέλλεις ... – ἅπερ ἀεὶ λέγω ... – ταῦτα μὲν τοίνυν προθυμησόμεθα ... οὕτω ποιεῖν· θάπτωμεν δέ σε τίνα τρόπον;

which resemble the case of τοίνυν with imperative, e.g. at 60 D 8

 εἰπὲ τί χρὴ λέγειν. – Λέγε τοίνυν ... τἀληθῆ, ὅτι ...

in two respects: first, the verbs communicate a volition;[3] secondly, they do so in response to another expression of will. This combination takes the form of an exploiting of the interlocutor's assent at 70 D 7 and 96 A 6:

70 D 7
 (C 4) σκεψώμεθα δὲ αὐτὸ τῇδέ πη, εἴτ' ἄρα ἐν "Αιδου εἰσὶν αἱ ψυχαὶ

---

[1] P. 568.
[2] Des Places 285-6, quoted *GP* 569.
[3] Alternatively, if παρακαλῶ at 89 C 9 is present indicative, as Robin and Gallop

154 CHAPTER FIVE

τελευτησάντων τῶν ἀνθρώπων εἴτε καὶ οὔ. ... – Πάνυ μὲν οὖν ... – Μὴ
τοίνυν κατ' ἀνθρώπων ... σκόπει μόνον τοῦτο ...

and 96 A 6

(95 E 9) ... δεῖ περὶ γενέσεως καὶ φθορᾶς τὴν αἰτίαν διαπραγματεύεσθαι,
ἐγὼ οὖν σοι δίειμι περὶ αὐτῶν, ἐὰν βούλῃ, τά γε ἐμὰ πάθη· ἔπειτα ἄν τί
σοι χρήσιμον φαίνηται ὧν ἂν λέγω, πρὸς τὴν πειθὼ περὶ ὧν δὴ λέγεις
χρήσῃ. – Ἀλλὰ μέν, ... βούλομαί γε. –Ἄκουε τοίνυν ὡς ἐροῦντος. ἐγὼ
γὰρ ...

The two volitional characteristics are not inseparable, and neither of them
is all-pervasive. The second one, response *to* will, is found without the
first at 99 D 4, 110 B 5, and 108 E 4 – 109 A 9:

99 D 4

βούλει σοι ... ἐπίδειξιν ποιήσωμαι ...; – ὑπερφυῶς ... ὡς βούλομαι. –
ἔδοξε τοίνυν μοι ...

at 110 B 5

... ἄξιον ἀκοῦσαι ... – ... ἡδέως ἂν ἀκούσαιμεν. – λέγεται τοίνυν ...

and at 108 E 4, 109 A 6, 9

... οἵαν πέπεισμαι εἶναι ... οὐδέν με κωλύει λέγειν. – (Ἀλλ') ... καὶ
ταῦτα ἀρκεῖ. – πέπεισμαι τοίνυν ... ἐγὼ ὡς πρῶτον μέν, ... πρῶτον μὲν
τοίνυν ... τοῦτο πέπεισμαι. – καὶ ὀρθῶς γε ... – ἔτι τοίνυν ... (followed
by an accusative-cum-infinitive depending on πέπεισμαι)

The first one, communication *of* will, is found without the second at 72 A
11, 90 D 9, and 104 B 6:

72 A 11

ὁμολογεῖται ἄρα ἡμῖν καὶ ταύτῃ ..., τούτου δὲ ὄντος ἱκανόν που ἐδόκει
τεκμήριον εἶναι ὅτι ἀναγκαῖον ... – δοκεῖ μοι ... ἐκ τῶν ὡμολογημένων
ἀναγκαῖον οὕτως ἔχειν. – ἰδὲ τοίνυν οὕτως ... ὅτι οὐδ' ἀδίκως ὡμολο-
γήκαμεν, ὡς ἐμοὶ δοκεῖ. εἰ γὰρ μὴ ...

90 D 9

(C 8) οὐκοῦν ... οἰκτρὸν ἂν εἴη τὸ πάθος, εἰ ... – ... οἰκτρὸν δῆτα. –
πρῶτον μὲν τοίνυν ... τοῦτο εὐλαβηθῶμεν ...

and 104 B 6

... συγχωρεῖς ἢ οὔ; – πῶς γὰρ οὔκ; ... – ὅ τοίνυν ... βούλομαι δηλῶσαι,
ἄθρει.

---

construe it ("Bon, je t' appelle! Fis-je". – "'All right,' I said, 'I summon you,' ..."), rather
than future indicative, as Hackforth does ("'Yes, I will,' I replied, ..."), it may be classified
as a performative. And formally it could of course be present subjunctive.

At 71 C 9 too, in

> (C 1) Τί οὖν; ἔφη, τῷ ζῆν ἐστί τι ἐναντίον, ὥσπερ τῷ ἐγρηγορέναι τὸ καθεύδειν; – Πάνυ μὲν οὖν. – ... – Τὴν μὲν τοίνυν ἑτέραν συζυγίαν ὧν νυνδὴ ἔλεγον ἐγώ σοι, ἔφη, ἐρῶ, ὁ Σωκράτης· σὺ δέ μοι τὴν ἑτέραν.

the presence of τοίνυν is partly motivated by the element of will: not just that represented in the surface structure by ἐρῶ, but more particularly that which might be supplied explicitly to the elliptic δέ-clause, in the form of an imperative or a second person future indicative such as '... and you <(will) tell> me the other one'.

This presupposes that the force of the particle extends over the entire period introduced by it, including the directive second half. I submit that it does so likewise at 104 E 7 and at 92 C 8:

104 E 7

> (D 5) ἃ ἂν ἡ τῶν τριῶν ἰδέα κατάσχῃ, ἀνάγκη αὐτοῖς οὐ μόνον τρισὶν εἶναι ἀλλὰ καὶ περιττοῖς ... (D 9) ἐπὶ τὸ τοιοῦτον δή ... ἡ ἐναντία ἰδέα ἐκείνῃ τῇ μορφῇ ἣ ἂν τοῦτο ἀπεργάζηται οὐδέποτ' ἂν ἔλθοι ... (D 14) εἰργάζετο δέ γε ἡ περιττή ... ἐναντία δὲ ταύτῃ ἡ τοῦ ἀρτίου ... (E 1) ἐπὶ τὰ τρία ἄρα ἡ τοῦ ἀρτίου ἰδέα οὐδέποτε ἥξει. – οὐ δῆτα. – ... – ... – ... – ναί. – ὃ τοίνυν ἔλεγον ὁρίσασθαι, ποῖα οὐκ ἐναντία τινὶ ὄντα ὅμως οὐ δέχεται αὐτό, τὸ ἐναντίον ... ἀλλ' ὅρα δὴ εἰ οὕτως ὁρίζῃ ...

where, after a parenthesis of three lines, δή at 105 A 1 comes to reinforce the appeal announced by τοίνυν.[1]

92 C 8

> (C 2) ... οὗτος οὖν σοι ὁ λόγος ἐκείνῳ πῶς συνᾴσεται; – οὐδαμῶς ... – καὶ μήν, ... πρέπει γε εἴπερ τῳ ἄλλῳ λόγῳ συνῳδῷ εἶναι καὶ τῷ περὶ ἁρμονίας. – πρέπει γάρ ... – οὗτος τοίνυν ... σοι οὐ συνῳδός· ἀλλ' ὅρα πότερον αἱρῇ τῶν λόγων ...

It turns out that an affinity of τοίνυν with the communication of will could account for a considerably greater proportion of its occurrences than even the frequency of its coincidence with imperative and hortative subjunctive—which is high in itself—would lead us to expect, and it is worth noting that the element of exploiting assent, which was found at 70 D 7 and 96 A 6,[2] is present in most, if not all, of these instances.

---

[1] As Professor C.J. Ruijgh points out (personal communication).
[2] P. 154 above.

2. *In arguments in* Phaedo

2.1. *In formal conclusions*

We have seen[1] that the ascription of a 'logical force' to τοίνυν in *GP* is
not without reservations. Among the classes distinguished there we shall
concentrate on those which promise to yield the clearest examples of it.
This would seem to apply first of all to I.(2), τοίνυν 'in conclusions of
formal syllogisms'.[2] Two out of three examples given here are from the
Sophist.

At 238 B 2:

μὴ ὄντι δέ τι τῶν ὄντων ἀρά ποτε προσγίγνεσθαι φήσομεν δυνατὸν εἶναι;
– καὶ πῶς; – ἀριθμὸν δὴ τὸν σύμπαντα τῶν ὄντων τίθεμεν. – εἴπερ γε καὶ
ἄλλο τι θετέον ὡς ὄν. – μὴ τοίνυν μηδ' ἐπιχειρῶμεν ἀριθμοῦ μήτε πλῆθος
μήτε ἓν πρὸς τὸ μὴ ὂν προσφέρειν. – οὔκουν ἂν ὀρθῶς γε, ὡς ἔοικεν,
ἐπιχειροῖμεν, ὥς φησιν ὁ λόγος.

Here it would perhaps be more accurate to say that a formal syllogism is
easily distilled from what we actually find:

'if no ὄν can be added to μὴ ὄν, and all number is ὄν, then no number can be
added to μὴ ὄν'.

But what the guest from Elea says is

'... then *let's* not *try* to bring any number to μὴ ὄν',

which is a proposal rather than a proposition; τοίνυν, I submit, hints that
Theaetetus is bound by his earlier admissions to consent to it. Accordingly Theaetetus' reply is not 'You're right' or 'That's true', simply granting the visitor's point, but 'No: we could never do so correctly ...', responding to the visitor's appeal.

255 B 5 is closely parallel:

ὅτιπερ ἂν κοινῇ προσείπωμεν κίνησιν καὶ στάσιν, τοῦτο οὐδέτερον αὐ-
τοῖν οἷόν τε εἶναι. – ... – ... – κομιδῇ γε. – μετέχετον μὴν ἄμφω ταὐτοῦ
καὶ θατέρου. – ναί. – μὴ τοίνυν λέγωμεν κίνησίν γ' εἶναι ταὐτὸν ἢ θάτε-
ρον, μηδ' αὖ στάσιν. – μὴ γάρ.

'What may be predicated of both motion and rest cannot be identical with
either' – 'Quite so' – 'Now both partake of sameness and otherness' – 'They
do' – 'Let's not identify either of them with these, then!' – 'No, let's not';

---

[1] P. 152 above.
[2] *GP* 571.

again, the use of τοίνυν rather than ἄρα is motivated precisely by the personal element which distinguishes the conversation from a formal argument.

The third example in GP[1] is rather different:

Charm. 159 D 10

> φαίνεται ἄρα ... κατά γε τὸ σῶμα οὐ τὸ ἡσύχιον, ἀλλὰ τὸ τάχιστον καὶ ὀξύτατον κάλλιστον ὄν. ἦ γάρ; – πάνυ γε. – ἡ δέ γε σωφροσύνη καλόν τι ἦν; – ναί. – οὐ τοίνυν κατά γε τὸ σῶμα ἡ ἡσυχιότης ἄν, ἀλλ' ἡ ταχυτὴς σωφρονέστερον εἴη, ἐπειδὴ καλὸν ἡ σωφροσύνη.

> 'It appears that, as far as the body is concerned, what is finest is not what is quiet but what is quickest and keenest. Or isn't it?' – 'It is' – 'And σωφρο-σύνη is something fine?' – 'So it is' – 'Not τοίνυν as far as the body is concerned is it quiet which is more σῶφρον, but speed, given that σωφρο-σύνη is fine'.

Here we have no sign of a volition. If we retreat to the position that τοίνυν serves to remind the interlocutor of his commitment to the earlier statements on which the next one is based, we owe an explanation *why* Plato's Socrates should particularly choose to do so here; but the supposition *that* he does so is confirmed by his repetition of the second premiss in the clause ἐπειδὴ καλὸν ἡ σωφροσύνη.

In view of the peculiar characteristics of these three examples which set them apart from the majority of conclusions of formal syllogisms, it comes as no surprise that the occurrence of τοίνυν in such conclusions is 'rare', as Denniston[2] notes.

2.2. *Not so formal*

So far we have suggested that (1) the observation that τοίνυν often accompanies an imperative or an hortative subjunctive may be generalized to a statement of the affinity of the particle with communications of will, and (2) that such an affinity is still not sufficiently general to account for all its occurrences even within our limited sample; and we have hinted that (3) the notion of the particle's exploiting the interlocutor's previous assent might take us further in the direction of a comprehensive explanation. We shall apply these generalities to the principal subspecies of 'logical τοίνυν' distinguished in *GP* and to the remaining instances of the particle found in the *Phaedo*.

---

[1] Ib.
[2] Ib.

The most general use of 'logical τοίνυν' dealt with in *GP* is one in which Denniston himself concedes that 'the logical force is often not very strong'.[1] This is in dialogue, introducing an answer, which the particle 'represents as springing from the actual words, or general attitude, of the previous speaker'.[2]

I submit that this description fits some of the eight Platonic examples in *GP*[3] better than others. At

Charm. 162 B 4

οὐκ ἄρα ... τὸ τὰ τοιαῦτά τε καὶ οὕτω τὰ αὑτοῦ πράττειν σωφροσύνη ἂν εἴη. – οὐ φαίνεται. – ᾐνίττετο ἄρα, ὡς ἔοικεν, ὅπερ ἄρτι ἐγὼ ἔλεγον, ὁ λέγων ...· οὐ γάρ που οὕτω γε ἦν εὐήθης. ἢ τινος ἠλιθίου ἤκουσας τουτὶ λέγοντος ...; – ἥκιστά γε, ... – παντὸς τοίνυν μᾶλλον, ὡς ἐμοὶ δοκεῖ, αἴνιγμα αὐτὸ προύβαλεν, ... – ἴσως, ἔφη.

'It appears he was speaking in riddles, as I told you just now (...) for he was not such a fool. Or was he?' – 'Far from it!' – '*There, you see?* Speaking in riddles, I'm sure (...).' – 'It looks like it.'

Socrates exploits Charmides' admission that his spokesman was no fool, to make him subscribe to Socrates' own account.[4] It is his presupposition that this is the only alternative: either a fool, or speaking in riddles. The only difference with the example (159 D 10) from the same dialogue quoted in the last section,[5] is in the logical structure of the argument; in its linguistic expression the particle serves the same use of exploiting, and at the same time stipulating for, assent. This applies to both contexts, which are of what may be called the 'propositional', as opposed to the volitional[6] variety.

By contrast, none of the other examples belonging to the present section is very similar to these two. An element of assent, now in a more or less volitional context, is still operative in two of them. One of these,

Ion 542 B 3

ἑλοῦ οὖν πότερα βούλει νομίζεσθαι ὑπὸ ἡμῶν ἄδικος ἀνὴρ εἶναι ἢ θεῖος. – πολὺ διαφέρει, ὦ Σώκρατες· πολὺ γὰρ κάλλιον τὸ θεῖον νομίζεσθαι. – τοῦτο τοίνυν τὸ κάλλιον ὑπάρχει σοι παρ' ἡμῖν, ὦ Ἴων, θεῖον εἶναι καὶ μὴ τεχνικὸν περὶ Ὁμήρου ἐπαινέτην.

---

[1] P. 569-70.

[2] P. 569.

[3] P. 570-1.

[4] The inference is made with ἄρα; with τοίνυν Socrates throws in what weight his own conviction may carry ('just believe me ...'), cf. ὡς ἐμοὶ δοκεῖ, as opposed to (οὐ φαίνεται in the reply following the first ἄρα, and ὡς ἔοικεν after the second ἄρα.

[5] P. 157 above.

[6] 1.2 above, p. 153-5.

'You choose whether you wish to be regarded as unjust or as inspired' – 'Oh! Socrates. it's much finer to be considered inspired' – 'All right then, this finer thing is yours in my eyes ...' (end of dialogue)

provides some justification for our use of the term 'volitional' to cover both communication *of* and response *to* will, by being ambivalent between the two; at the same time it throws doubt upon the notion that τοίνυν 'represents the answer as springing from the ... words or ... attitude of the previous speaker' *alone*. The relevant context extends backwards to Socrates' own invitation, which it reinforces because Ion has not yet formally accepted but only expressed a preference. 'You had a choice; now take it', '... well, here you are'.

The other instance of assenting τοίνυν from among the class in question likewise combines expression *of* with response *to* will, though in a context which is even less explicit:

Charm. 156 A 1

καὶ ἐγὼ εἶπον ὅτι αὐτὸ μὲν εἴη φύλλον τι, ἐπῳδὴ δέ τις ἐπὶ τῷ φαρμάκῳ εἴη, ... · ἄνευ δὲ τῆς ἐπῳδῆς οὐδὲν ὄφελος εἴη τοῦ φύλλου. καὶ ὅς, ἀπογράψομαι τοίνυν, ἔφη, παρὰ σοῦ τὴν ἐπῳδήν.

'And I told him this was an herb, but there was a spell belonging to it, and without the spell the herb was no use. And he said, "All right then, I will copy the spell from you" ...'

It is hard to see the use of logic here. Charmides makes it clear that he has taken the point of Socrates' words and intends to act as they suggest.

3. *Remaining instances in* Phaedo

Before turning to some uses of τοίνυν which we have not yet been prepared for, it is convenient to insert the remaining five examples from the *Phaedo*, all found in non-volitional contexts. Note that they all figure in statements which contain nothing new (contrast ἄρα), yet cannot be taken for granted (contrast δή) but derive support from the interlocutor's preceding admission.

59 B 3:

καὶ πάντες ... σχεδόν τι οὕτω διεκείμεθα ... εἷς δὲ ἡμῶν καὶ διαφερόντως, Ἀπολλόδωρος. – οἶσθα γάρ που τὸν ἄνδρα ... – πῶς γὰρ οὔ; – ἐκεῖνός τε τοίνυν παντάπασιν οὕτως εἶχεν, καὶ αὐτὸς ἔγωγε ἐτεταράγμην καὶ οἱ ἄλλοι.

'He had it particularly badly – you know him?' – 'I do' – 'Well, he had it all over, but we had it too'.

61 C 8

... οὐδ' ὁπωστιοῦν σοι ἑκὼν εἶναι πείσεται. – τί δέ; ... οὐ φιλόσφος Εὔηνος; – ἔμοιγε δοκεῖ. – ἐθελήσει τοίνυν καὶ Εὔηνος ...

('Tell him to follow in my footsteps' –) 'He'll never be willing to do as you say' – 'Why, isn't he a seeker after wisdom?' – '*I* think he is' – 'Well, then he too will be willing'.

62 C 6

οὐκοῦν ... καὶ σὺ ἂν τῶν σαυτοῦ κτημάτων εἴ τι αὐτὸ ἑαυτὸ ἀποκτεινύοι, μὴ σημήναντός σου ὅτι βούλει αὐτὸ τεθνάναι, χαλεπαίνοις ἂν αὐτῷ ... – πάνυ γ', ἔφη. – ἴσως τοίνυν ταύτῃ οὐκ ἄλογον μὴ πρότερον αὐτὸν ἀποκτεινύναι δεῖν, πρὶν ἀνάγκην τινὰ θεὸς ἐπιπέμψῃ ...

('It is forbidden to do violence to oneself' – 'How is that?'–) 'You too would be angry if a creature of your possession killed itself without your authority, wouldn't you?' – 'Certainly' – 'Well, there you see why it's not unreasonable that a man should not kill himself before a god sends some necessity'.

The thesis is first mentioned at 61 C 9-10 by Socrates, who at the request of Cebes establishes it in an argument *ad hominem* rounded off by τοίνυν.

83 E 5

(82 C 2) ἀλλὰ τούτων ἕνεκα ... οἱ ... φιλόσοφοι ἀπέχονται ... (83 A 1) ... γιγνώσκουσιν οἱ φιλομαθεῖς ὅτι ... – ἀληθέστατα ... λέγεις ... – τούτων τοίνυν ἕνεκα ... οἱ δικαίως φιλομαθεῖς κόσμιοί εἰσι καὶ ἀνδρεῖοι, οὐχ ὧν οἱ πολλοὶ ἕνεκά φασιν· ἢ σὺ οἴει; – οὐ δῆτα ἔγωγε.

'This is why philosophers abstain ...' – 'Very true' – 'Well then, this is why philosophers are orderly... or do you disagree?' – 'No I don't'.

The insight was expressed at 82 C 2, but it has now been established to the partners' mutual satisfaction.

The last example from the *Phaedo* raises again[1] the question of the position and scope of the particle:

100 C 9

φαίνεται γάρ μοι, εἴ τί ἐστιν ἄλλο καλὸν πλὴν αὐτὸ τὸ καλόν, οὐδὲ δι' ἓν ἄλλο καλὸν εἶναι ἢ διότι μετέχει ἐκείνου τοῦ καλοῦ ... τῇ τοιᾷδε αἰτίᾳ συγχωρεῖς; – συγχωρῶ ... – οὐ τοίνυν ... ἔτι μανθάνω οὐδὲ δύναμαι τὰς ἄλλας αἰτίας τὰς σοφὰς ταύτας γιγνώσκειν· ἀλλ' ... τοῦτο δὲ ἁπλῶς καὶ ἀτέχνως καὶ ἴσως εὐήθως ἔχω παρ' ἐμαυτῷ, ὅτι οὐκ ἄλλο τι ποιεῖ αὐτὸ καλὸν ἢ ἡ ἐκείνου τοῦ καλοῦ εἴτε παρουσία εἴτε κοινωνία εἴτε ὅπῃ δὴ καὶ ὅπως † ... †

'A thing is beautiful because it partakes of the Beautiful, do you agree?' – 'I agree' – 'Well then, I no longer understand ..., but to this I am perhaps

---

[1] Cf. p. 155 above.

naively attached, that what makes it beautiful is nothing but the presence or communion or whatever of that Beautiful'.

On the strength of the four preceding instances I submit that τοίνυν here is less closely connected with the negative first half of the period, in which it is found, than with the positive second half, which contains the emphatic reassertion of a thesis which has now been established for the purposes of the debate and is expected to be conceded.

These instances from propositional contexts in the *Phaedo*, then, may be classed with *Charm.* 162 B 4 quoted in the last section.[1]

4. *In arguments from other Platonic dialogues*

The remaining examples of the use of 'logical' τοίνυν 'introducing an answer'[2] confront us with yet another and a still wider conception of logic. What sets them apart from those quoted earlier is that they are all used not in assenting but in contradicting. Several times in the *Republic* especially the particle appears in fairly emphatic denials of what was stated or suggested or implied or presupposed in a more offhand way:

Resp. 358 A 4

ἐν ποίῳ (εἴδει ἀγαθοῦ, 357 C 5) τὴν δικαιοσύνην τιθεῖς; – ἐγὼ μὲν οἶμαι ἐν τῷ καλλίστῳ ... – οὐ τοίνυν δοκεῖ ... τοῖς πολλοῖς, ἀλλὰ τοῦ ἐπιπόνου εἴδους ...

'In which class do you put justice?' – 'Well, I think in the finest' – *You had better realize* that's not the common suffrage'.

Resp. 450 D 8

ὦ ἄριστε, ἦ που βουλόμενός με παραθαρρύνειν λέγεις; – ἔγωγε. – πᾶν τοίνυν τοὐναντίον ποιεῖς.

'My friend, I think you are trying to encourage me?' – 'Oh yes I am!' – 'I tell you you are doing just the opposite'.

In the last two quotations the interlocutor is invited to make his assumption explicit before this is contradicted. In the next two the assumption is insinuated rather than stated, and the denial with τοίνυν follows at once:

Resp. 398 C 7

ἆρ' οὖν οὐ πᾶς ἤδη ἂν εὕροι ...; καὶ ὁ Γλαύκων ἐπιγελάσας, ἐγὼ τοίνυν, ἔφη, ὦ Σώκρατες, κινδυνεύω ἐκτὸς τῶν πάντων εἶναι· ...

'Surely everybody is now able to find out ..., isn't he? – Glaucon laughed

---

[1] P. 158 above.
[2] *GP* 569-71; cf. 2.2 above, p. 158.

162 CHAPTER FIVE

and said 'Believe me, Socrates, it looks as if your "everybody" might not include me'.

Resp. 430 D 6

πῶς οὖν ἂν τὴν δικαιοσύνην εὕροιμεν, ἵνα μηκέτι πραγματευώμεθα περὶ σωφροσύνης; – ἐγὼ μὲν τοίνυν, ἔφη, οὔτε οἶδα οὔτ' ἂν βουλοίμην αὐτὸ πρότερον φανῆναι, εἴπερ μηκέτι ἐπισκεψόμεθα σωφροσύνην· ἀλλ' εἰ ἔμοιγε βούλει χαρίζεσθαι, σκόπει πρότερον τοῦτο ἐκείνου ...

'How then may we find out justice – not to bother about σωφροσύνη any longer?' – 'Now listen', he said, 'I neither know nor would choose to have this made clear first, if it means we're not going to inspect σωφροσύνη after that: if you'll do me a favour, look into that first'.

This quotation shows what we may call dissenting τοίνυν in a context which begins as propositional and continues as volitional. The one remaining example in *GP*,[1] not from the *Republic*, confirms that dissenting τοίνυν is at home in contexts of will:

Euth. 15 E 3:

εἰπὲ οὖν, ὦ βέλτιστε Εὐθύφρων, καὶ μὴ ἀποκρύψῃ ὅτι αὐτὸ ἡγῇ. – εἰς αὖθις τοίνυν, ὦ Σώκρατες· νῦν γὰρ σπεύδω ποι, καί μοι ὥρα ἀπιέναι.

'Tell me, dear Euthyphron! Don't deny me your opinion.' – 'Some other time, please, Socrates. I'm in a hurry now'.

In *GP*[2] this passage is cited under 'apparently superfluous connectives', a heading in which 'apparently (superfluous)', is surprisingly paraphrased as 'strictly speaking (unnecessary)'. In Des Places we learn that τοίνυν here 'does not entirely lose its logical force',[3] a view implicitly countenanced by Denniston in his classification of this example in the main text of his *GP*.[4]

With reference to the dissenting use of τοίνυν I submit that it is not merely vain but quite perverse to invoke the name of logic, and plainly absurd to claim that the particle 'represents the answer as springing from the actual words, or general attitude, of the previous speaker' (*GP* 569).

I shall end with an example of the other use distinguished in *GP*[5] under 'logical τοίνυν in general', i.e. that in continuous speech. This is found 'rare in Plato'; three other examples are all drawn from the *Laws*. The one that concerns us is at *Symp.* 178 D 4:

---

[1] P. 570.
[2] P. xlvi.
[3] 'sans toutefois perdre entièrement sa valeur logique' p. 295-6.
[4] P. 570.
[5] P. 569.

ὃ ... χρὴ ἀνθρώποις ἡγεῖσθαι ... τοῖς μέλλουσι καλῶς βιώσεσθαι, τοῦτο
οὔτε συγγένεια οἷα τε ἐμποιεῖν οὕτω καλῶς ... οὔτ' ἄλλο οὐδὲν ὡς ἔρως.
λέγω δὲ δὴ τί τοῦτο; τὴν ἐπὶ μὲν τοῖς αἰσχροῖς αἰσχύνην, ἐπὶ δὲ τοῖς
καλοῖς φιλοτιμίαν· οὐ γὰρ ἔστιν ἄνευ τούτων ... καλὰ ἔργα ἐξεργάζε-
σθαι. φημὶ τοίνυν ἐγὼ ἄνδρα ὅστις ἐρᾷ, εἴ τι αἰσχρὸν ποιῶν κατάδηλος
γίγνοιτο ... οὔτ' ἂν ὑπὸ πατρὸς ὀφθέντα οὕτως ἀλγῆσαι ... οὔτε ὑπ' ἄλλου οὐδενός ὡς ὑπὸ παιδικῶν.

'Love, more than anything, is capable of providing us with the incentive
towards a good life. What I mean by that? Being ashamed of behaviour that
is shameful. Now my claim is that a lover would choose to be caught in
some shameful action by anyone sooner than by his beloved'.

The substitution of the label αἰσχύνη for the unique description ὃ ... χρὴ
... ἡγεῖσθαι scarcely amounts to a *logical* step; it merely helps to establish the terms of the proposition. With φημὶ τοίνυν ἐγώ Phaedrus proceeds to make his statement: '*Here I* am telling *you*', '*Now you* listen to
me'. Without the φημί we might have expected οὖν, which would not so
much have brought the act of assertion into relief, as directed the hearer
from the preliminary specifications to the content of the proposition they
were relevant to.

5. *Towards a synthesis*

We have encountered τοίνυν in a baffling diversity of applications, and
have not found modern scholarship illuminating. It strikes me that we
should begin by heeding the etymology of the particle, which it is safe to
assume is a compound of enclitic τοι, in origin dative of σύ, and enclitic
νυν. The derivation from demonstrative (locative) *τοῖ, relating it to τοίγαρ and compounds, was refuted more than one hundred years ago by
Wackernagel,[1] but continued to be defended by Kühner-Gerth, Brugmann-
Thumb, and Des Places, and was abandoned only by Denniston and
Schwyzer-Debrunner. I submit that we could make one small concession
to it: the resemblance to τοίγαρ etc. may have furthered the use of τοίνυν
in the context of consequence by a kind of unconscious popular etymology, just as it has probably helped to remove τοίνυν *to*, and τοιγαροῦν
from, the first place in the sentence in later authors.

Etymology, then, suggests that τοίνυν is not in origin a connecting
particle at all, whether logical or, even more improbably, transitional, but
a sentence particle, or perhaps 'utterance particle' rather, used as an aid
to present a communication to its addressee with some insistence. Natu-

---

[1] *IF* 1 (1891) 377.

rally such an aid is less often required in continuous speech than it is in dialogue. Here its divergent and apparently contradictory uses may perhaps be reduced to the following categories: the particle is employed either to *correct* or to *forestall* a disrepancy between the pragmatical information or practical disposition of the partners. The corrective use is obviously the more emphatic one, and provides the link between two extreme cases found above: at one end τοίνυν marks a compliance even beyond the demands of the interlocutor (*Charm.* 156 A 1, *Ion* 542 B 3),[1] at the other end it puts in a laboured plea for a dissenting view (*Resp.* 430 D 6).[2] The preventive use, in which the speaker's aim is to have his point or his wish granted, is the commoner and the less specific of the the two. Here we may distinguish between cases in which the point to be granted has been made before and the *sole* use of repeating it is to enlist the other's support (*Charm.* 162 B 4, *Phaedo* 83 E 5),[3] and cases in which it is intimated that the other participant cannot, in view of his own admissions, reasonably deny a point or reject a proposal which is now to be made (*Charm.* 159 D 10, *Phaedo* 90 D 9).[4] The motives for bolstering up one's thesis in this way may vary with the cogency of the argument; to return to the explanation of *Charm.* 159 D 10 demanded earlier,[5] I suggest that Socrates is there trying to make the rules of the game, the mechanics of the dialogue as it were, as explicit as possible out of consideration for a favourite novice.

---

[1] P. 158-9 above.
[2] P. 162 above.
[3] Pp. 158 & 160 above respectively.
[4] Pp. 157 & 154 above respectively.
[5] P. 157 above.

INDEX LOCORUM

Aeschylus

Persians	159	53
Prom.	521	62
	1064	63[2]

Aristophanes

Ach.	186	38
	693	53
Birds	100	35
	179	64
Clouds	69	63
	126	35
Eccl.	327	64
Frogs	33-4	56
	103-4	56
	106	54
	171	34 f.
	258	54
	285	54
	288	54[1]
	803	56
	814	57
	907	54[2]
	1036	54
	1119	54[2]
	1198	54[2]
	1249	54[2]
	1263	54[2]
	1470	56, 56[2]
Lys.	1089	62
Plut.	698	62
Thesm.	9	35
	63	62
	457	35, 38

Aristoteles

Rhet.	1358 a 37-b 2	51
	1372 a 8	37

Euripides

Bacch.	939	62
	1118	64
El.	293	37
	1123	38
Hel.	1465	62[2]
Heraclid.	55	62
Herc.	138	40[1]

Hipp.	51	39
Med.	68	53

Herodotus

1.18.4	57
1.24.7	133[1]
1.27.1	132
1.43.2	53[3]
1.86.3	132
1.77.4	118[1], 127
1.111.1	136
1.111.5	126
1.112.2	122[1], 133
1.119.2	57
1.141.2	125
1.178.1	57
1.184.1	57
2.28.5	128[3]
2.49.1	138[1]
2.58	138
2.140.1	133[1]
2.141.3	133
3.14.8	136
3.34.3	122 f.
3.34.4	122 f., 124, 124[1], 134
3.45.4	131[2]
3.64.4	122[1], 134
3.65.3	122, 122[1], 124, 134
3.70.1	122[1], 136
3.72.1	59
3.134.1	132[1]
4.32	128
4.134.1	125
4.45.4	122[1], 134 f.
4.45.5	135
4.64.3	122[1], 137
4.189.1	134[1], 137 f.
4.205	124[2], 133, 134[1]
5.1.3	57
5.49.8	120, 138
5.87.2	133
5.92 γ 2	135 f.
5.106.4	128
5.124.2	131
6.11.1	57

ANALYTICAL INDEX

English

Greek

SUPPLEMENTS TO MNEMOSYNE

EDITED BY A.D. LEEMAN, C.J. RUIJGH AND H.W. PLEKET

4. LEEMAN, A.D. *A Systematical Bibliography of Sallust (1879-1964)*. Revised and augmented edition. 1965. ISBN 90 04 01467 5
5. LENZ, F.W. (ed.). *The Aristeides 'Prolegomena'*. 1959. ISBN 90 04 01468 3
7. McKAY, K.J. *Erysichthon. A Callimachean Comedy*. 1962. ISBN 90 04 01470 5
11. RUTILIUS LUPUS. *De Figuris Sententiarum et Elocutionis*. Edited with Prolegomena and Commentary by E. BROOKS. 1970. ISBN 90 04 01474 8
12. SMYTH, W.R. (ed.). *Thesaurus criticus ad Sexti Propertii textum*. 1970. ISBN 90 04 01475 6
13. LEVIN, D.N. *Apollonius' 'Argonautica' re-examined*. 1. The Neglected First and Second Books. 1971. ISBN 90 04 02575 8
14. REINMUTH, O.W. *The Ephebic Inscriptions of the Fourth Century B.C.* 1971. ISBN 90 04 01476 4
16. ROSE, K.F.C. *The Date and Author of the 'Satyricon'*. With an introduction by J.P. SULLIVAN. 1971. ISBN 90 04 02578 2
18. WILLIS, J. *De Martiano Capella emendando*. 1971. ISBN 90 04 02580 4
19. HERINGTON, C.J. (ed.). *The Older Scholia on the Prometheus Bound*. 1972. ISBN 90 04 03455 2
20. THIEL, H. VAN. *Petron. Überlieferung und Rekonstruktion*. 1971. ISBN 90 04 02581 2
21. LOSADA, L.A. *The Fifth Column in the Peloponnesian War*. 1972. ISBN 90 04 03421 8
23. BROWN, V. *The Textual Transmission of Caesar's 'Civil War'*. 1972. ISBN 90 04 03457 9
24. LOOMIS, J.W. *Studies in Catullan Verse*. An Analysis of Word Types and Patterns in the Polymetra. 1972. ISBN 90 04 03429 3
27. GEORGE, E.V. *Aeneid VIII and the Aitia of Callimachus*. 1974. ISBN 90 04 03859 0
29. BERS, V. *Enallage and Greek Style*. 1974. ISBN 90 04 03786 1
37. SMITH, O.L. *Studies in the Scholia on Aeschylus*. 1. The Recensions of Demetrius Triclinius. 1975. ISBN 90 04 04220 2
39. SCHMELING, G.L. & J.H. STUCKEY. *A Bibliography of Petronius*. 1977. ISBN 90 04 04753 0
44. THOMPSON, W.E. *De Hagniae Hereditate*. An Athenian Inheritance Case. 1976. ISBN 90 04 04757 3
45. McGUSHIN, P. *Sallustius Crispus, 'Bellum Catilinae'. A Commentary*. 1977. ISBN 90 04 04835 9
46. THORNTON, A. *The Living Universe. Gods and Men in Virgil's Aeneid*. 1976. ISBN 90 04 04579 1
48. BRENK, F.E. *In Mist apparelled. Religious Themes in Plutarch's 'Moralia' and 'Lives'*. 1977. ISBN 90 04 05241 0
51. SUSSMAN, L.A. *The Elder Seneca*. 1978. ISBN 90 04 05759 5
57. BOER, W. DEN. *Private Morality in Greece and Rome*. Some Historical Aspects. 1979. ISBN 90 04 05976 8
61. *Hieronymus' Liber de optimo genere interpretandi (Epistula 57)*. Ein Kommentar von G.J.M. BARTELINK. 1980. ISBN 90 04 06085 5
63. HOHENDAHL-ZOETELIEF, I.M. *Manners in the Homeric Epic*. 1980. ISBN 90 04 06223 8
64. HARVEY, R.A. *A Commentary on Persius*. 1981. ISBN 90 04 06313 7

65. MAXWELL-STUART, P.G. *Studies in Greek Colour Terminology. 1.* γλαυκός. 1981. ISBN 90 04 06406 0

68. ACHARD, G. *Pratique rhétorique et idéologie politique dans les discours 'Optimates' de Cicéron.* 1981. ISBN 90 04 06374 9

69. MANNING, C.E. *On Seneca's 'Ad Marciam'.* 1981. ISBN 90 04 06430 3

70. BERTHIAUME, G. *Les rôles du Mágeiros.* Etude sur la boucherie, la cuisine et le sacrifice dans la Grèce ancienne. 1982. ISBN 90 04 06554 7

71. CAMPBELL, M. *A commentary on Quintus Smyrnaeus Posthomerica XII.* 1981. ISBN 90 04 06502 4

72. CAMPBELL, M. *Echoes and Imitations of Early Epic in Apollonius Rhodius.* 1981. ISBN 90 04 06503 2

73. MOSKALEW, W. *Formular Language and Poetic Design in the Aeneid.* 1982. ISBN 90 04 06580 6

74. RACE, W.H. *The Classical Priamel from Homer to Boethius.* 1982. ISBN 90 04 06515 6

75. MOORHOUSE, A.C. *The Syntax of Sophocles.* 1982. ISBN 90 04 06599 7

77. WITKE, C. *Horace's Roman Odes.* A Critical Examination. 1983. ISBN 90 04 07006 0

78. ORANJE, J. *Euripides' 'Bacchae'.* The Play and its Audience. 1984. ISBN 90 04 07011 7

79. STATIUS. *Thebaidos Libri XII.* Recensuit et cum apparatu critico et exegetico instruxit D.E. HILL. 1983. ISBN 90 04 06917 8

82. DAM, H.-J. VAN. *P. Papinius Statius, Silvae Book II.* A Commentary. 1984. ISBN 90 04 07110 5

84. OBER, J. *Fortress Attica. Defense of the Athenian Land Frontier, 404-322 B.C.* 1985. ISBN 90 04 07243 8

85. HUBBARD, T.K. *The Pindaric Mind.* A Study of Logical Structure in Early Greek Poetry. 1985. ISBN 90 04 07303 5

86. VERDENIUS, W.J. *A Commentary on Hesiod: Works and Days, vv. 1-382.* 1985. ISBN 90 04 07465 1

87. HARDER, A. *Euripides' 'Kresphonthes' and 'Archelaos'.* Introduction, Text and Commentary. 1985. ISBN 90 04 07511 9

88. WILLIAMS, H.J. *The 'Eclogues' and 'Cynegetica' of Nemesianus.* Edited with an Introduction and Commentary. 1986. ISBN 90 04 07486 4

89. McGING, B.C. *The Foreign Policy of Mithridates VI Eupator, King of Pontus.* 1986. ISBN 90 04 07591 7

91. SIDEBOTHAM, S.E. *Roman Economic Policy in the Erythra Thalassa 30 B.C.-A.D. 217.* 1986. ISBN 90 04 07644 1

92. VOGEL, C.J. DE. *Rethinking Plato and Platonism.* 2nd impr. of the first (1986) ed. 1988. ISBN 90 04 08755 9

93. MILLER, A.M. *From Delos to Delphi.* A Literary Study of the Homeric Hymn to Apollo. 1986. ISBN 90 04 07674 3

94. BOYLE, A.J. *The Chaonian Dove.* Studies in the Eclogues, Georgics, and Aeneid of Virgil. 1986. ISBN 90 04 07672 7

95. KYLE, D.G. *Athletics in Ancient Athens.* 2nd impr. of the first (1987) ed. 1993. ISBN 90 04 09759 7

97. VERDENIUS, W.J. *Commentaries on Pindar. Vol. I. Olympian Odes 3, 7, 12, 14.* 1987. ISBN 90 04 08126 7

98. PROIETTI, G. *Xenophon's Sparta.* An introduction. 1987. ISBN 90 04 08338 3

99. BREMER, J.M., A.M. VAN ERP TAALMAN KIP & S.R. SLINGS. *Some Recently Found Greek Poems.* Text and Commentary. 1987. ISBN 90 04 08319 7

100. OPHUIJSEN, J.M. VAN. *Hephaestion on Metre.* Translation and Commentary. 1987. ISBN 90 04 08452 5

101. VERDENIUS, W.J. *Commentaries on Pindar. Vol. II.* Olympian Odes 1, 10, 11, Nemean 11, Isthmian 2. 1988. ISBN 90 04 08535 1
102. LUSCHNIG, C.A.E. *Time holds the Mirror. A Study of Knowledge in Euripides' 'Hippolytus'.* 1988. ISBN 90 04 08601 3
103. MARCOVICH, M. *Alcestis Barcinonensis.* Text and Commentary. 1988. ISBN 90 04 08600 5
104. HOLT, F.L. *Alexander the Great and Bactria.* The Formation of a Greek Frontier in Central Asia. Repr. 1989. ISBN 90 04 08612 9
105. BILLERBECK, M. *Senecas Tragödien: sprachliche und stilistische Untersuchungen.* Mit Anhängen zur Sprache des Hercules Oetaeus und der Octavia. 1988. ISBN 90 04 08631 5
106. ARENDS, J.F.M. *Die Einheit der Polis. Eine Studie über Platons Staat.* 1988. ISBN 90 04 08785 0
107. BOTER, G.J. *The Textual Tradition of Plato's Republic.* 1988. ISBN 90 04 08787 7
108. WHEELER, E.L. *Stratagem and the Vocabulary of Military Trickery.* 1988. ISBN 90 04 08831 8
109. BUCKLER, J. *Philip II and the Sacred War.* 1989. ISBN 90 04 09095 9
110. FULLERTON, M.D. *The Archaistic Style in Roman Statuary.* 1990. ISBN 90 04 09146 7
111. ROTHWELL, K.S. *Politics and Persuasion in Aristophanes' 'Ecclesiazusae'.* 1990. ISBN 90 04 09185 8
112. CALDER, W.M. & A. DEMANDT. *Eduard Meyer.* Leben und Leistung eines Universalhistorikers. 1990. ISBN 90 04 09131 9
113. CHAMBERS, M.H. *Georg Busolt. His Career in His Letters.* 1990. ISBN 90 04 09225 0
114. CASWELL, C.P. *A Study of 'Thumos' in Early Greek Epic.* 1990. ISBN 90 04 09260 9
115. EINGARTNER, J. *Isis und ihre Dienerinnen in der Kunst der römischen Kaiserzeit.* 1991. ISBN 90 04 09312 5
116. JONG, I. DE. *Narrative in Drama.* The Art of the Euripidean Messenger-Speech. 1991. ISBN 90 04 09406 7
117. BOYCE, B.T. *The Language of the Freedmen in Petronius'* Cena Trimalchionis. 1991. ISBN 90 04 09431 8
118. RÜTTEN, Th. *Demokrit — lachender Philosoph und sanguinischer Melancholiker.* 1992. ISBN 90 04 09523 3
119. KARAVITES, P. (with the collaboration of Th. Wren). *Promise-Giving and Treaty-Making.* Homer and the Near East. 1992. ISBN 90 04 09567 5
120. SANTORO L'HOIR, F. *The Rhetoric of Gender Terms.* 'Man', 'woman' and the portrayal of character in Latin prose. 1992. ISBN 90 04 09512 8
121. WALLINGA, H.T. *Ships and Sea-Power before the Great Persian War.* The Ancestry of the Ancient Trireme. 1993. ISBN 90 04 09650 7
122. FARRON, S. *Vergil's Aeneid: A Poem of Grief and Love.* 1993. ISBN 90 04 09661 2
123. LÉTOUBLON, F. *Les lieux communs du roman.* Stéréotypes grecs d'aventure et d'amour. 1993. ISBN 90 04 09724 4
124. KUNTZ, M. *Narrative Setting and Dramatic Poetry.* 1993. ISBN 90 04 09784 8
125. THEOPHRASTUS. *Metaphysics.* Introduction, Translation and Commentary by Marlein van Raalte. 1993. ISBN 90 04 09786 4
126. LEVENE, D.S. *Religion in Livy.* 1993. ISBN 90 04 09617 5
127. THIERMANN, P. *Die 'Orationes Homeri' des Leonardo Bruni Aretino.* Kritische Edition der lateinischen und kastellanischen Übersetzung mit Prolegomena und Kommentar. 1993. ISBN 90 04 09719 8
128. PORTER, J.R. *Studies in Euripides'* Orestes. 1993. ISBN 90 04 09662 0
129. SICKING, C.M.J. & J.M. VAN OPHUIJSEN. *Two Studies in Attic Particle Usage.* Lysias and Plato. 1993. ISBN 90 04 09867 4